Sea Kayaking
Along the
New England Coast

2nd Edition

Tamsin Venn

APPALACHIAN MOUNTAIN CLUB BOOKS
BOSTON, MASSACHUSETTS

Front cover photograph: Knubble Light, York, ME © Dennis Welsh
Back cover photographs: Young kayakers paddling © Tamsin Venn
                            Plover chick © Don Sias
                            Kayaker along the shore © Tamsin Venn

All interior photographs by the author unless otherwise noted.
Cover design: Kala Sabel
Book design: Kristin Sperber
Map design: Carol Bast Tyler
Interior images scanned by Jay's Publishing Services

Sea Kayaking Along the New England Coast, 2nd Edition
© 2004 by Tamsin Venn. All rights reserved.

Distributed by The Globe Pequot Press, Inc., Guilford, CT.

For Library of Congress Cataloging-in-Publication Data, contact AMC Books.

The paper used in this publication meets the minimum requirements of the American
National Standard for Information Sciences—Permanence of Paper for Printed
Library Materials, ANSI Z39.48–1984.∞

Printed on recycled paper using soy-based inks. ✪
Printed in the United States of America.

**Due to changes in conditions, use of the information
in this book is at the sole risk of the user.**

10 9 8 7 6 5 4 3 2 1   04 05 06 07 08 09

To Lilly and Anton

"Even if I knew tomorrow the world would go to pieces,
I would still plant my apple tree."
—Dr. Martin Luther King, Jr.

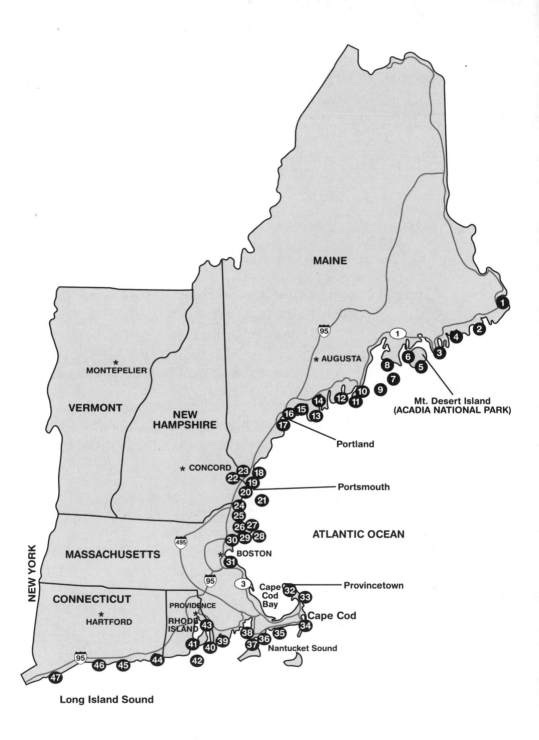

CONTENTS

FOREWORD

It's a pleasure to introduce the second edition of Tamsin Venn's *Sea Kayaking Along the New England Coast*. What changes we have witnessed in the world of sea kayaking since the AMC published the first edition in 1991! It was the first comprehensive guide to sea kayaking trips on the East Coast. Now there are guides for every New England coastal state.

Despite its origins in the ancient craft of the Arctic Inuit, sea kayaking as a recreational pursuit was a newcomer to the outdoor scene when Tammy's first edition appeared. Sea kayaking for pleasure began in the mid- to late nineteenth century in Europe with the pioneering efforts of Rob Roy MacGregor and Johannes Klepper, but it remained a fringe activity for only a dedicated few. In the 1940s and 1950s, Franz Roemer and Hannes Lindemann demonstrated the ultimate functionality of these early boats by crossing the Atlantic Ocean in Kleppers. Most of the converts to paddling on the ocean during the 1970s and 1980s were also primarily interested in adventure expeditions, including trips around Cape Horn and Paul Caffyn's circumnavigations of the islands of New Zealand and even Australia.

Throughout the 1990s, sea kayaking's popularity grew exponentially. Longtime friends who only wondered at my paddling the Maine coast have now joined the legions of recreational paddlers plying the ocean—only twenty years late by my reckoning. Of course, with so many more paddlers, kayak manufacturers have increased in numbers, companies have merged, and I believe the basic sea kayak hull design has been sliced into so many variations on the theme that you can pick any numbers for hull dimensions and certainly find a boat that matches them. One worrisome addition to the fleets of new designs is the "recreational touring kayak." This class came into being more for profit than for performance and is decidedly unfit for ocean use. Nevertheless, new paddlers with these kayaks who, lacking in requisite skill, knowledge, experience, and judgment, tend to move to the ocean once they feel the urge to quit the quiet environs for which the boat was designed.

Despite the number of guidebooks that have appeared, there is still a need for one that not only takes a regional perspective, but also contains the wisdom gained only by paddling the coast for more than twenty years. A new dimension to Tammy's experience arrives through her family, which also has been added since the first edition. Her recommendations for family trips are genuine and tested by her, her husband David, and her two children, Lilly and Anton.

Other, not-so-pleasant changes have occurred in sea kayaking since the first edition of this guide. One of these is the overuse of Maine's islands. In 1988, through Dave and Dorrie Getchell's vision, steadfast efforts, and a collaboration with the state of Maine and the Island Institute of Rockland, Maine, the Maine Island Trail was established. This first coastal island ocean trail for small boaters encompasses lands from the state's extensive island holdings as well as generous offerings from private island owners—it's a unique partnership. The establishment of this trail for use by all small-boat owners provided an added incentive to kayakers to come to Maine for a paddling vacation. Unfortunately, other New England states have not followed suit, and access remains a deterrent outside Maine. In my foreword to the first edition, I expressed the hope that publication of the guidebook and establishment of the Maine Island Trail would allow the inevitable attraction of new paddlers to the area and increased use of the islands and water trails of New England to occur gracefully. Well, it has not been so graceful. The Maine Island Trail Association (MITA) has had to build platforms on selected islands to ease the camping impact and was forced to establish absolute limits on numbers of overnight campers and maximum stay limits to combat the overuse of the most popular islands. The number of individual kayakers using the islands has increased dramatically, but the number of outfitters using the islands has increased even more. I have witnessed more than fifty paddlers from three different outfitters or summer camps overnighting on Fort Island near the mouth of the Damariscotta River. It is a foregone conclusion that we will eventually have a reservation system to ease such abusive excesses. Some private islands are no longer accessible to the public because of owners' concerns about overuse.

The other unhappy result of more paddlers is what I call the pariah stigma. At the time of Tammy's first edition, paddlers were new, a bit of an oddity, and viewed as pioneers at best, or tolerated as eccentrics at worst. As this new edition arrives, paddlers have earned an unjust reputation among lobster fishermen, small-boat operators, and coastal property owners as either an accident waiting to happen or as intruders into their once exclusive domains. This reputation arrived because of the thoughtless actions of a very few. If this reputation ever fades, it will be only through the actions of most of us practicing absolute safety and being thoughtful, respectful interlopers.

The emphasis of the second edition is less to stimulate new participation in sea kayaking or to attract paddlers to New England while the sport is still growing; rather it is to guide those who come to enjoy the fruits of Tammy's research on where and how to enjoy the New England coast. The guidebook will also encourage the development of skill, knowledge, experience, and judgment. This will help in the long run to remove the pariah stigma as we gain a reputation for safe and sensible seamanship.

New England paddlers have been leaders in developing sea kayaking with an emphasis on education and safety. We were the first to develop the symposium concept in 1982. The sea kayaking symposium provided the educational, social, and promotional formats so essential to a healthy growth of the sport. The symposium structure is acknowledged as a responsible means of introducing new paddlers to the sport and has been adopted nationally. Many readers of this guidebook may have participated in one or more sea kayaking symposia.

The rampant growth over the last half of the 1990s underscores the sustained popularity of sea kayaking and its broad appeal to and accommodation of all ages and abilities. Despite so many new paddlers hitting the water, our safety record remains remarkably good for a sport in which the participant in New England waters is always attended by the risk of immersion hypothermia. On any given day, the paddling conditions can range from benign to severe—often within a short distance or period of time. The challenge for a sea kayaking guidebook writer is to provide the necessary balance between the siren song and cautions. In keeping with this philosophy, this second edition emphasizes the safety considerations for ocean paddling. Tammy is a serious paddler and capable writer who has worked hard to provide the details for that perfect trip, but she wisely has avoided any attempt at a rating system for any trip. There are three good reasons for not rating trips. These are: (1) there is too much subjectivity in assessing paddler skill and experience; (2) the wind, wave, and current climates impose objective complexity onto any ocean trip and can't be accommodated by a rating; and (3) a rating tends to remove individual and collective responsibility for matching ability to oceanographic conditions, coastal physiography, and weather forecasts. Instead, Tammy Venn elected to indicate the general, potential hazards of any trip on the ocean in New England, under what conditions these hazards become extreme, and those specific sections of a trip requiring careful planning. Users of the guide should know something of wave dynamics, tides and tidal currents, local weather patterns, and interactions of waves, currents, and coastlines. Chance will always favor the prepared paddler!

The trips Tammy has included are but a sampling of the many paddling experiences that New England has to offer the wandering ocean kayaker. You can explore or surf expansive sand beaches, go bird watching in vast marshes, tour in near-wilderness estuaries, or challenge your skills along the wild and rocky shorelines. You'll find whatever appeals to you. In addition, I'll reiterate something I said in the foreword to the first edition: "Don't worry about repeating your favorites; no stretch of coast ever seems the same twice!"

—*Kenneth Fink*

PREFACE TO THE SECOND EDITION

Sea kayaking in New England has developed rapidly over the twelve years since this guidebook was first written (this is the second edition), and almost everyone who lives near the New England coast has tried kayaking at least once; many own their own craft. Over the past decade-plus, much has changed in the sport, and the contents of this book—fourteen new trips are included—reflect those changes. But the number of places to paddle isn't the only change. In this section, I've included a few thoughts on the development of the sport over the past dozen years.

In regard to safety—an issue important to anyone venturing out on the water—the network of kayakers sharing safety information has grown considerably larger. We are much more aware of the effects of coldwater immersion, hypothermia, and cold shock, and as a result coldwater workshops offered in the off-season abound. Use of safety equipment such as personal flotation devices (PFDs), wetsuits, and weather radios is now quite standard for the knowledgeable kayaker.

A dozen years ago, we only paid lip service to low-impact camping as we humorously figured out ways of carrying human waste off the islands. Now our self-imposed low-impact values are more clearly spelled out and spearheaded by a national organization called Leave No Trace. Limits on the number of people at camping sites have been set, and the rule now understood is: move on if campsites are already occupied.

Kayaking clubs have grown and matured; most now have their own websites. Clubs are a good place for companionship, instruction, safety information, and trips—some even have a healthy cash flow and have bought their own real estate. Today show-and-go club trips are a thing of the past. Trips are organized and fill up well in advance, and everyone participating must sign liability waivers.

The gap between trained instructors and beginner kayakers eager to learn is lessening. Now almost everyone who has been kayaking for a few years moves into a British Canoe Union or American Canoe Association certification course, even if they don't do any professional guiding or teaching.

Another change in the sport is that a dozen years ago, one or two people paddled with Greenland paddles, and they were considered very strange, maybe even a liability. Would they be able to keep up with those using wide Euro blades? In fact, Greenland paddlers often leave the others behind and amaze us all with an array of rolling techniques, documented by Greenland historians. These days the Greenland Kayak Club is open to foreigners, who can also now participate in the annual championships in Greenland.

When the first edition of this book was published, the 14-foot recreational kayak barely existed (the Keowee was the notable exception). The 17-foot fiberglass ocean kayak with deck rigging and a custom-built day hatch made us all ready for a circumnavigation of Great Britain. Today a whole length range of kayaks exists, from 12 to 20 feet; it's not an either–or proposition anymore. Plastic is a good alternative to fiberglass—and you can haul it across the rocks with no damage.

Once paddlers had to drive three hours to the nearest kayak store to special-order from a paddle sports catalog, but now kayak stores ring major cities and towns and are even located in remote outposts. These days you can always find a place to buy a compass, charts, or a well-made paddle.

Only one Atlantic Coast–oriented guidebook existed when I wrote *Sea Kayaking Along the New England Coast*, while today more than a dozen cover the coves and islands of this region, not counting those for Lake Champlain and the Connecticut and Charles Rivers.

A dozen years ago, only a few kayaking instruction and safety manuals, mainly by British authors, were available. Now new ones come out every year, not to mention the array of instructional videos that have appeared. All these are produced to satisfy the insatiable need of kayakers for more information on the sport they love and continue to develop.

In 1991, the Internet did not exist for use by the general public, but today more than 5,000 sea kayaking websites offer information to the paddler. The use of digital cameras makes it easy to display adventures online for everyone to share.

The water trail movement has also grown substantially. The Maine Island Trail has matured, and now even provides island caretakers and tent platforms for paddlers—not to mention its progress in fund-raising. This association continues to involve island owners and users in a successful reciprocal agreement to use and take care of the many pristine islands of Maine. The Maine Island Trail was the catalyst for a national water trail movement.

Women are now a much bigger part of this sport than in the past.

Families with children are finding safe and enjoyable ways to explore the marine wilderness.

Other changes of note include the advent and use of GPS (Global Positioning System), which continues to alter navigation knowledge and technique; the use of digital maps to load into your GPS; and the proliferation of personal watercraft, which quietwater users such as kayakers continue to help regulate.

But some aspects have not changed. The New England coast continues to be an ideal place for this sport in terms of challenging water, relaxing quiet coves and estuaries, historic appeal, scenery, nature preserves, and working harbors. The sport has uncovered a new environment for exploration and enjoyment. Because sea kayakers can travel in 6 inches of water or less, they have access to a coastal margin not easily explored in any other manner. The sea kayak's speed and low wind resistance allow for travel over great distances and exploration in familiar neighborhoods perhaps previously visited only by sailboat or motorboat.

This book draws on the expertise and experience of longtime paddlers along the New England coast. Their input has been invaluable, and includes advice on tides, currents, headlands, harbor rules, other oceangoing craft, weather, seasons, wildlife, campsites, launch spots, and land-use permission along this coast.

This guide is written for those paddlers who crave the freedom of putting a seaworthy boat on top of the car and exploring a coastal zone that has never before been experienced in this manner—and whose use of such will promote its preservation at a time when coastal zones are increasingly threatened. It is written for those individuals who have a passion for wild places, are in reasonably good physical shape, and are deeply interested in conservation and exploration.

Such kayakers enjoy the companionship that sea kayaking generates. They seek and enjoy a challenge. They find satisfaction in relying on their own emotional, physical, and mental resources, as well as on their own judgment in the wilderness. They are ultimately aware of the risks involved.

The book is also for those who enjoy an intimate relationship with the moods and currents of the sea that kayaking allows us to experience. It is for the Appalachian Mountain Club (AMC) members and other naturalists who simply enjoy being outdoors.

Sea Kayaking Along the New England Coast consists of a general introduction on equipment, clothes, technique, and safety, but the bulk of the book describes forty-seven recommended trips on the Northeast Coast, from Maine to Connecticut.

Readers should be keenly aware that in every case, wind and weather conditions will differ radically, altering each trip's nature. For example, some people have paddled around Small Point in Maine in millpond conditions and loved the experience. Others found conditions on the same route such that they swore they would never make the trip again. I don't recommend paddling up a river against the wind when small-craft warnings are in effect or making a long crossing in breaking beam seas. I also don't like paddling in the fog. The ocean's conditions are constantly and quickly changing, and a great deal of stamina and courage may be required in many situations. But the opening of a new coastal world makes the challenge worthwhile.

ACKNOWLEDGMENTS

This guide reflects the knowledge, expertise, humor, advice, encouragement, and wisdom of New England paddlers from Maine to Connecticut. Each one has been more than helpful in providing knowledge of local waters and even exposing favorite put-in spots in a spirit of generosity for sharing this special sport.

In particular I would like to thank Ken Fink for writing an inspired foreword. I would also like to thank my family for going on many trips with me and staying in bleak commercial campgrounds in the off-season. My husband, David Eden, was especially awesome for his willingness to check out one more launch. He also worked dutifully on the maps. Also thanks to Martin Fox at Maptech for providing the charts and Beth Krusi and the publishing crew at AMC Books for the great job they've done. And thanks to my staff at *Atlantic Coastal Kayaker* for filling in during my absence. To all of the above, one million thanks plus one.

—*Tamsin Venn*

HOW TO USE THIS BOOK

Organization

This book's sea kayaking trips are organized by state, north to south. There are nineteen trips alng Maine's coast, four trips along New Hampshire's small coastline, sixteen trips in Massachusetts, and four trips each in Rhode Island and Connecticut. Each state has individual qualities that make it unique. Preceding the descriptions of the areas in each state is a brief summary of the characteristics of that state, including information on physiography (physical geography), geological setting, camping, access, launch and parking, trip planning, weather conditions, coastal wildlife, living off the wild, and special safety considerations.

Trip Descriptions

The suggested routes for the trips in this book are not meant to be definitive. Wind and wave conditions are the ultimate route deciders, and many interesting islands, estuaries, channels, and inlets may draw the kayaker away from the main route. Rather, these are general routes, merely suggestions over very large, watery, undefinable trails.

Note that under no circumstances should the maps that are provided with each trip be used for navigation. Always consult a regular marine chart of the area.

Each trip description includes the following information:

Trip Mileage: The mileage, in statute miles, is an estimate from the charts and does not take into account detours into inviting inlets and bays or how far inshore or offshore you might travel. If you calculate that the average sea kayaker travels 3.5 nautical miles an hour, you can reasonably estimate how long it will take to paddle from point A to point B, assuming favorable winds and tide. We also list whether the mileage is for a one-way, round-trip, or loop trip.

Tidal Range: This refers to average difference between high and low water over a year's time as provided by the *Eldridge Tide and Pilot Book* (see the bibliography). Where no figure is available for a specific area, the closest recorded range is given. Remember that specific tidal range varies throughout the lunar month, seasonally, and according to wind direction and barometric pressure. Last night's high-tide line is no guarantee that the next high tide won't be considerably higher.

Charts and Maps: The recommended maps are marine charts issued by the National Oceanic and Atmospheric Administration (NOAA). Most kayakers find the scale of 1:40,000 suitable. If you paddle long distances at a good pace, then the standard 1:250,000 USGS topographic maps are useful, despite their lack of the usual navigational aids found on the NOAA charts.

Caution Areas: Often, these are narrow passages, headlands, tide rips, exposed crossings, and areas with ledges or great variation in water depths. In summer, heavy boat traffic including personal watercraft is always a consideration, if not a major hazard, when considering caution areas and is not always referred to in this guide.

Access: Normally, only one or two access spots are described, but note that many more are usually available in any given area. Some of those are described at the end of the route description, along with other options.

Getting There: This section provides directions to the launch point, and any other information that might help you along the way.

Trip Map: Each trip includes a map that shows nearby towns, roads, parking, and boat access as well as the paddling route and campgrounds. These maps make planning easy but should not be used for navigation.

Other Options: These include both other launch spots and other trips, possibly extensions of the one recommended or day trips from a particular camping spot. Much of an itinerary is determined by prevailing winds and tide as well as the group's mood.

Camping: Where appropriate, either islands or saltwater mainland campgrounds are mentioned. Because the sport has grown so popular, it is in your best interest to have a backup camping plan before you get on the water. As you travel south, camping options diminish, and most trips are day trips.

WELCOME TO
THE WORLD OF SEA KAYAKING

Equipment, technique, navigation, safety, camping, paddling with kids, and Leave No Trace: In the past decade, paddlers have written or produced at least two dozen books and videos covering these topics. (One video set is a ten-volume kayak training series!) Consult the bibliography. Therefore, this book covers information only as it pertains specifically to paddling in New England. Remember that as you develop skills, you need to learn what works best for you from the school of experience, the sea itself (see appendix B for an equipment checklist).

Equipment

Choosing a Boat

As one experienced paddler pointed out when asked for advice on choosing a kayak, he has yet to find the right sea kayak—even though he has had ten years of paddling different boats and family ownership of seven kayaks. The lesson here is not to expect a perfect solution but to decide on the best compromise.

Some good ways to try boats are to attend sea kayak symposiums or paddle sport shows, borrow friends' boats, or visit a sea kayak dealer. The larger the symposium, the more opportunity you will have to paddle a large variety of craft provided by the manufacturers and distributors. Paddle shops sponsor demo days, usually early in the season, with the store's models available to try. Some, especially those on the water, offer that as an ongoing service. Also try boats through the classifieds of magazines and club newsletters and websites.

Probably the best way to select your craft is to begin with the boat of a friend whose size, stamina, and trip interests match yours. Find out what he or she likes about the kayak. Then try it for yourself, preferably in strong winds when the boat will reach the limits of its ease. Kayaks perform very differently in various conditions.

Also, try to spend at least a day in the kayak. Paddling a kayak is all about repetition over a long period of time, so little things that bother you on a test paddle around the cove may turn into significant drawbacks on a longer stretch.

One good way to try a boat before buying is to attend a sea kayak symposium.

Types of kayaks cover a wide spectrum: single cruising, single special purpose (including surfing), double, racing, and folding. With more than 200 manufacturers selling kayaks, how do you know what boat is best to buy for New England waters? The kayaking world could be divided roughly in half in the way it has developed over the past decade. For most of us, the choice is between what are loosely described as recreational and as touring kayaks—that is, boats for light cruising in protected waters on day trips versus those for ambitious voyages involving long distance on exposed water with changing conditions.

Figure out what kind of paddling you wish to do: short trips in estuaries, protected paddling behind barrier beaches, longer voyages across exposed water to delectable islands, large New England lakes, or small Jet Ski–free ponds? Most of those starting out opt for the recreational kayak, a short, stable, polyethylene boat that is readily available and inexpensive. The boat is best suited for protected waters such as marshes behind barrier beachers, where you don't need to paddle very far to get home. Inevitably, however, the same adventurous spirit that drove you to buy a kayak will drive you to the sea—say, as part of an AMC trip in Knubble Bay in Maine or out to Monomoy Island on Cape Cod. And you may get into trouble.

Why?

The recreational boat is short (average 12 to 14 feet), wide (more than a 24-inch beam), and stable (flat bottomed). It turns easily because it's short and is great for poking around ponds and marshes. The cockpit tends to be roomy, and often a cupholder is molded into the seat between your legs.

The touring kayak is longer (average 17.5 feet) and narrower (average 21- to 22-inch beam) and is designed for trips ranging from an overnight to several months in the wilderness. Its length gives it greater speed and tracking ability, something you appreciate on long trips, so your energy is spent propelling the boat forward and not correcting its course. The kayak can be all but useless in narrow channels such as you find on Cape Cod because you can't maneuver it well around corners. Who needs all that storage space for a picnic?

However, in a place where wind and tide can churn the water into a washing machine in a very short time and short distance—on a trip out to the Porcupines in Bar Harbor, Maine, or at the mouth of the Essex River, Massachusetts, say—you need the touring boat's seaworthiness. Its length, width, and hull shape all are suited to paddling in breaking waves and strong winds. The speed with which you can paddle to safety and your ability to stay on course if worsening conditions arise should not be underestimated. The shorter kayaks get tossed around in the waves, don't move fast, and feature a large cockpit that can get filled with water and make the boat sink, literally.

Within the dichotomy of recreational versus touring, however, the spectrum continues to widen, and choices are many. The key factor to consider is weight. Women in particular should buy a boat that weighs 40 pounds or less. Unfortunately, that immediately puts you into a higher price range. The rotomolded plastic boat tends to weigh more but also cost less because of the manufacturing process—it's easy to churn out the hulls once you've got the mold. In general, polyethylene kayaks can add 20 percent to a kayak's weight.

A fiberglass boat, which weighs less, is built individually with its own laminate, fabric, and resin combination. Hence, you can gear up with an entry-level plastic boat for less than $500 (if the store is having a deal on paddles and PFDs at the same time), whereas you can pay up to $2,000 for a fiberglass model, without the paddle. That surges upward as you select the seductive lightness of fabrics and layups, such as Kevlar and carbon, which weigh up to 25 percent less than regular fiberglass. Bottom line: The less the boat weighs, the more it costs. The upside is, you'll be able to paddle by yourself because you can lift the boat onto your car and then get it down to the beach without trolley wheels. Also, trips to massage therapists or chiropractors are reduced. (Note that car rack manufacturers continue to improve systems for easy kayak loading atop your car.)

The downside of fiberglass is that you can't bang around in rock gardens or scrape the hull across mussel beds. On an expedition, if the boat breaks, you will have to know fiberglass repair (although duct tape does well in a pinch). Plastic boats need no repair, and you can drag them over the rocks guilt-free. I once paddled with a friend who rammed straight into a piling in Provincetown, Massachusetts, in his plastic boat. Solution? Pour boiling-hot water into the bow. Voilà! The bow popped back into shape.

It used to be that fiberglass models had cleaner lines and more design finesse, but that has changed, and some of the polyethylene boats are very performance oriented. One other downside of plastic: in heat, sitting on car racks, they tend to oil-can or warp.

Another consideration in the recreational-versus-touring debate is that many recreational boats are sold without bulkheads. Bulkheads divide the kayaks into different compartments and are glued into place. The space created is critical for the boat to float. If the entire boat fills with water, it can easily sink or wallow to the point of being unmanageable. It is important to have a cockpit that is easy to empty of water. Another solution manufacturers use to provide what they think is sufficient flotation is simply to place a bulkhead fore or aft—but such a boat can do a Cleopatra's needle, with one end sinking while the other dangles on the surface. If you buy a boat without bulkheads (always ask the retailer if the boat has bulkheads!), use flotation bags you can fill with air and place in the bow or stern.

The single cruising models vary according to length and width. The narrower boats tend to have rounded or shallow-arched hulls for speed and stability, upturned bows and sterns to ride easily over waves, and short waterlines; they also sacrifice storage space for speed. Since beam measurements average 22 inches, the boats are relatively tippy and demand a certain repertoire of bracing strokes. While the boats have low initial stability (they feel tippy when you first sit in them), their proponents claim that they have more final stability because the rounded hull enables a kayaker to lean more smoothly into the wave. Their low profile minimizes wind interference. Some have chines—that is, several flat-hull surfaces. That enables the boat to track, to turn, and to stabilize at certain angles for bracing.

The wider boats are typically stable, slower, and have lots of storage space. The wide beam and flat hull make them initially very stable; you feel very much at ease when first stepping in, and they don't tip over easily, but they can be harder to roll back up when they do. The cockpits tend to be roomy, making them more suitable for larger people. They have long waterlines, flat midsections, and high-peaked decks, and on high seas are known to tip and wallow because of their flat hulls.

If you will be practicing a lot, you may want to go with the sporty boat. If you want the kayak for occasional weekend gunkholing or wandering, binoculars and bird book on your lap, a wider, more stable boat is appropriate. In the final analysis, think of your first boat as one of many boats that you will own as you change habits, skills, needs, and desires on the water. Don't worry. The market for second-hand boats is a robust one, because kayaks hold up well over time.

Aside from general hull design, several other details need to be considered. To provide tracking in cross winds, you drop a skeg out of a recessed box in the rear or lower a rudder via cables over the rear stern (several variations exist). The choice of a rudder or skeg is personal preference (cables can break; skegs can get jammed). More experienced kayakers use them very little, if at all, preferring paddle strokes and body lean to adjust and hold course, without the annoyance of moving parts.

Other considerations in choosing a boat include the size and shape of cockpits (finding, for example, a compromise between ease of entry and the volume of water the cockpit will collect in a capsize), the size of hatches (the larger the diameter, the easier to load and unload gear), and the nature of hatches (how watertight).

Other basic elements to think about are seat comfort (greatly refined); material (Kevlar, fiberglass, plastic molds, canvas, nylon, wood); the deck shape, flat or peaked; and design aesthetics overall (how does it look?).

Single-purpose boats include various surfing kayaks and surf-skis of Hawaii and California, and recessed-hull kayaks that you can clamber back onto or snorkel from. Build-at-home wood kayaks draw aficionados who appreciate the beauty and lightness of wood, not to mention the satisfaction of building their own boat (just don't count the hours of work too carefully). Wood builders will even pull off the road to check out the craft of a fellow builder. For travel, inflatable kayaks are a less expensive but seaworthy alternative to folding boats.

Paddler Audrey Sutherland has made those models popular through extended trips in Hawaii and Alaska. Racing kayaks produced by both Olympic medalists and amateur racers (Epic, Futura, West Side Boat Shop) are swift, light, and narrow.

Folding boats, which you can break down into a carrying package and ship anywhere in the world, come in one to three bags. Typically, they have wood or aluminum tubing frames with canvas or nylon deck fabrics, rubber hulls, inflatable sponsons for extra buoyancy, and rudder assembly; they're also very stable and are available in single or double models. The precursor for folding kayaks and the best known is the Klepper, created in 1907 by the German tailor Johann Klepper. These boats are particularly popular in urban areas, where apartment dwellers can store them in their closets, take taxis to launch sites, or carry them to the nearest airport for some exotic travel. The Klepper has made two transatlantic crossings (one successful) with the use of a sailing rig. Other popular folding boats include the French-made Nautiraid, Canadian Feathercraft, U.S. Folbot, and several others.

Finally, double kayaks that feature two people paddling from their own stations in the same kayak serve several purposes. Expedition paddlers in remote places use them as a safety measure—one paddler may become incapacitated yet can still be paddled to safety by a partner. In racing, two strong paddlers in a double can always outpaddle a single kayak. Families like them for carting small children, dogs, or lots of camping gear around. In general, double kayaks are fast, safe, stable, and can store a lot of gear. Often those paddling to far offshore islands on the New England coast, such as Matinicus (20 miles) or Monhegan (10 miles), use them to share the exertion over a four-plus-hour trip on exposed seas. The downsides of the double kayak are the need for a partner when you want to go paddling and the need for compatibility with such a partner. Double kayaks have earned the nickname *divorce boats* for failure in the latter case.

Choosing a Paddle

The aim of a paddle, like the paddle stroke itself, is efficiency. Lifting and holding unnecessary weight is a waste of energy, admonished one major paddle manufacturer. So as with your boat, lighter is best. Many people spend hours agonizing over the choice of a boat, then buy the first paddle they see on the rack. Save room in your checking account for a very good paddle. It will add a lot to your enjoyment.

Choose the paddle that you feel most comfortable with in terms of balance and shaft size and shape. Your first decision will be between wood and fiberglass. Wood has a pleasing aesthetic feel and more flexibility over the length of the shaft, resulting in less tendon fatigue on a long trip. Wood suffers wear from launching off the rocky beaches of Maine, but it can be easily repaired with sanding and varnishing. Fiberglass can be more durable but not as easily repaired if broken. Like kayaks, paddles now are available in superlight space-age materials that make you feel you could fly them like a kite from a kayak. One manufacturer makes a paddle with a wood shaft and carbon blade, combining the best of both materials.

For the ease of a forward stoke with less fatigue and aches, shorter paddles (212 centimeters for a paddler between 5 foot 4 and 5 foot 6) are becoming more popular, as are narrower shafts. While a larger blade gives you power to get out of the surf, on long hauls it is more tiring. Crank shafts move your hand in front of the blade face.

The Greenland narrow-blade paddle is increasingly popular. Almost all of those available commercially are made of wood, but some fiberglass models exist. Once you become accustomed to the stroke's shortened radius and lower hand position, you will keep up with paddlers with wider blades. Paddlers have spawned a repertoire of rolling and bracing skills borrowed from the native Greenlanders and take great delight in practicing, teaching, and gathering to share those maneuvers—all activities part of Club Qajak USA (U.S. Chapter of the Greenland Kayak Association). Some Americans even participate in Greenland's paddling championship, recently opened to foreigners.

A spare paddle, a two-piece, take-apart model that can be conveniently stored, is essential for safety. The pieces are also useful as probes to get you through the sandbar you didn't see in time and, in the case of a four-piece take-apart, can be packed in your suitcase. The most important element in the take-apart paddle is that it has a proper fit—not too tight or loose. Some models have a special locking mechanism to prevent play between the pieces.

Other Equipment

Sprayskirts. The sprayskirt is intended to prevent water from entering the cockpit; to achieve this, it must stay in place when you lean or roll. A snug shock-cord fit on the coaming (the cockpit's raised rim) is essential, yet it should be loose enough to yank off via a grab loop (the

Sprayskirts prevent water from entering the cockpit; the shock-cord fit should be loose enough to yank off via an always-accessible grab loop.

grab loop should always be accessible; some tie plastic Wiffle balls to the loop for an easy-to-find handle) if you need to get out of your boat. More experienced kayakers use a tight sprayskirt, but the novice should opt for a looser one to gain confidence in wet exits. The sprayskirt is available in different sizes to match cockpit size. Neoprene versions are very waterproof (good for when a wave breaks in your lap) and have various waist sizes to ensure a snug fit. You can also get a better fit, tighter or looser, through straps or a Velcro adjustment. Coated nylon models are lighter, cooler, less expensive, and come with shoulder straps to help keep the sprayskirt in place. A combination of neoprene and nylon is also available. A pocket is often added to carry items such as emergency flares, suntan lotion, sunglasses, and bug repellent. In New England, some paddlers opt for two versions, neoprene in the colder season and nylon in hot months.

Drysuits and Wetsuits. Water carries heat away faster than air—cold water can kill you. Drysuits and wetsuits are essential for protection from immersion but are not totally effective: they simply afford you time to get out of cold water as quickly as possible to prevent death from hypothermia.

Drysuits are generally made of pack cloth specially coated for waterproofing. They are sealed around the neck, wrists, and ankles with latex gaskets, and have either a rear or a front zipper. A drysuit will keep you dry and warm in winter paddling conditions, with a pile liner underneath for warmth and perspiration absorption. Common complaints about drysuits include overheating, fragile latex ankle seals, and the disintegration of latex seals from perspiration, suntan lotion, or insect repellent. Most companies will repair or replace seals for a fee.

Wetsuits are generally made of about 0.13-inch-thick neoprene (a lighter weight than those used by skin divers). Generally, they consist of a "farmer john," which covers the legs and torso. You then wear a paddling jacket on top for wind and spray protection. Some argue the farmer john does not provide arm protection. Wetsuits insulate against cold water by trapping a thin layer of water, which is then warmed by the body. Several companies will custom-make wetsuits for a slight surcharge. Drawbacks to wetsuits include overheating and chafing. Recently, paddlers have started using "fuzzy rubber," a wetsuit that combines stretch waterproof material and a "plush" insulation, recommended for wear by itself in all seasons except winter.

Gear for the Head, Toes, and Eyes. Footwear ranges from neoprene booties to a high-tech array of water shoes made of neoprene or nylon mesh with sturdy soles, both recommended for warmth, grip, and protection on rocky shores. Add neoprene socks for extra warmth in winter. While many wear water sandals, they are not recommended because a strap can get caught in a foot pedal, which can lead to entrapment in the cockpit. A visor works to keep away the sun. Broad-brimmed floatable hats or explorer hats with a neck flap provide even more protection to neck and ears—remember, you're exposed to both overhead and water-reflected sun rays. It's best to wear sunglasses with UVB and UVA protection. To save your sunglasses in a capsize, a floatable security strap is the answer.

Gear for Winter Paddling. Sea kayaking in winter can be benign, with few other boats and lovely snow-covered scenery. In crashing surf, it can be deadly. Preparation for frigid water and air tempera-

Winter paddling can be benign, with few other boats and lovely snow-covered scenery.

tures includes a drysuit (see pages 8 and 9), pogies (tubular mitts that attach to the paddle), and neoprene gloves or mitts. Neoprene hats and hoods are advisable, particularly for surfing. Dress warmly but not too heavily so you don't overheat. A complete change of everything you are wearing should be in the kayak. A stainless-steel (not glass) thermos with a hot drink, such as cider or tea, is a good idea. Many of these items also make sense on a blustery summer day, especially in Maine's cold, 50-degree waters.

Gear for Summer Paddling. Several companies make outdoor clothes with built-in sun protection factor (SPF), good for sun protection in summer and while paddling in the Tropics. Waterproof suntan lotion of 30 SPF or higher with UVA and UVB protection (look on the label) is recommended.

Outfitting Your Kayak

Custom-fitting your kayak is increasingly popular for both safety and comfort. Knee and thigh braces cut from closed-cell foam and glued onto the boat can greatly enhance rolling and bracing technique. You can buy seats made of gel, foam, or inflatable material to replace the traditional plastic sea kayak seat or to slip over the seat to increase

Almost all outfitters, kayak shops, and clubs offer instruction.

your comfort, especially over long hauls. Deck lines wear out over time, and they are easy to replace by buying nylon line or bungee cord in bulk and restringing through deck fittings already in place or ones you add, both around the perimeter and on the deck (fore and aft) of the cockpit. For greater visibility at night, you can add self-adhesive reflective tape directly onto your boat or slip reflective covers over your deck line.

Technique

Paddle Strokes

Most paddling skills are easy to learn. Your goal is efficiency of paddle stroke, not muscling your way through the water until your arms fall off or shoulders lock into armor. The paddle should act like a magic wand, held lightly in your hands, swirling away in seawater.

Wedge your knees firmly underneath the deck by adjusting the foot braces. Your paddle will usually be feathered for a right- or left-hand control. A fully feathered paddle has blades at right angles to each other, which helps reduce wind resistance. The control hand holds the paddle and rotates while the other hand stays in one position, letting the paddle turn in it. To find the optimum position, hold

In a high brace, push your paddle facedown into the oncoming wave.

your paddle above your head. Place your hands on the shaft of the paddle where your elbows form right angles.

The basic stroke requires moving your paddle at a slight angle over the front of your boat (as opposed to up and down), punching out with your leading arm almost completely extended, and pushing forward with your other arm as the paddle moves through the water. The upper body and shoulders should rotate with each stroke. Rely on your stomach muscles to propel the stroke (your arms actually do very little of the work). That is the paddle stroke in its simplest form, but experts can—and do—write volumes on the simple movement.

When you reverse the paddle stroke, you go backward. Other maneuvers include the draw and sculling draw strokes, which pull your boat sideways—useful for maneuvering to docks and beaches or over to your paddling companion. The sweep stroke turns your boat. Stabilizing maneuvers include the low brace, where the paddle is held flat on the water with the spoon concave facing up; and the high brace, used primarily in big waves, in which you hold your paddle above your shoulders (but not above your head) and jab the paddle, spoon concave facing down, into the wave as you lean into it.

Depending on the wind, current, and heading, you will "correct" your strokes. If you are paddling without a rudder or retractable skeg, you can lengthen the paddle shaft to one side and provide more paddling power on that side by adjusting your hands. In a following sea, when the waves are coming from behind, your boat will tend to turn in one direction or another. By dragging the back of your paddle to one side, you can keep the boat tracking, prevent it from broaching (turning sideways), and then paddle quickly to catch some surf, which means a free ride.

Almost all outfitters, kayak shops, and clubs offer instruction. Since no umbrella organization in the United States monitors sea kayak instruction, ask the outfitter if the organization follows the guidelines of either the ACA (American Canoe Association) or BCU (British Canoe Union).

Rescue Techniques

One of the biggest controversies among kayakers is whether it is necessary to know how to execute an Eskimo roll, in which you right yourself following a capsize by using your basic paddle stroke on top of the water and lift your body to the surface without coming out of the boat. The basic Eskimo roll has many variations, the most common of which are the Pawlata, Screw, Put-Across, C to C, and Steyr. For a complete discussion of the technique, see Derek Hutchinson's *Eskimo Rolling* or one of the several excellent videos that cover this complicated maneuver: Performance Video's *The Kayak Roll*, University of Sea Kayaking's *Capsize Recoveries & Rescue Procedures*, or Nigel Foster's instructional series (see the bibliography).

You will need rescue skills less if you stay away from breaking waves, avoid headlands, or go out only in fair weather. But the debate notwithstanding, the aim is to get out of cold water as soon as possible, and the Eskimo roll is the most efficient method for doing so. The energy exerted in rolling back up is much less than that of twisting back into the boat and pumping out an unstable water-filled craft that can tip you over again. If you learn the Eskimo roll, it will improve your bracing technique to such an extent that you may not need to know how to roll. Individuals, clubs, and outfitters hold pool sessions throughout the year to practice rolling and deepwater rescue techniques.

Another self-rescue technique is the Paddle Wing, in which a float is tied to the paddle, providing flotation on the paddle to simulate an outrigger. This allows you to crawl back into your boat without it tipping over. The effectiveness of swimming to shore, if you are near the

In an Eskimo roll, following a capsize, right yourself by using your basic paddle stroke on top of the water and lift your body to the surface without coming out of the boat.

shore, alone, and your self-rescue is not effective, should not be underestimated as a rescue technique.

In group rescues, the rescuers raft up to their capsized colleague, collect the stray paddle, pull the boat up on the rescuer's deck to empty the water, and then hold the boat at the coaming while the colleague climbs back in using paddles that have been placed across the back of the cockpit for leverage. The rescuers continue to hold the boat while the water is pumped out. This rescue can also be performed by only one rescuer, but do not hesitate to take advantage of two other paddlers by placing the swamped boat between their boats.

In an Eskimo-bow rescue, the capsized paddler remains upside down and strikes his or her upturned hull to attract attention. Then the capsized paddler holds both hands in a fixed position in the air until the rescuer nudges his or her boat up to the extended hands. The paddler then pulls to the upright position while holding on to the bow of the rescuer's boat. Obviously, this technique requires proximity to the paddling companion.

For more on assisted rescues, consult the videos mentioned on the previous page. Kayakers are continually developing new techniques. For example, there's the Hand of God, in which you reach underwater and pull a capsized paddler back to the surface; and the Reenter and Roll, which involves sliding your legs back into your kayak and using a paddle float to raise yourself back up to the surface.

The point is, you should have your safety covered with a first line of defense for deepwater rescue—that is, an efficient technique such as an Eskimo roll—followed by a series of techniques that definitely work for you as a second line of defense.

Navigation

Equip yourself with NOAA (National Oceanic and Atmospheric Administration) charts or USGS (United States Geological Survey) maps and a compass, both mounted on your deck, and know how to use them. New developments in charting and navigation include the use of the handheld GPS (Global Positioning System) and loading digital charts into a pocket PC that can be read by the GPS while on the water. GPS tells you where you are on the water by giving longitude and latitude points. You can load "waypoints" into the PC/GPS and take advantage of a fully programmed route.

Note that NOAA makes significant changes yearly to its maps, so it's worthwhile to keep up to date, both to know where to paddle and to realize where you can expect the larger sailboats and powerboats to be, more or less.

Sea conditions are variable and, more important, are quickly variable. For example, you may find yourself suddenly enveloped in fog and going in circles. It is important to have the navigational tools and know how to use them. Many clubs and shops offer navigation courses throughout the year.

Most coastal paddlers in New England find a 1:40,000 scale on charts suitable, although a 1:20,000 is nice for greater detail, particularly in harbors. The ratio is inches on sea to inches on land. The larger the second number, the smaller the scale. Some paddlers, however, have settled on a 1:250,000 scale on a USGS map. That allows them to see distant points for correct orientation and navigation and to avoid paddling off one chart and onto another too quickly. You can buy charts and a chart kit—many are now waterproof—in any marine store, or you can order charts, both paper and digital, online (see appendix A).

For tides and currents, consult the annual *Eldridge Tide and Pilot Book*, by Robert E. White (see the bibliography). This book is particularly useful if you are paddling in river estuaries and plan to go into and out of a river's mouth.

Be aware that headlands pose the greatest challenges for sea kayakers, be they rock cliffs in Maine or long, narrow sand spits on the Cape. Here the current runs strongest and closest to shore, and winds can stir up a chop and turbulence way out to sea. Wherever water narrows into a passage, particularly if it has come from a very large body of water, such as Cobscook Bay or Harpswell Island in Maine, be aware of strong currents and possible whirlpools. Lean downstream in the same direction as the current is flowing when crossing a strong eddy line; otherwise the current flow will grab the hull and possibly capsize you.

Don't forget to look over your shoulder to see what the coastline will look like on your return trip. That applies to both remote coastlines dotted by trees and boulders, and suburban shorelines with a jumble of houses. Mark in your memory any outstanding landmarks, such as a lone tree, a rocky outcrop, or a church steeple. One of the best primers on sea kayak navigation is still David Burch's *Fundamentals of Kayak Navigation* (see the bibliography).

Safety Considerations

Always wear your PFD. It is nearly impossible to put on and zip up a PFD in the water while holding on to your boat and paddle. Federal law requires every boater to have a life jacket on the boat. Statistics have proven many times over that PFDs save lives by keeping the person in the water afloat. The wetsuit/drysuit and PFD are probably the two most important safety items a kayaker can use to buffer cold water's risks.

All boats have the right of way except sea kayaks, which are difficult to see and not detected by radar. When crossing busy channels, do so at a right angle, in a group, and quickly. Stay out of boating channels, which run between red and green buoys into harbors. Larger-draft-boat skippers who know what they are doing need to use the deeper passage. By staying out of the channel and in the shallow water, the kayaker avoids not only the worry but also any actual collision. In case of trouble, contact the Coast Guard (see appendix C) on either a VHF radio or cell phone.

Operate within a margin of safety. You may want to keep things exciting by pushing your limits, but be cautious by waiting out conditions for a few hours until the tide changes, or a day or two if the weather deteriorates: you can't afford to be on a deadline to get somewhere if the waters are getting hazardous.

People often capsize because they stop paddling when another person in the group has tipped over. When you stop paddling, the dynamic balance you had established while paddling is disrupted, possibly causing you to upset. Capsizes also often occur late in the afternoon when paddlers are tired, during launching and landing, in overfalls or tide rips, and while playing in surf. Learn to anticipate potential capsizes; they usually occur because of the momentary conditions or the skill level of one or more paddlers in the group.

One of the keys to safety, especially when paddling in groups, is communication. The group should have a paddling plan. Decide where you plan to go, where you plan to gather, where you plan to turn around, and what to do in case of emergencies. These decisions are much easier to make beforehand than they are on the water during a crisis. It's a good idea to have a meeting before the trip to discuss such matters. File a float plan (see appendix D) with a responsible, calm friend or relative back home.

Designate one person in your group to be leader, and another to be sweeper (the last boat); frequently switch positions to maintain morale. Paddle to accommodate the ability of the weakest or slowest paddler. Establish group horn or whistle signals—say, one for attention, two to raft up. Also set up paddle signals in the event of group separation—a common occurrence when the weather turns bad or conditions intensify.

Be aware of how well you know the person or people with whom you are paddling. Do they know how to do self- or group rescues? How often do they go kayaking? Is this their first trip by kayak? How will they react if the wind and waves kick up? Clubs have refined the requirements for trips over the past decade, making it easier to judge the skill level of yourself and/or enthusiastic companions.

Make sure your boat has securely fixed flotation/bulkheads in both bow and stern. Swamped boats usually sink at only one end. Wear a whistle; if you need help, it's easier to blow a whistle than to yell.

Other safety equipment includes a spare paddle in case yours breaks or floats away. Carry a compass and/or GPS, marine charts in a waterproof chart case on the deck, and a weather radio. Obtain a weather check before any long crossings, and check the Beaufort wind scale (see appendix E).

Additional items include a hand pump (if a foot or hand pump is not built into your boat), sponge, loud horn, at least three emergency marine flares (smoke flares for day use), first-aid kit, waterproof flashlight, strobe light, towrope, waterproof bags, and complete set of spare clothes. Rig your kayak with nonstretch lines around the perimeter so you can grab easily it in a capsize. Reflective tape on the boat allows you to be seen easily at night. By law, you must have a white light on your boat visible from 200 feet when paddling between sunset and sunrise. Some paddle with a bike flag mounted on the rear deck for increased visibility, but nowhere is that mandated by law.

Coast Guard regulations require the wearing or possession of a PFD and use of a light at night. For more information on regulations for PFDs, visual distress signals, sound signals, or navigation lights, go to www.uscgboating.org.

You may feel safe just because you are in a group; however, that is false security. The most important thing to remember is that you are solely responsible for your own safety. You need to be self-sufficient, know your limits, have your own gear, and, most of all, exercise sound judgment. Don't go out if you are worried about the weather; be aware of bail-out points; and go with an experienced group.

Be aware that many grassy areas harbor the Lyme tick, a tiny insect that carries a virus that can cause debilitating arthritis and even heart disease. Always wear boots or pants tucked into shoes when walking in the grass. Check for small dark spots on your skin. Should you develop a circular rash or flulike symptoms, seek medical attention immediately. In its early stages, Lyme disease is curable by a cycle of prescription medicine.

For a list of gear suggested for day trips and overnights, see appendix B.

Hypothermia

Hypothermia can develop rapidly if an individual is not properly dressed for immersion. Cold water removes heat from the body 25 times faster than cold air. Approximately 50 percent of that heat loss occurs through the head. Physical activity, such as swimming, increases heat loss and decreases survival time.

Survival curves show that an adult dressed in average clothing and wearing a personal flotation device (PFD) may remain concious for an hour at a water temperature of 40 degrees Fahrenheit and for perhaps two to three hours at 50 degrees Fahrenheit. Without a PFD, the effects of coldwater immersion—cold shock symptoms such as gasping, hyperventilation, and limb paralysis—are immedate and can result in drowning long before hypothermia sets in.

Even with a wetsuit/drysuit on, the hands rapidly become useless in water in the low 40s. Protective gloves and a hood are important. Shivering occurs as body temperature drops from 97 degrees Fahrenheit down to approximately 90. Muscle rigidity and loss of manual dexterity—physical helplessness—occurs at about 93 degrees Fahrenheit. Mental capacity also deteriorates at this point. Loss of consciousness occurs when the body's core temperature reaches approximately 86 degrees Fahrenheit.

Dressing for the possibility of immersion can buy you time to work out a rescue in the event of an accident. Warm weather does not cancel the danger of cold water. Hence, wearing lighter clothing on warm days may increase risk.

Once in the water, try to get back in or on your boat immediately. Do not leave the boat. If you are not wearing thermal protection and can't get out of the water, stay as still as possible. Fold your arms, cross your legs, and float quietly on the buoyancy of your PFD until help arrives (this is known as the Heat Escape Lessening Posture or HELP). If two or more people are in the water, put your arms around one another. Stay still and close together (huddle posture).

In cases of severe hypothermia, shivering may have stopped and the victim may resist help or be semiconscious or unconscious. The victim must be kept prone and immobile on his or her back and handled gently. Cover torso, thighs, head, and neck with dry covers to stop further heat loss. Arms and legs must not be stimulated in any manner, as cold blood in extremities that suddenly returns to the core may induce cardiac arrest. Seek medical attention immediately.

To plan ahead, check the weather forecast for the day. Wear clothing that permits safe coldwater immersion and a PFD. This is the only way to combat the risk posed by cold water. Wear a wetsuit or drysuit with warm layers underneath. Carry dry clothing in a waterproof bag. Tell someone where you are going and when you will return, and inform them of your return. While on the water, watch the boats around you: you are all depending on one another for prompt rescue in case of an accident. Learn more about coldwater paddling at www.enter.net, where you can find the brochure "Off-Season Boating, Cold Shock, & Hypothermia," by Chuck Sutherland, the source for this information about hypothermia.

Camping

The great advantage of sea kayak camping over backpacking is that you can carry lots of gear and not have to worry about weight. Heavy loading can actually enhance a kayak's stability. Luxury items such as sun showers, lanterns, canned or fresh food, nature books, camp stools, or two-burner stoves are all admissible. Also, you can bring plenty of fresh water. Unless you have watertight hatches, you will need waterproof bags, which are available in various sizes.

Always take your boat above the high-tide mark and tie it in place so it won't blow or drift away at night. Put on a cockpit cover to keep out sand fleas and other unwanted creatures—and also to prevent an unnecessary search and rescue should your kayak float away.

Increasingly, as more of us take to the wilderness for breaks from busy lives, our natural places are being trampled. Please read the Leave No Trace guidelines provided in this book (see pages 25 to 28).

Paddling with Kids

Sea kayaking is a great way to share the marine environment as a family. In a two-parent family, the best way to start is to put the child in the middle hatch of a double kayak. If you're paddling with your child by yourself in a single kayak, sit the small child in your lap—although be aware you can get tired holding your arms up above the child's head. You can place the child in the rear hatch with lots of padding to sit on. That strategy works best for quiet children. Rambunctious toddlers are best placed in the middle hatch of a double. When they reach 30 to 35 pounds, they make the boat unsteady when riding in the rear hatch.

If you're placing a child in the front paddling station, it's best to have a compact lightweight double that lets you to do most of the paddling on your own.

My husband and I have tried different arrangements as our two children have grown. We placed our six-month-old daughter in the middle hatch of our seaworthy and fast double. She slept most of the time but also spent time throwing things out of the boat. You need to be prepared to retrieve overboard items (true with any arrangement). We removed the bulkhead between the middle hatch and the rear cockpit to be able to grab her if seas got too rough (we've never actually

After a trip, be sure to rinse off all your gear in fresh water.

had to use this safety measure). When my son came along, Lilly went into the front cockpit and basically waved her paddle around in the air; Anton went into the middle hatch; Dad huffed and puffed the whole contraption around Penobscot Bay. I paddled a single as the support boat, picking up overboard items such as bottles and hats, adjusting straps, providing snacks, and giving general encouragement.

The next step came when Lilly was old enough to paddle her own boat, at about the age of seven. Determining when the child is old enough to paddle his or her own boat is the biggest decision you will make in family paddling.

Our current arrangement is that Mom and Dad paddle the fast, stable double, so we can get to places directly if need be; Anton, age six, sits in the middle hatch; and Lilly, age ten, paddles her own boat but still gets towed a lot. A towrope is probably the single most important item you can own in family paddling. The good news is that it's easier to tow than to paddle a child's weight. Anton has graduated to Lilly's old kayak—a Wilderness System Poquito (designed by paddling dad Andy Singer)—and Lilly has graduated to a 13-foot Pygmy Osprey, which her father made for her (more on boats on the next page). The towrope allows you to cover greater distances than you could if the child were paddling the whole way on his or her own. In terms of safety, when towing in rough seas, have the child keep a paddle on the water surface for balance and readiness to brace.

Although children can love kayaking, it is not necessarily their first choice as an activity. To mitigate the whine factor, a good plan for very young children is to paddle out to a place for an hour, picnic and beachcomb, then paddle back. If you're on a longer expedition, plan on stops every hour. Don't overcommit yourself in terms of time and distance. Get out on the beach to hunt for shells and crabs and to have a picnic. Swims, hikes, and nature exploration are as big a part of the trip as the actual paddling. A great resource book for onshore exploration is the AMC's *Seashells in My Pocket*. For the sake of safety and visual interest, paddle close to shore.

Don't ever count on actually getting someplace. Plan a slow-moving expedition. Keep it short to account for children's shorter attention spans and safety factors.

On the water, the trip's success in keeping a child entertained is inversely proportional to the amount of wildlife you see. Seals and dolphins are the best entertainment, but loons, guillemots, and ospreys work; seagulls will do in a pinch. Snacks help as a reward system. ("If you paddle five more minutes, you can have five M&Ms.") Singing songs passes the time. Best of all is bringing a friend of the child's ability along. That alone is the greatest motivator and the most fun for the child. Paddling with another family makes a big difference in terms of your children's stamina and enthusiasm for the trip.

As with adults, dress kids for coldwater immersion. Several manufacturers make children's wetsuits. Kokatat makes a kid's drysuit (note that children need help to get a drysuit on correctly). Always wear a PFD. Many manufacturers make children's PFDs. For the smaller children, it is best to have a collar that helps keep the head out of the water—it also has a handy grab loop. Make sure all straps are secure. Give the kids their own whistle and tell them to use it only in an emergency, not for play! In spring and fall, children should wear pogies to keep their hands warm (kids don't do well with cold, wet hands).

Other gear includes thermal underwear, surf shoes or water sandals (surf shoes are better protection, and the child doesn't have to deal with annoyance of pebbles getting stuck underfoot). Check for blisters and bandage quickly before they get too raw, or switch to another shoe right away. Bring sunglasses with a floating security strap, along with a wide-brimmed hat attached to the child in some way (it will blow away). Use waterproof sunscreen and apply one hour before going out. Keep sunscreen off the forehead to avoid stinging eyes. The child should have his or her own water bottle and be reminded to drink constantly (plan pee stops accordingly). Binoculars are helpful for entertainment (again, secure to the child or boat). Pack lots of snacks and drinks—don't let the child throw trash or juice boxes into the water or leave them on the island. Onshore, you might provide a disposable camera so the child can take his or her own nature shots.

Into a small dry bag (separate from yours) goes hypothermia treatment clothing—a fleece top and bottom, wool hat, socks, and rain gear to protect against spray if need be (and in case of rain).

As with adults, watch for onshore hazards. Kids should always wear shoes to avoid cutting their feet on shells, sharp rocks, and barnacles exposed at low tide. The most useful tool in your first-aid kit is bandages, both for protection and as a placebo. Also, carefully monitor any climbing on steep rocks or cliffs. Tie up the sprayskirt (these tend to be oversized) so the children don't trip on it. Don't sit on PFDs; it wears down the flotation.

Children should also practice low-impact techniques, stay on paths, and not climb on banks that might be prone to erosion. They should respect wildlife.

For entertainment, try flying a kite from your kayak or towing a toy boat; onshore, use a pail or plastic bag for collecting items. Prepare shelves at home for growing rock and shell collections.

How to choose a boat for your child? Be sure to choose a child's boat and not a small-sized adult boat, which is too heavy, wide, and deep. The child's kayak is both short and narrow, with a beam of 22 inches or less. Perception's Umiak, Wilderness Systems' Tchaika or Piccolo, and EPI Englehart Products' Epibrat are all good options. Wood boat manufacturers like Pygmy and Chesapeake Light Craft provide kits for children's kayaks. Wood is light, and the design is suited for small bodies. A sit-on-top such as those Ocean Kayak makes is definitely a good way to get children started; if they tip over, they just climb back on. Smaller-sized folding kayaks work as well as inflatables.

A well-designed children's paddle makes a huge difference in the child's ability to propel the boat and in enjoyment. Werner, Swift, Sawyer, and L. L. Bean all make children's paddles. Some parents make their children small Greenland paddles, which work well. Catch abrasion early to avoid blisters.

Before heading out on the ocean, practice wet exits and rescues in a warm pond or lake. Make sure the child can pop off the sprayskirt and do a wet exit. Play games to make rescue practice fun. Swimming lessons are useful for everyone's comfort level in the water, but in a rescue situation, getting out of the cold water fast is far more important than knowing how to swim. Both the adult and the child should always wear a PFD—this is a point worth repeating. It has been proven over and over that PFDs save lives.

Children are just natural paddlers, so you don't have to explain too much about technique. Just make sure hands are equidistant on the paddle (to keep them paddling in a straight line) and that the spoon blades are right side up. Make sure foot pegs are properly adjusted. In deep kayaks, provide a cushion to sit on so the child doesn't have to lift and dip the paddle—too tiring. The wilder the seas, the more many children seem enjoy the experience, which is very helpful for anxious parents.

If you are not an experienced paddler yourself but want to paddle with your child, book a family trip with an outfitter or nature organization. The outfitter does all the work, and you can reserve your energy for paddling and exploring tidal pools—especially on camping expeditions. Or sign your child up for a kayak camp; most start at age ten. If you're an experienced paddler and want to make some distance or be challenged, leave your child at home.

What a thrill it is for a child to be kayak camping! Get the children involved in camp chores such as gathering wood or water. Never leave children alone around cookstoves or open fires. Girls with long hair should keep it tied back. Don't forget a book, sketch pad, teddy bear, camp slippers, and the child's own flashlight. Bring a hammock and marshmallows. Tell ghost stories.

Involve the children in the trip planning and destination. Children love maps; they can measure trip distance. They also like knots.

Ultimately in family paddling, it's best not to try to get anywhere. Just experience the sea and sights, and make enjoyment the primary goal.

Leave No Trace

Leave No Trace, Inc., is a nonprofit organization dedicated to establishing a nationwide code of outdoor ethics by which to shape a sustainable future for natural lands. With recreational use soaring, the LNT ethic has never been so needed. There are seven important

LNT principles to help ensure that seagoers minimize their impact on fragile ecosystems. In the following sections, LNT principles have been adapted to apply to the coastal environment.

Plan Ahead and Prepare

Kayaking the coastline in a responsible way requires forethought and planning on the part of each individual.

- Every island and piece of shoreside property is owned by someone; you must have the owner's permission to land. State lands are generally open to the public. See appendix A for information about landowners and access.
- Consider shoreside campgrounds and/or B&Bs as alternatives to island camping.
- Many areas have regulations or recommended guidelines that limit camping, the use of fire, and other recreational activities.
- To help reduce your impact, keep your group size to six people or fewer.
- To reduce potential litter at the source, remove excess food packaging before you leave home.

Travel and Camp on Durable Surfaces

Shoreside soils are often shallow, easily eroded, and quickly compacted. Once an inch of soil layer is lost, it can take centuries to replace. Vegetation is intrinsic to healthy soil, holding it in place and preventing erosion.

- Onshore, travel on sand, stone, resilient grassy areas, and established trails.
- Avoid scrambling over dirt banks or shrubby ledges; these are easily eroded and rarely recover. Please do not walk in wet, boggy areas, and avoid trampling mosses and lichens.
- Please do not cut or clear vegetation, trees, or limbs—dead or alive—for any purpose.
- Use existing campsites; do not expand established sites or clear new sites. If the campsites are already in use, squeeze into an existing site or bivouac on smooth granite, sand, or gravel.
- Limit your stay to two nights. The longer you stay, the more impact you create.
- When leaving, restore your campsite to its natural state.

Dispose of Waste Properly

Exposed waste is unhealthy for humans and wildlife. Digging cat holes to bury waste is not appropriate in seacoast areas because the soils are so often shallow and easily eroded. It is illegal to discharge human waste into U.S. waters, including the intertidal zone.

Solid human waste should thus be carried off and disposed of in an appropriate receptacle on the mainland (toilet, RV campground waste facility, sewage treatment plant, or marine pump-out station). Toilet paper should also be packed out. Recommended carry-off methods include:

- Portable toilet or boat holding tank.
- The Boombox, a compact, washable, reusable toilet system. Contact GTS Inc. at 316-682-4037.
- Bucket with tight-fitting lid (seawater, sand, or lime minimize odor).
- Small Tupperware quarter-filled with seawater or other inert material.
- Double plastic bag or milk carton with kitty litter.

  As for trash and garbage:

- Carry out all trash and garbage—both your own and any you find—and dispose of properly.
- Food scraps should be picked up and packed out. Reducing food waste helps prevent animals from becoming attracted to humans as a food source.

Leave What You Find

People come to seaside wildlands to enjoy them in their natural state. Allow others a sense of discovery by leaving rocks, plants, and other objects of interest as you find them.

- Minimize campsite alterations. Consider the idea that good campsites are found and not made. Leave the area as natural as (or even more so than) you found it.
- Avoid damaging trees and plants. To prevent damage to greenery, use freestanding tents when possible. A coastal visitor picking flowers, leaves, edible berries, or plants may seem harmless, but the cumulative effect of many visitors doing so becomes quite damaging.

- Don't dig up someone's hidden past. Ancient stone walls, cellar holes, shell heaps, and other markers of past inhabitants can provide important archaeological information when excavated properly.

Minimize Campfire Impacts — Kindle No Fires

Seaside campfires have a high risk of spreading due to changeable winds, interconnected root systems, organic soils, and the lack of services. The wisest policy is to kindle no open fires at any time. If you must have a fire, use a camp stove below the high-tide line for cooking. The following techniques will ensure that you leave no trace:

- Use established fire rings. If no fire rings are present, build your fire on sand or use a fire pan below the high-tide line. Fires on granite leave permanent scars.
- Make your fires small and safe.
- Use only driftwood from below the high-tide line.
- Use extreme caution! Have a bucket of water nearby at all times.
- All fires should be dead out and cleaned up before you leave camp.

  In case of emergency, call toll-free 888-900-FIRE.

Respect Wildlife

We are all visitors to the seacoast, many of whose inhabitants are wild—deer, seabirds, ospreys, and seals. If we think of ourselves as guests when using wildlands, we can't go too far wrong.

- Leave all pets at home.
- Please avoid seabird nesting sites from early April to mid-August. If your presence is causing birds to leave their nests, you are too close.
- Avoid areas with eagles entirely.
- Seals bear their young between mid-May and mid-June. Disturbance can cause seals to flee, leaving pups exposed and vulnerable. Stay far enough away from the ledges so that the seals do not flee into the water.

Be Considerate of Others

When you paddle the New England coast, you are among thousands of other boaters.

- If there are other people in an area, respect their privacy. Look for a landing site some distance away, or find another site.
- Help preserve the wilderness look of the shoreline by keeping your visual impact low. Pull small boats out of sight on durable surfaces and pitch tents inconspicuously in established campsites.

For more information about Leave No Trace, see appendix F, or contact LNT, Inc., P.O. Box 997, Boulder, CO 80306; 800-332-4100; www.lnt.org.

Maine

Down East Paddling

CRUISING SAILORS HAVE LONG recognized the appeal of Maine's geography and expanses of almost deserted waters even during tourist season. For the sea kayaker, the real appeal lies in the inner coastal zone, where only a few inches of water off granite-ringed islands allow the paddler to pick a path between foundered boulders to reach protected coves and harbors. The sea kayaker's vantage point allows plucking of mussels off a low-tide shelf, watching a seal's nose sink out of sight, or pulling up to the smoothest of warm ledges for a picnic.

The more you paddle in Maine, the more distinctive each area becomes. Traveling in and out of harbors and paddling along the more populated shores, you can observe the coastal economy, past and present, of lobster and fishing industries, quarrying, shipping, ship-building, tourism, summer retreats, harbor defenses, and marinas.

Maine sea kayakers have the privilege of public access to more than 1,500 state-owned, mostly uninhabited islands, although in reality kayakers use no more than 100 of those islands. They make for both short and long hopping distances between landfalls up the coast. Described below are nineteen trips along the Maine coast that take advantage of some of those public islands. Destinations range from deserted outposts in remote Cobscook Bay to unpopulated oases in the midst of busy waters surrounding Portland.

Physiography

Although the straight-line distance of Maine's coast is 250 miles, it twists and turns into inlets, harbors, bays, and coves for 3,478 miles. Add the permutations of nearly 3,000 islands lying just offshore and you have an almost endless number of paddling trips.

The Maine coast is divided by large bays, all with good sea kayaking routes. Some of the major bays include the busy Casco Bay off Portland, inland Knubble Bay, quiet lobster-buoy–studded Muscongus Bay, 20-mile–wide Penobscot Bay, island-dotted Merchant Row off Deer Isle, Blue Hill Bay, and Frenchman Bay. Moving farther east, the tides and fog become factors in Pleasant, Englishman, and Cobscook Bays. Paddling in any one of these areas, you can usually dodge into a cove out of the wind or make for an island without too long a crossing. Traveling from one bay to another usually involves passing a headland or cape—both well known for turbulent water—such as Small, Pemaquid, or Schoodic Points, or Mosquito Head.

Geological Setting

The 3,000-odd Maine islands are topographic high points of a previous mountain range formed 500 million years ago by a continental collision, worn down by erosion, then scoured and scraped by Pleistocene glaciers. Only 170 of these islands are inhabited, creating a true coastal wilderness.

The geologic and physiographic settings have contributed to the distinct character of each Maine island. Some have long histories of year-round communities, such as those at Vinalhaven, Monhegan, Matinicus, and Swans. Many islands, such as Matinicus Rock and Eastern Egg Rock, are unique seabird nesting sites. Some islands, such as Crotched Island in Stonington Harbor, are only a few minutes' paddle from shore. Others, such as Monhegan, 10 miles offshore, take hours to reach.

Helpful Guides to Maine's Islands

The main source for information on paddling Maine's islands is the Maine Island Trail Association (MITA), with offices in Portland and Rockland. MITA manages recreational use of about a hundred private and public islands along more than 300 miles of the Maine coast, from Portland to Machias. Each year MITA publishes the *Stewardship Handbook and Guidebook* (the sixteenth edition as of this writing). The association's goal is to help provide an exceptional recreational experience through careful and vigilant stewardship, with the emphasis increasingly on the latter as MITA tries to conserve the islands' fragile nature against increasing assault from island lovers.

Maine's Bureau of Parks and Lands' brochure "Your Islands and Parks on the Coast" describes 64 of the 300 state-owned islands that BPL manages. To request a copy, contact the Maine Bureau of Public Lands, 22 State House Station, Augusta, ME 04333-0022; 207-287-3821. Many state-owned islands have the standard blue BPL sign posted on trees, and allow camping.

Four new guidebooks on paddling in Maine have come out since the first publication of this book. See "Guides" in the bibliography at the back of this volume.

The Appalachian Mountain Club owns Knubble Bay Camp in Georgetown, which serves as a launch for the 60-acre Beal Island, a mile away in Knubble Bay. Both are used by sea kayakers and tidewater canoeists along the Midcoast. The AMC publishes a tidewater map for the area.

Many islands are owned by nonprofit agencies. The Maine Chapter of The Nature Conservancy is the largest nonprofit owner and manager of islands on the coast. The Nature Conservancy allows day use on its islands. Many of them are located in the Jonesport and Vinalhaven area, and many are seabird nesting islands, off-limits to visitors from March 15 through August 15. The Nature Conservancy provides a complete list and regulations for all its islands.

The Maine Coast Heritage Trust protects 325 islands along the coast, including the recently acquired Jordan's Delight in Milbridge. Maine Audubon, National Audubon, and the Department of Inland Fisheries and Wildlife own many islands critical to breeding and migrating of seabirds and ducks, off-limits to visitors until August 15. Other island owners include Acadia National Park, U.S. Fish and Wildlife, the Island Institute, and ninety local land trusts in the state. Varying environmental philosophies rule island use; consult the appropriate organizations before you visit.

Camping Considerations

In the decade since I first wrote this book, camping is no longer the Robinson Crusoe–inspired experience it once was. So popular has sea kayak camping become that the very existence of many fragile islands is threatened by overuse. Where once pine needles or meadows acted as tentsites, tent platforms are increasingly in use, MITA has set voluntary camping capacities on nearly forty state-owned islands, and three popular islands in Casco Bay—Jewell, Little Chebeague, and Crow—have an island caretaker who helps monitor low-impact camping from Memorial Day through Labor Day. It is important to check on these island capacities before visiting the islands, and to be prepared to move on if they have been reached.

I hesitate even to sing the praises, as I once did, of visiting a public island, open to all, with a gravel beach or smooth granite shelves to land on, grassy tentsites on the edge of spruce forest, trails, and views of the ocean and other islands when you emerge from the trees. Cooking on a gravel beach, enjoying the sunset, or exploring the island is now more a privilege than a right. All those activities come with the expensive price of potential environmental damage, and low-impact camping is a requirement for any visitor (see "Leave No Trace" on pages 25 to 28). Fires on islands are things of the past; fire trucks don't make it to the islands, and entire ecosystems can burn down.

Access, Launching, and Parking

Maine is the most accommodating New England coastal state in terms of public access to the water. All of Maine's coastal towns have public landings available, with few seasonal restrictions, fees, or sticker requirements for the nonresident. Some towns, however—such as Falmouth Foreside or Pretty Marsh on Mount Desert—are restricting parking at their launch sites to town residents. Some of the more popular areas like Stonington rely on ferry or school parking lots. Marinas, boatyards, saltwater campgrounds, and entrepreneurs with a spare field are taking up the slack with launching facilities and safe parking lots, for a fee. As has always been true, parking at southern coastal beaches is open only to town residents.

Out of courtesy, you should park your vehicle as far from the ramp as possible to allow space for commercial fishermen and local residents. If you will be spending a few days on the water, it is a good idea to inform the local police or town officials so that they will know why the car is there.

The Maine Bureau of Parks and Lands and Maine Department of Inland Fisheries and Wildlife provide access to lakes, ponds, rivers, and the coast at almost 400 locations. Sites may have gravel or hard-surfaced ramps and may include boarding floats, restrooms, and picnic tables. A few sites have canoe or carry-in access only. Some ramps on tidal waters may be usable only at high tides and are designated "part-tide" facilities. A brochure listing all the boat launches is available by calling 207-287-4952; you can view an online version at www.state.me.us/doc/parks/programs/boating.

You can also consult the DeLorme Publishing Company's *Maine Atlas and Gazetteer*, which identifies launch sites through a red boat symbol (handheld sites are simply outlined in red). The maps are updated regularly, but if you have an older edition, note that some launch sites may no longer be available. Also, note that even though a spot may be a public launch, community aversion to traffic might keep it fairly inaccessible.

Coastal areas in Maine are still covered by a colonial law that allows fishing, fowling, and launching or landing of boats for everyone between the high- and low-water marks. In 1986, that law was challenged by private property owners in the Maine Supreme Court to determine whether the right of access to the intertidal portion of Moody Beach in Wells, Maine, included recreational activities. The high-court ruling determined that people using the area in Wells must prove the use of fishing, fowling, or navigation; beach recreation was not considered a legitimate use for access, given changes in public activities since colonial days. Although the case was applied to one specific beach, the law could eventually have ramifications for all Maine coastal areas in the future.

The tradition in Maine coastal areas and on islands has been a friendly, hospitable one allowing strangers the use of islands. However, as expensive real estate investment (retirees are building bigger waterside mansions than ever before) and disregard for others' property increases, that age-old hospitality is becoming strained. Thus, you should not picnic or camp on private islands unless you have secured permission from the owner in advance; don't assume that because there is no obvious dwelling, the island is available for your use.

An increasingly attractive alternative, to spare the fragile islands from yet more kayakers' booties and to cater to aging baby boomers' increasing need for creature comfort, is to stay onshore in a comfortable B&B or inn. Lee Bumsted's *Hot Showers! Maine Coast Lodgings for Kayakers and Sailors* will help you find a spot on the water that's friendly to kayakers, with a launch spot and hot running water.

Trip Planning

Trips can range from a day to a month, depending on your time restrictions, ability, sea conditions, and route length. You can start and end the trip at the same launch spot by making a loop, so you will not have to paddle the same waters twice. Bring an old bicycle in your car so you can ride from the parking area to the launch site after leaving your boat. (Be creative in hiding the bicycle while you are off paddling.)

The first decision to be made is whether to stay close to shore, go island to island, or go to an offshore island. Next, identify state-owned islands, public campgrounds, or coastal inns and B&Bs. Always set reasonable goals—no more than 8 miles per day—with a backup plan for alternate sites should bad weather deter you. If fog sets in, there is absolutely no reason to pack up and go. Be sure to bring a good book to read, or a journal or sketchbook. If you need to land on a private island, ask for the owner's permission. On an extended trip (a week or more), it is a good idea to plan a few layover days to rest, enjoy the beach, and hike. Although clamming, fishing, and foraging can greatly enhance your dinner menu, be sure to bring adequate food and lots of fresh water—there is no drinkable water on the islands.

If you'll be traveling to an offshore island by ferry, inquire about ferry requirements for taking kayaks, and be sure to make ferry reservations well in advance, particularly on holiday weekends and in July and August. Some ferries don't allow hand-carried kayaks.

Weather Considerations

The best time for kayak travel is early morning or late evening. Daily onshore breezes generated by the sun begin in the late morning and are at their strongest between 1:00 and 4:00 P.M., so be prepared for choppy conditions in longer crossings or plan to make longer crossings very early in the morning.

The prevailing winds in summer are the southwesterlies, caused by the clockwise rotation of high-pressure centers sitting out in the western Atlantic. The counterclockwise-rotating low-pressure systems that cause coastal storms are usually trailed by a high-pressure air mass with winds from the northwest, which brings on clearing and colder air. That cold front is responsible for those crystal-clear blue skies in summer. Most notably, the northwest wind is the strongest; it's also an offshore wind, with very high risks for kayakers in terms of being blown offshore. The summer easterlies are rarely strong, with the exception of northeasterlies. Whether storm winds blow from the southeast, east, or northeast depends on the exact track taken by the storm relative to Portland, Maine (a convenient marking point), according to oceanographer Ken Fink. For example, if storm winds blow east of Portland, a good portion of those winds will be out to sea.

Rapid changes in the weather are typical of coastal Maine; a bright blue August sky may swiftly become enshrouded in heavy fog. You may find yourself in cloudy conditions with visibility of a mile or so, plan a trip out to an island, then change direction fifteen minutes out and barely be able to see from one side of a cove to the other—a distance of less than 0.3 mile. You may find yourself hugging the shore for dear life. Use and knowledge of a map and compass are critical here. Remember this simple rule in the fog: The mainland is always to the west. Set your compass accordingly. As you travel farther Down East, the tidal range will become more important in your travel plans. To avoid a long trek through the muck or a steep ledge to negotiate, you will have to avoid launching or landing at low tide.

One of the Atlantic puffin's only native breeding sites in the United States is at Matinicus Rock, 18 miles out to sea.

Coastal Wildlife

The relatively unpopulated coast is a great place for spotting birds and mammals. One of the rarest birds in Maine's coastal waters is the Atlantic puffin (although it is quite common in Canada). One of this alcid's only native breeding grounds in the United States is on Matinicus Rock, 18 miles from the mainland at Sprucehead. Attempts to restore the puffin to its breeding ground in the United States have been remarkably successful over the past twenty years. Through the Puffin Project, Steve Kress of the National Audubon Society and Cornell University's Ornithological Lab have successfully reestablished a puffin colony on Eastern Egg Rock in Muscongus Bay (four pairs in 1981; fifty-two pairs in 2002), using such techniques as bird recordings and puffin decoys to entice returning former fledglings. He attempted a similar colonization program on Seal Island, another historic breeding ground, 6 miles to the east of Matinicus Rock; the colony has succeeded—179 pairs in 2002. Meanwhile, Matinicus Rock had more than 200 pairs in 2002. The projects used hatchlings from Newfoundland's Bird Island, where about 160,000 pairs nest. Puffins now also nest on Petit

Manan (twenty pairs). The project is based in Ithaca, New York, and the Todd Wildlife Sanctuary in Midcoast Maine. For more information, contact Project Puffin, 159 Sapsucker Woods Road, Ithaca, NY 14850; 607-257-7308; puffin@audubon.org; www.audubon.org/bird/puffin.

Roseate, arctic, and common tern colonies live on several bald Maine islands, usually with gulls. (One way to distinguish among terns is the bill color: roseate is all black, arctic is all red, and common is red tipped by black.) Common terns are by far the most numerous. The roseate is a federally endangered species. In recent years, the National Audubon Society's Seabird Restoration Program has developed Eastern Egg Rock into the largest common, arctic, and roseate tern colony in Maine. Similar restoration techniques have also helped to protect the terns at Matinicus Rock and to establish new tern colonies at Seal Island, Stratton Island (Saco Bay), Jenny Island (Casco Bay), and Pond Island (Kennebec River). The program has also reestablished a common tern colony (eleven pairs nesting in 2002) on Outer Green Island in Casco Bay—an amazing feat considering that the common tern last nested there in 1914.

Restoration of seabird colonies takes years, even decades, of persistent work. Please respect that effort and stay off nesting islands when the conservation organizations ask you to—usually from spring through the end of July or mid-August.

Leach's storm petrels nest on about a dozen barren outer islands. Colonial seabirds like eiders occupy entire islands such as the White Islands east of Inner Heron Island off South Bristol. Bald eagles breed in Cobscook Bay and are steadily moving farther south, with 200 nesting pairs identified throughout the state in 2002. The osprey has made an explosive comeback along the coast since the elimination of DDT; more than 2,000 pairs now nest in Maine, both inland and along the coast. The more common double-crested cormorants, eiders, and black guillemots occupy coves and inlets of the jagged coastline and are also the primary colonial nesters on coastal islands. Common loons nest on freshwater lakes, then move to coastal waters in late summer, where they winter. The least terns and piping plovers nest on specific beaches—Seawall, Popham, and Reid. Those nesting places are roped off and flagged by signs during breeding season, which starts at the end of March and should be respected.

Harbor seals and harbor porpoises are plentiful in summer, and you may spot the less common, larger gray seal (distinguished by its horse-shaped head) farther north or on far offshore ledges. Avoid disturbing seals and their young during pupping season. Typically, seals give birth to one pup in the upper reaches of quiet bays from the middle of April to the middle of June. Although seals can swim after they're born, the trauma comes when the approach of kayakers elicits an alarm response, causing seals to rapidly enter the water. The 150-plus-pound mother seals can trample and suffocate the pups in their frantic attempts to reach the safety of water when startled off haul-out ledges. The pups are usually weaned within a month, but during that time they remain vulnerable to separation from the mother. Continued disturbance of mother-pup pairs could lead to abandonment and subsequent mortality of the pup, according to the Northeast Region Stranding Network.

If your presence causes any of the following reactions, you are too close: increased vocalizations by seals; movement back into the water (a single animal or the herd); all eyes on you (a single animal or several in the herd); disturbance from normal resting position (lifting their heads to watch you). One of the best ways to protect coastal wildlife is to keep your distance and satisfy your curiosity by using binoculars.

Report sick or injured seals to the appropriate agency. From Camden north, call the College of the Atlantic at 207-288-5644. From Rockland south, call the Marine Animal Lifeline's twenty-four–hour rescue hot line: 851-6625 (do not dial 207 in Maine) or 207-773-7377; mal@stranding.org; www.stranding.org. You can also call New England Aquarium in Boston at 617-973-5247.

Living Off the Wild

No license is required to fish the ocean, but new laws do require a license for brown trout, brook trout, and landlocked, and Atlantic salmon (it is possible to catch them in the estuaries). Heavy fines will result if you tamper with lobster traps.

Local laws regulate clamming. Big tides cover and uncover an extensive littoral reef life with mussels, periwinkles, and sea urchins. Do not eat clams or mussels during a red tide, which causes paralytic shellfish poisoning (PSP). The NOAA weather channel and local radio news broadcasts will note clamming areas that are closed. Sea urchin roe served on crackers makes a delicious hors d'oeuvre; the prime time for this delicacy is before the spawning season, from April to June. For mussels, carry a string or onion bag and drag the mussels behind your boat or let them drift in a tidal pool for three to four hours to filter them. The mussels will clean themselves of grit.

Keeping Safe

Maine islands tend to have names such as Crow, Crotch, Long, Sheep, Hay, and Heron—all of which denote features that can be helpful when trying to site the island from the water. Black Islands tend to be covered in spruce, for example, while Sheep Islands are bald due to grazing. Those general terms may help you locate them, along with the blue-and-white BPL signs.

Narrowing channels where huge volumes of water are constricted or get churned up in opposing wind and tide are particularly risky for kayakers: the mouth of the Kennebec River, the Sasanoa Hell Gates. Exposed headlands where water speeds up and refracts off rock cliffs, with no safe landing for several miles, are also dangerous: Pemaquid Point, Schoodic Head, Mosquito Head. The farther Down East you travel, the more fog becomes a factor in longer crossings.

If you need help, use the flares or smoke signals you have brought along to signal help from a passing boat. To launch a search for a missing companion in adverse conditions, call the Coast Guard by cell phone or VHF radio—if you're not carrying one, a passing lobster boat probably will be (see appendix C). Also see "Safety Considerations" in this book's introduction, and read "Caution Areas" for each trip listed below.

Down East Canoe Trail

Many thanks are due to enthusiastic tidewater canoeists for charting the first canoe trail along the Maine coast, the Down East Canoe Trail. During the summer of 1979, the Beal and Tidewater Islands Committee of the Appalachian Mountain Club laid out an extended canoe trail of 63 miles from Spring Point Ledge in South Portland to Fort William Henry, just short of Pemaquid Point at the edge of Muscongus Bay. Canoeists began exploring the tidewater rivers and the coast east of Bath during the early 1960s. The exploration included Beal Island, which the club bought in 1967, as well as Knubble Bay Camp, also owned by the AMC, on the mainland.

In 1913, Maine state legislators halted the sale of state-owned islands in the interest of preserving those remaining for public use. In 1973, the Bureau of Public Lands (BPL) set up the Coastal Island Registry to determine legal ownership of the islands, setting a two-year deadline; any islands not registered by 1975 would be held in state trust. In 1979, the BPL offered leases on several of those islands—and the idea was hatched to use those newly identified public islands for outdoor recreation. The Down East Canoe Trail was born. It should be noted, however, that these waters were canoed nearly 400 years ago by the Indians on fishing and foraging expeditions; a resurgence in the interest in heritage trails may lead to the remapping of some of these ancient trails.

Appalachian Mountain Club members have access to one of the most beautiful spots in Maine's tidewater rivers at Knubble Bay Camp in Georgetown, south of Bath, and Beal Island, a fifteen-minute paddle from Knubble Bay. Both serve as launch spots for paddling in this area, which includes several major rivers and the magnificent Hockomock Bay, which resembles a large inland lake more than a tidewater bay. Fort Island and Swan Island, both owned by the state, are nearby and convenient for camping. The entire route can be plotted on a single NOAA chart: #13288, Monhegan to Cape Elizabeth.

Maine Island Trail Association (MITA)

In spring 1988, David Getchell, under the aegis of the Island Institute, a nonprofit organization dedicated to the preservation of Maine islands and their traditional uses, organized the Maine Island Trail Assocation (MITA). Getchell aimed to call attention to the availability of islands owned by the Maine Bureau of Public Lands for public recreation and identify a serious small-boat waterway in which members agreed to use a low-impact approach to camping. Of about 1,500 state-owned islands, Getchell identified those that provided a logical meander up the coast and compiled a booklet with chartlets locating those islands. MITA currently directs the care or monitoring of more than fifty state-owned islands as well as a growing number of privately owned islands (also about fifty). *The Maine Island Trail Guidebook*, the stewardship handbook, is full of information about low-impact use, access, and boating on the trail.

Kayakers have spent anywhere from a week to a couple of months traveling this magnificent coastal route, which some have likened to the beginnings of an Appalachian Trail on water. Most would agree

Cape Rosier is one of the prettiest spots to paddle along the 325-mile Maine Island Trail that travels from Casco Bay to Machias Bay.

that the public islands are some of the best recreational resources in New England.

The waterway winds up the Maine coast for 325 miles, extending from Casco Bay off Portland on the west to Machias Bay on the east, generally passing by the headlands. Islands are spaced less than a day's paddle away from each other, generally making for easy travel. As you travel farther Down East, however, there are fewer islands and rougher landing spots on the rugged, foggy coast, especially in the Frenchman Bay and Gouldsboro Bight regions. (Huge tides of 18 feet or more that bring strong currents and rough waters when the wind kicks up are other deterrents this far east.)

Getchell was confident that small boaters' enthusiasm for this recreational opportunity would be matched by their willingness to volunteer for the islands' welfare. What he may not have envisioned was the enthusiasm with which private island owners embraced MITA, generously donating use of their islands, initially for safe navigation on the waterway, but ultimately for the sake of stewardship. Nearly half of MITA's islands are privately owned, and the membership is engaged in a variety of stewardship programs that include coastal use logs, adopt-an-island programs, island cleanups, and island monitoring.

Also, along with their membership cards, paddlers carry a commitment to practice low-impact use. That means restoring a campsite to near-pristine conditions and boating out all refuse, including human waste. (See "Leave No Trace" on pages 25 to 28.)

The most obvious benefit of MITA is its handbook (grown from 100 to nearly 400 pages since its inception), which includes chartlets identifying and locating MITA islands along with firsthand descriptions of landing spots, camping conditions, wildlife, emergency numbers, and caution areas. The chartlets are reduced versions of the NOAA marine charts and are by no means substitutes for those navigational charts. MITA holds an annual meeting to update members on island use and to foster a sense of camaraderie in using and protecting Maine's islands.

Yearly, MITA adds islands or mainland sites to the trail due to generosity of private landowners. In addition, islands may be removed from the trail because of overuse, change of ownership, or wildlife considerations.

Note: The following trips are arranged north to south. That means Cobscook Bay is the first trip described. Wild, remote, beautiful, seldom visited, Cobscook Bay is a wonderful paddling destination. Still, it would not be the first choice a lot of paddlers, even if driving distance were not a consideration. Because of tides of up to 20 feet, the bay dries out at low tide, leaving acres of mud to hike across for launching. Also, whirlpools, overfalls, and major tidal rips caused by the huge volume of water flowing in and out of the bay make paddling conditions challenging here, to say the least. In summary, the trip is a reminder that sea kayaking can be a very challenging sport and should not be attempted by anyone who is not fully prepared, equipped, and aware of the challenges involved.

TRIP 1

Cobscook Bay

COBSCOOK BAY STATE PARK TO SEAL ISLAND

Trip Mileage: 10.5 miles round trip

Tidal Range: 18.2 feet at Eastport

Charts and Maps: NOAA #13328 at 1:44,900

Caution Areas: Cobscook Reversing Falls is a 0.5-mile–long set of falls between Mahar Point and Falls Island. The tidal flow passes through a 300-yard gap between Cobscook and Whiting Bays. Water rushes through here at 10 to 14 knots and should not be paddled except at slack tide, which lasts only a few moments, and by experienced paddlers only. Paddling with current tidal information is a must, due to long stretches of mud at low tide. Novice paddlers will do well to plan day trips at slack water, because tide rips and whirlpools do form around the headlands, Cobscook Falls, and narrows. You must be prepared for cold water (40 degrees in mid-May), hard-running tides, and upswellings, and have knowledge of the tidal conditions.

Access: Cobscook Bay State Park. South Edmonds has an all-tide ramp, picnic tables, Adirondack shelter, and latrine; there's no fee. There's also a launch at Whiting.

Getting There: To reach Cobscook Bay State Park, take I-95 to Bangor, then ME 9 east to Wesley, ME 192 south to Machias, and US 1 north to Whiting; then head north to the park, located off US 1. Watch for the sign. To reach the South Edmonds launch, follow directions into park, then proceed about a mile past the park entrance. The launch at Whiting just north of town puts you into the southern reaches of Whiting Bay.

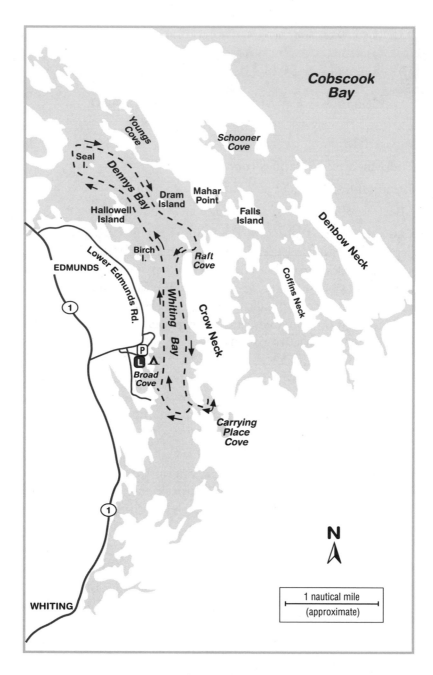

Cobscook Bay

QUIETUDE IS COBSCOOK BAY'S great attribute. Sit still and listen. No cars, no boat engines, no voices—only the sound of the wind in the trees and the birds, maybe a loon's gurgle, maybe a clammer in an aluminum skiff, and no sense of imminent intrusion. You feel like you've dropped off the edge of the coastal waterfront into paradise. The entire area is as remote as you can get on the East Coast, short of going to the Maritimes.

Whiting Bay is in the innermost reaches of Cobscook Bay, which in turn is folded into Passamaquoddy Bay. Whiting is a long, protected arm of water; it resembles an inland lake but gets tides of 24 feet twice a month and rises a foot every fifteen minutes, according to local sources. It is possible to step into your kayak from dry land, wait five minutes or so, then float off, avoiding wet feet altogether. Catch the tides right, and you can paddle up to 20 miles a day with little effort. A good option is to camp at Cobscook Bay State Park, located on Whiting Bay. It is quiet, isolated, beautiful, and uncrowded, and provides a good base for several interesting and sheltered day trips.

Cobscook is a Maliseet-Passamaquoddy word meaning "boiling tide," while *Passamaquoddy* means "people of the undertow." It is the spot of water Franklin Delano Roosevelt, who summered on nearby Campobello Island, wanted to harness to produce electric energy during the 1930s. The volume of water flushing in and out and up and down in deep columns twice daily provides very interesting currents, eddies, and boils. On a map, note how Cobscook Bay funnels into two large westernmost inland bays that stretch far to the north and south—Dennys and Whiting Bays. All the water from Cobscook Bay must funnel through two passages, each about 200 yards in width. The passage to the north is known as Cobscook Reversing Falls, located between Mahar Point, a long mainland peninsula, and Falls Island. The falls run up to 10 to 14 knots and are such a spectacular sight that the state has set up Cobscook Reversing Falls Park just so spectators can eat their sandwiches and watch the show.

It is best to paddle near the falls at slack water, but it is difficult to judge when slack water occurs because the waters do not conform to the tide tables. One kayaker determined that slack water occurred for about fifteen minutes, "and then the water went nuts" with standing waves and whitewater conditions. Another paddler reported that a good hour's window at slack allows passage through the falls but stressed that good navigation skills are critical at all times so kayakers won't get sucked into the falls. Still another noted that the trip through the falls even at slack is not recommended, because slack lasts only a few minutes and eddies continue to shift. And one experienced paddler said that the falls are no worse than many a whitewater run in the Kennebec Gorge.

The falls are even more impressive because the rushing water pushes against a large rock and so divides into two standing waves, then hits a rock on the mainland point and swells into another standing wave. You can feel the current's effects as far away as the campground, 3 miles south. You can hear the falls from several miles away.

The bay's cold, nutrient-rich waters, strong tidal currents, and extensive intertidal flats create critical breeding and feeding grounds for many different animals. It is home to a wide variety of marine species, bald eagles, migratory shorebirds, and waterfowl. A shallow 40-square-mile estuary with 200 miles of rugged, rocky convoluted shoreline, Cobscook Bay has avoided the heavy development experienced by most estuaries on the eastern seaboard and remains a relatively intact marine system. The bay provides prime habitat for sea scallops, sea urchins, and soft-shell clams.

Cobscook Bay is part of Moosehorn National Wildlife Refuge, whose federal officials have worked for several decades on eagle recovery in the salmon-rich area. A dozen nesting pairs of eagles live here. Once you become familiar with the eagle's soar height, white head, and dark body, you are bound to see several. Seals and loons are also common.

Paddle out of Broad Cove and follow the permutations of the shore, which is both forest- and farmland. In about 0.5 mile, a no-name island near shore has an eagle's nest. Paddle past the Birch Islands, then to Hallowell, also known as Williams Island, owned by U.S. Fish and Wildlife. You can picnic on the gravel beach and walk around the perimeter (no interior trails). Then paddle up to Seal Island, where you are bound to see seals. Next paddle behind the Drams nearer to the falls, where you can play with your eddy turns and ferries—but keep your distance from the falls. It's best to do this around slack on an incoming tide. That timing provides a comfort zone, because the falls provide an onshore nudge. With whitewater skills, you can negotiate the eddies near Mahar Point and land close enough to Reversing Falls Park to get out and watch. The basic rule for paddlers is that you lean down into an eddy in the same direction

Beware of low tide in Cobscook Bay; even the ramps are too short.

as the current, contrary to a natural inclination to lean into it. Conditions are squirmy around south side of Falls Island.

In 2002, The Nature Conservancy acquired 140-acre Falls Island, a wild and rugged island at the geographic center of Cobscook Bay. Falls Island is one of the most productive bald eagle nesting sites in the state. Thanks in large part to landowners who have respected the eagles' needs for undisturbed habitat, pairs nesting on the island have produced nineteen eaglets in the last twenty years.

Head back down Whiting Bay following Crow Neck, an undeveloped wooded peninsula, with several interesting indentations. Closer to slack, you can paddle into the scenic Raft Cove and feel that you will be able to exit again. Three miles down Crow Neck is the entry to the lovely Carryingplace Cove (note that it empties at low tide), then paddle back across to your campsite.

Another option is to paddle south toward Whiting down the bay, which is sheltered and picturesque. Paddling south is just as interesting as paddling up the bay, with numerous coves and wildlife but decidedly weaker currents and less racing water around the headlands. You can explore Timber and Weir Coves; Commissary Point near Whiting is owned by the Maine Department of Inland Fisheries and Wildlife, which allows careful day use. Burnt Cove, along which several of the park's campsites are located, is worth a detour.

Low tide requires attention. Try to time your trips to get on and off the park's launch ramp with water still covering it (the launch ramp travels 30 feet down). At low tide, mud flats expand to about 15 feet before reaching the channel, and you easily sink up to your knees. Every green spot on the chart indicates mud at low tide, and all coves on the chart have generous washes of green. Also, because it moves so strongly, time your trips *with* the tide. Beware, in particular, of opposing wind and tide creating breaking waves—enough to keep you ashore.

One final note of caution: park your car well away from the ramp to avoid submersion while you are out paddling.

Other Options: State-owned Cat Island lies in the middle of Schooner Cove off Leighton Neck (not be confused with Leighton Point). For more paddling options, stay at the Machias Motor Inn in Machias, next to Helen's Restaurant, right on the Machias River. Moderately priced, it has kitchenettes and an indoor heated pool (207-255-4861).

Pembroke town officials have built a long road and picnicking area at the falls. Drive down as far as you can, then hike down to the rocky beach to watch the show. To get there, turn off US 1 in Pembroke. From the park entrance, go 9.4 miles north on US 1. At the gas station, bear right onto Leighton Point. Go 3.4 miles and take the right turn at the sign for the park. If wind pins you down, consider hiking the loop trail along the bold cliffs of Western Head off ME 191, 11 miles southeast of East Machias, for crashing surf and expansive views of the Atlantic.

Camping: Cobscook Bay State Park, open May 15 through October 15. Many of the one hundred well-spaced campsites are on the water, in three different areas—Whiting Bay, Broad Cove, and Burnt Cove; more than three-quarters are for tents. The park has its own ramp from which you can launch mud-free on the top two-thirds of the tide. It also has hot showers, a picnic area, hiking trails, and fresh water. Overnight parking is allowed for a small fee. For more information, contact Cobscook Bay State Park, RR 1, Box 127, Dennysville, ME 04628; 207-726-4412. Reserve a spot online through the Bureau of Parks and Lands at www.state.me.us/doc/parks/programs, or call 800-332-1501 within Maine, 207-287-3824 out of state.

TRIP 2

Englishman Bay

ROQUE BLUFFS TO HALIFAX ISLAND

Trip Mileage: 6 miles round trip (one overnight)

Tidal Range: 12.5 feet at Roque Island Harbor

Charts and Maps: NOAA #13326 at 1:44,900

Caution Areas: It is one thing to be traveling along the shoreline of this "rugged" water; it is another to head out into the open sea. You should proceed with caution in this area of big tides, swift currents, confused seas, ocean swells, fog, and little protection beyond the coastline. On any route east of Corea, the water can get wild and treacherous, and caution is advised. Conditions can vary quickly. For example, fog sits in the Bay of Fundy, and a change of wind direction to the south can bring it on to the Jonesport area. It's best to have your weather radio handy. Wind and waves can pound the shore at Roque Bluffs State Park in southerly winds. An underwater bar between Halifax and Green Islands (just north of The Brothers) can create breaking waves in opposing wind and tide.

Access: Roque Bluffs State Park has no launch ramp, but you can launch from the pebble beach on the south-facing shore. There's ample parking.

Getting There: To reach Roque Bluffs State Park, turn right off US 1 at the White House Diner in Jonesboro onto Roque Bluffs Road; at the intersection, bear right and follow the road all the way to end. Watch for signs for the park. It's about 6 miles from the turnoff. There is a $1 fee for day use. Restrooms, picnic tables, bathhouse, and a freshwater pond for swimming are available.

Englishman Bay

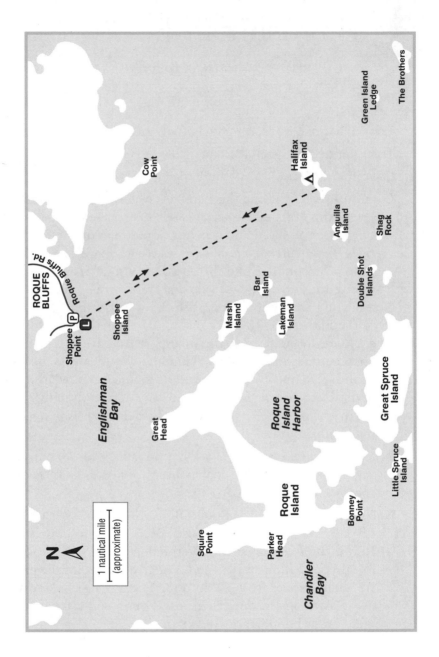

HALIFAX IS A BEAUTIFUL OUTER ISLAND that is part of the Petit Manan National Wildlife Refuge and managed by the U.S. Fish and Wildlife Service. It is open to the public for careful day use and for camping by prior permission. The island has two sections joined by a narrow neck; it's best to land on the southern peninsula. The interior of the larger northeast section of the island is closed to visitors due to the fragile plants growing in upraised bogs, a unique feature in New England. For hiking, stay on the rocky perimeter.

Wildlife includes harbor seals, bald eagles, black guillemots, great blue herons, common loons, gulls, terns, cormorants, and flocks of female eiders with their young in summer.

The trip starts on the large gravel spit of Roque Bluffs State Park. From the beach, Halifax looks like a spoon lying facedown, the south end rising into a hillock. Paddle along the east side of Shoppee Island out into Englishman Bay. A couple of handsome, freshly painted white lobster boats may putter offshore, noting your presence in the area but not disturbing your privacy.

To the south lies Roque Island. You are near one crossbar of the H-shaped island and the trio of Marsh, Bar, and Lakeman Islands. Privately owned Roque Island, about 1.5 miles offshore, is possibly the most beautiful spot on the Maine coast. Known for its bald eagles and 2-mile Great Sand Beach on the south side, it is a favorite mooring spot for luxury yachts, which treat it as a turnaround point to head back south. The Roque Island Archipelago is lovely, small-boat cruising territory, but most of the islands are owned by a family corporation or The Nature Conservancy. Together the islands form a sensitive ecological niche, and are often the subject of scientific study. The family therefore does not want anyone landing on the islands—or even paddling through them—without written permission. No Trespassing signs abound. Many of the ledges form a complex breeding ground for seals and should be avoided May through October.

When you reach Halifax, the best landing is on the northwest-facing gravel beach or at the south-facing cove on the smaller end, the spoon curve of the island to the south. Be aware that the southern cove can develop a nasty break in bad weather. From here you can climb a grassy hill for a spectacular view of the islands stretching to the south, including Anguilla and the Double Shot Islands. Halifax is the one place I've been where a mink sat up on its hind legs right next to me to inspect what I was having for lunch.

On Halifax, you get a view of Anguilla and Double Shot Islands stretching to the south.

On another trip, if weather permits, you might like to go out to Pulpit Rock and The Brothers. A good après-paddle spot is the friendly White House diner on US 1 in Jonesboro, which serves hefty portions to both truckers and families.

Other Options: The Maine Island Trail ends in Machias. Note that traveling farther Down East, from Cutler to West Quoddy Head, a distance of about 17 miles, you are entering truly open, unprotected waters known as the Bold Coast, which are not recommended for the casual or even adventure-bent kayaker, although paddlers have covered the distance. Sunrise County Canoe & Kayak, Machias, does offer a trip along the Bold Coast (see appendix A), however, if you want to tap into some local knowledge. Put-in spots in coves, around the corner from heads or points, appear every mile or so, most notably Moose Cove and Bailey's Mistake, but you need settled weather to make the trip. Refractions off tall cliffs create confused and gnarly water. Pond Point and Red Head are good examples of how exposed some of the coastline can be. At West Quoddy Head, marked by the red, candy-striped lighthouse, you've paddled to the easternmost point of the United States. In recent years much of this coast has been protected by various conservation organizations, a promise that this splendid area will stay wild forever.

Camping: Halifax Island. Get camping permission from USFWS, which has an office in Milbridge. Call 207-546-2124 weekdays to make a reservation. Day use is allowed without permission. The campsite is located on the gravel of the wash-over bar between the northeast-facing beach and the south-facing cove. Do not camp on the environmentally sensitive grassy hillside to the south.

TRIP 3

East of Schoodic

BIRCH HARBOR TO ROQUE BLUFFS

Trip Mileage: 52.5 miles one way (five days)

Tidal Range: 11.5 feet at Jonesport

Charts and Maps: NOAA #13324 at 1:40,000

Caution Areas: Petit Manan Point is one of the riskiest places on the Maine coast for all boaters, as are Pond Point and Red Head at the south end of Great Wass Island. Be prepared to carry over rockweed, and plan your trip around the tides, avoiding low-tide landings and launchings if at all possible. Because of high tides, take your boat much higher than you think you have to and tie it to a tree.

Access: Ocean Wood Campground

Getting There: To reach Ocean Wood Campground from West Gouldsboro on US 1, take ME 195 south to Prospect Harbor, then ME 186 to Birch Harbor. Watch for signs for the campground. Spot a car at Roque Bluffs State Park; see Trip 2, page 49.

———————

THE OUTER ISLANDS OF MAINE are special rocky thresholds where the full force of the Atlantic makes first contact with firm land. Paddling the Maine Island Trail east of Schoodic requires special attention. The fog is more frequent, crossings are longer, exposure to wind and waves is greater, the currents are stronger, the tides are bigger, and the need for wise decisions is critical. You can seem to move around so easily, but when things go bad, they go bad really quickly, said one longtime guide to the area.

Just beyond Ellsworth, the gateway to Acadia National Park, lies Schoodic Peninsula. Your trip starts on Schoodic's east side in Birch

East of Schoodic

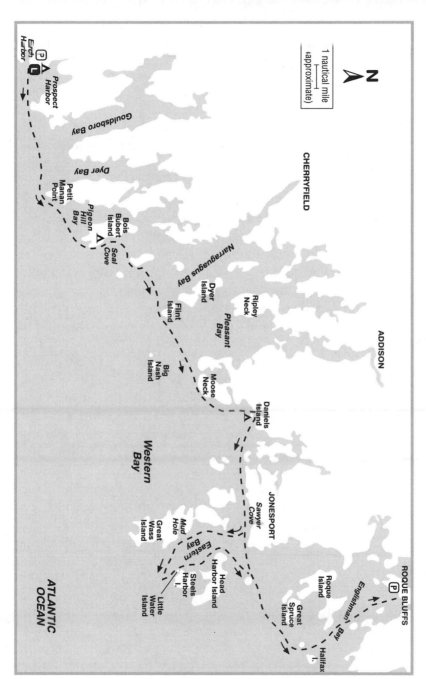

N

1 nautical mile
(approximate)

Eech
Harbor

Prospect
Harbor

Gouldsboro Bay

Dyer Bay

Petit
Manan
Point

Pigeon
Hill
Bay

Bois
Bubert
Island

Seal
Cove

CHERRYFIELD

Narraguagus Bay

Dyer
Island

Ripley
Neck

Pleasant
Bay

Flint
Island

Big
Nash
Island

ADDISON

Moose
Neck

Daniels
Island

Western
Bay

JONESPORT

Sawyer
Cove

Mud
Hole

Great
Wass
Island

Eastern Bay

Head
Harbor Island

Steels
Harbor
I.

Little
Water
Island

ATLANTIC
OCEAN

Roque
Island

Great
Spruce
Island

ROQUE BLUFFS

Englishman Bay

Halifax
I.

Harbor at the Ocean Wood Campground. Leave a car there and spot another one in Roque Bluffs. The launch is from the campground's cobble beach, which can be tricky. Carrying a loaded boat over rough cobblestones and into dumping surf can be a challenge. In a group, launch the less experienced first, with those still ashore offering steadying hands and a good push into the waves. The most experienced should go last. Once you've overcome this tricky launch, you are on the way.

Day One: Your first day will take you from Birch Harbor to Bois Bubert Island, a distance of 11 miles. Cross Prospect Harbor, round Cranberry Point, and paddle by the beautiful privately owned Sally Islands. The tide runs strongly—upwards of 2 to 3 knots—through the passages at the Sally Islands at the mouth of Gouldsboro Bay.

Paddle past Dyer Neck, across Dyer Bay; you are now headed for Petit Manan Point. It's a little more than 6 miles from Birch Harbor to Petit Manan. If you are in the fog, you can hear the bell buoy at Cranberry Point as you head out from Birch Harbor; your next sound reference will the surf crashing off the Sally Islands. Running Petit Manan Point's underwater bar is considered one of the most difficult negotiations on the Maine Island Trail. The good news is that you can pull over onto the beach and check out conditions before crossing. Crossing is best done at slack, early in the morning before the day's winds arise, and in settled conditions. On the chart, you can see that the bar's water depth measures 3 to 11 feet, while the surrounding water descends to 30 to 50 feet. Such a range is always bad news for kayakers. Swift tidal currents swell up over the bar, and in strong winds waves break across the entire length of the bar. The best passage for kayakers is through the inner bar, close to the point's southern tip. Avoid the water breaking over the ledges and steer your boat through the strong current. Go straight through any breaking surf you encounter; this is less risky than taking the waves sideways. We paddled through an hour after slack, and conditions were still on the mild side. You can relax on the beach on the other side.

To the south you can see the tall Petit Manan Lighthouse (Maine's second highest light at 119 feet) on Petit Manan Island, part of the Petit Manan National Wildlife Refuge. (This 3,335-acre refuge also includes Petit Manan Point, Bois Bubert, and Nash Islands.) Petit Manan Island has historically had one of the most important seabird colonies in Maine. Through the National Audubon Society's Seabird

Restoration Project, the endangered roseate tern (the one with the long black beak) breeds here, as does a colony of Atlantic puffins. Nesting puffins returned in 1992 after a 105-year absence.

The next part of the coast is spectacular. Cross Wood Pond Point, then head over to Bois Bubert Island, past Little Bois Bubert Harbor, around Big Head's ledges, and over to Seal Cove. The landscape here is as barren and rocky as a moonscape, and you probably won't see anyone else.

The U.S. Fish and Wildlife Service owns 90 percent of Bois Bubert as part of the Petit Manon National Wildlife Refuge. The northwest shore has several houses whose privacy you should respect. The island is big and brawny with a primeval interior forest braced by strong granite slabs. Wildflowers are plentiful. The most exquisite is the violet campanula, which grows on precipitous granite shelves at ocean's edge. Its fragility contrasts dramatically with the deep green sea that thrashes onto the cliffs, sending up spray and noise. It grows just beyond the 12-foot tides that rise dramatically over the enormous curves of cobblestone beaches.

Trails run through the island, marked by cairns and tree gashes, but it is easy to get disoriented. The interior has a freshwater pond.

To camp on Bois Bubert, you need permission from the USFWS, which has an office in Milbridge. Call 207-546-2124 to make a reservation. No more than ten people are allowed in the party, and you can stay no longer than two nights. Day use is allowed without permission. The landing and campsite are located in a grassy meadow off Seal Cove, about halfway down the east side of the island.

The surrounding islands are gorgeous. The trio of Douglas Islands rise vertically out of the sea, with wonderful shapes and angles and an almost Oriental feel—good places for eagles. Pond Island has an abandoned lighthouse. Recently bought by the Maine Coast Heritage Trust and USFWS, 27-acre Jordan's Delight is key breeding habitat for guillemots, eiders, and storm petrels.

Day Two: You are now entering Narraguagus and Pleasant Bays. Paddle over to Shipstern Island. Ocean swells clash against the high cliffs, which tower nearly 100 feet, sending salt spray 20 feet into the air with tremendous booms. Only the hardy black guillemot floats comfortably in this tidal surf zone. Paddle to the south of Flint Island, which is owned by The Nature Conservancy, where you are allowed to land after August 15. The Nash Island lighted buoy lies to the west

USFWS owns 90 percent of Bois Bubert as part of the Petit Manan National Wildlife Refuge.

of Nash Island, part of the refuge. Paddle past the Ladle Ledges. Check out the rams if they are still there. Paddle to the south of Norton (watch for breaking water on Norton Island Reef) and on to Cape Split, around Moose Neck, and north into Wohoa Bay and Daniels Island. From Bois Bubert to Daniels is 16 miles.

Daniels Island is owned by the BPL and is open to the public. Eight people (maximum) may camp there. After the turbulence of the outer islands, you will appreciate the quietude of the 2-acre inner island of Daniels, just across from Bare Point and 3 miles west of Jonesport. Note that you can land only at the top half of the tide. While you may expect a small lump of inner island, you have a spacious raspberry-bush-laden paradise with a fabulous view of Wahoa Bay. At sunset and low tide, you can watch terns, herons, greater yellowlegs, and sandpipers stalk and skip around extensive tidal flats on the north side. Foraging on Daniels can be very successful with a dinner of mussels and raspberries. According to MITA, Daniels is marked by a low hill covered with an open meadow and a small copse of poplar trees. Note that MITA provides several private camping options in this area. A public alternative is Indian River, a small, thickly wooded island, open to two people, located well into the

Indian River on a cove to the north of Crowley Island. It dries out completely at low tide, but you may have the island to yourself.

Day Three: The next day, paddle through the Moosabec Reach, past the fishing community of Jonesport (which spreads out for a mile along the shore), and under the bridge to stop at the town-owned Henry Point Campground. The current constricted in Moosabec Beach at the bridge can run as high as 6 knots with strong eddies developing under the bridge, so it is best to travel with the tide; avoid opposing wind and tide, which can create nasty waves. While few sailboats can get under the bridge, lobster and fishing boats, Jonesport's livelihood, make good use of the reach, so keep heads-up for busy traffic. On July 4, the reach is site for the famous Jonesport lobster boat races.

The campground is located on the east side of Sawyer Cove. You can land your kayak at the small beach. From here you can walk into town (street signs are in the shape of lobster boats) to get more food, make phone calls (at the fire station), and take a shower at the friendly Jonesport Shipyard (bring your quarters), located a few docks east of the town landing. The campground has picnic tables and is kayak friendly and a good place to compare notes with other kayakers (see "Camping" at the end of this trip description).

Next, head south to gunkhole away the afternoon in Great Wass, a splendid area to do so. The Nature Conservancy owns or protects nearly a third of the islands in the Great Wass Archipelago and allows day use—but only after August 15, when seabirds are no longer nesting. The USFWS also owns several islands and ledges, with landing restrictions up until July 31 and August 31. You will see eagles and dozens of seals. Camp on Little Water. Paddle along the east shore of Great Wass and into Mud Hole, one of the most scenic spots on the Maine coast. Mud Hole has a walking trail that starts at the head of the hole and travels along the south shore.

Little Water is a small grassy island that is very exposed to the weather and off-limits during seal pupping season. The low-tide landing had us hefting our kayaks up a 15-foot vertical rockweed-covered ledge; not an easy task. Reward yourself with cold drinks and fresh supplies from Jonesport. Since Little Water allows only two campers, there is a good chance you will have to go elsewhere. It's about 10 miles from Daniels to Little Water with a stop in Jonesport.

Day Four: You may be awakened early by the blaring Mistake Island foghorn—thick fog is common in this area. Pack up, then head north back through Mistake Harbor, past the Hardwoods and Spectacle Island in Eastern Bay, and around the north of Head Harbor Island. Then paddle over to Mark Island.

Note that the recommended trip is back through Eastern Bay and not around the south end of Head Harbor Island. The south ends of these peninsulas receive the full force of sea surges and can be white-knuckle affairs to paddle; they may even have you looking for the sky-hook to get yourself out of there. Of Pond Point and Red Head, at the south end of Great Wass Island, the MITA guidebook says: "Just about everything said about Schoodic and Petit Manan applies equally well here: swift currents, confused seas, ocean swells, and not much protection. Handle with great care." When I made this trip several years ago, wind was never a factor, but we had fog on two out of five days and required steady navigation.

You are now headed for Englishmen and Chandler Bays and the Roque Island Archipelago with a final camping night on Halifax (see Trip 2). It's 12 miles from Little Water to Halifax.

Day Five: Your final destination is Roque Bluffs State Park, a distance of about 3.5 miles from Halifax.

The Maine Chapter of The Nature Conservancy owns 1,540 acres of Great Wass, which has several hiking trails (posted trail map); the southern portion is known for its rare peatlands. If you get a chance after your trip, return to Great Wass Island to hike this splendid area.

Jonesport's public boat launch is at the end of Sawyer Street, which leaves the highway opposite the T. A. King & Son building supply store, if you're interested in gunkholing for a day around Beals and Great Wass Islands.

Camping: Ocean Wood Campground, P.O. Box 111, Birch Harbor, ME 04613; 207-963-7194; www.jabinc.org/oceanwood/ow_camp ground.htm. Ocean Wood has 50 tentsites, 20 on the water. Island camping is on Bois Bubert (USFWS, permission needed), Daniels (BPL), Little Water (BPL), and Halifax (USFWS, permission needed).

An option farther Down East in Jonesport is the municipal campground on Henry Point at Sawyer Cove, Kelley Point Road, Jonesport, ME 04649; 207-497-9633. A fee is charged. Tenters can use any of the forty sites, most on the waterfront. Pit privies. No running water, but both shade and sun are available, and the campground is on the water. To reach the campground from the mainland, look for a road labeled Kelley Point, which starts where the saltwater bay almost touches the highway. You can get drinking water from a tap on the south side of the fire hall in Jonesport, which is on the west side of the highway.

TRIP 4

Pleasant Bay

MILBRIDGE TO MINK ISLAND

Trip Mileage: 14 miles round trip (one overnight)

Tidal Range: 11.2 feet at Milbridge

Charts and Maps: NOAA #13323 at 1:44,900

Caution Areas: There are large breaking waves on several shoals off Ripley Neck, so careful route picking is needed. Also watch out for refracting waves and confused water in and out of Harrington Bay between Strout Island and Ripley Neck.

Access: Milbridge town ramp; launch ramps at Addison, South Addison at Cape Split Harbor, and the Harrington River at Ripley Neck. The word is to ignore all the other launch spots in the DeLorme *Gazetteer* as inaccessible for one reason or another.

Getting There: To reach the Milbridge town ramp, take US 1 north to Milbridge. Just north of the green bridge on US 1A, make the first right-hand turn and follow the road to the dock. A paved ramp gives access to the Narraguagus River.

As you head east of Bar Harbor and Acadia National Park, the territory becomes a lot wilder—higher tides, stronger currents, fewer boats, less people, more solitude. That means small-boat navigation requires some extra care but also is rewarded with a slower and quieter tempo.

Some lovely towns east of Acadia National Park give access to great paddling in less crowded coastal waters, with few whale-watching boats, ferries, or yachts, and only a handful of lobster and fishing boats. You virtually have the place to yourself. A good resting place on longer voyages is the aptly named Pleasant Bay, into which the

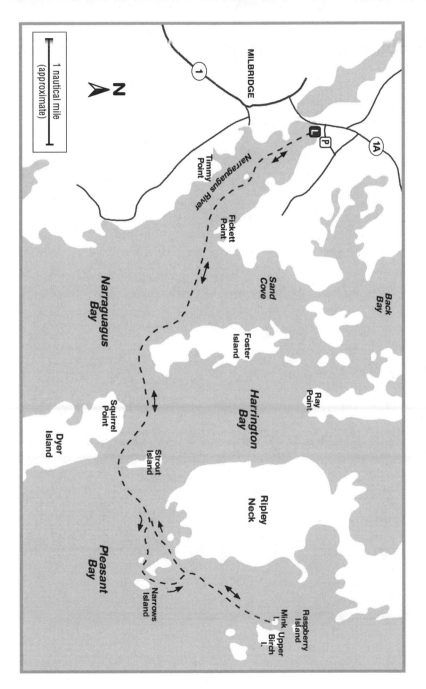

Pleasant Bay

Harrington and Pleasant Rivers empty. The shoreline is rural, and the paddling is mostly protected island-hopping and shore-hugging in bays and rivers. An overnight is possible on Mink Island, which is a high, wooded island populated mostly with hardwoods and located just south of Raspberry Island in Pleasant Bay. You can identify Mink by the large boulder at the edge of the trees. The best landing spot is on the northwest side, and camping, restricted to a party of two, is in the middle of the island.

From the Milbridge town launch, paddle south down the Narraguagus River; large schools of herring may leap in front of your bow. Views to seaward include the islands of Tommy and Shipstern. At low tide, stay in the channel to avoid getting stuck on mussel shoals. Town-owned McLellan Park at Baldwin's Head on the west side of the river has unusual red stones and is a good place for a picnic on a bluff overlooking the river. Head past Fickett Point and make the long crossing to Foster Island, past Squirrel Point on Dyer Island. Then paddle to the south of Strout Island, around Ripley Neck, to Pleasant Bay. At Ripley Neck, large breaking waves on several rock outcrops can be fairly dramatic. Be on the lookout for the rare, gigantic gray seal.

It is possible to pass between Narrows and Bar Islands at near-low tide, then head up the wide Pleasant River, now protected under the Maine Rivers Act. You are surrounded by 180 degrees of fir-clad shoreline with only an occasional house and one or two boats at mooring. Surfing is possible on long waves that break over Bunker Ledge. Just north of the ledge and the Birch Islands is Mink Island.

After a picnic or overnight, head back around Willard Point and the beautiful Inner and Outer Willards, around Ripley Neck, and so back to Milbridge, following the white church steeple, framed by the high, sloping humps of mountains in Franklin beyond.

Other Options: If you spot a car in Addison, about 5 miles north of Carrying Place Cove on the Pleasant River, you can get a full taste of the river without having to backtrack to Milbridge.

Camping: BPL Mink Island. On the mainland, McClellan Park on Narraguagus Bay offers eleven campsites that accommodate both tents and small to medium RVs. Camp facilities include fire rings, running water, bathrooms, picnic tables, and trails. The fee can be paid to the camp attendant or at the Milbridge town office, 207-546-2422. Go 4 miles from the junction of US 1 and the Wyman Road in Milbridge. In Milbridge, the Bayview Campground (fee), just up Fickett Point Road from the town launch site, has shower facilities and an easy launch that involves carrying your boat down a gently graded bluff. Launch on the top half of the tide. Call 207-546-2946.

TRIP 5

Acadia National Park

SOUTHWEST HARBOR TO LITTLE CRANBERRY

Trip Mileage: 13.8-mile loop

Tidal Range: 10.2 feet at Southwest Harbor

Charts and Maps: NOAA #13318 at 1:46,500

Caution Areas: From Seal Harbor on the south coast of Mount Desert, you are in exposed waters without the off-lying islands for protection, so be prepared for rough conditions. In July and August, the sea breezes fill in by 11:00 A.M. and summer calm can be replaced by a 20-knot onshore breeze, so anticipate a good following sea coming home. Off Bar Point on Little Cranberry are ledges over which waves build. Bass Harbor Bar gets strong current and large waves.

Access: Southwest Harbor town dock; an alternative launch site is at Manset, with a concrete ramp and more parking.

Getting There: To reach the Southwest Harbor town dock from US 1 at Ellsworth, take ME 3 south to ME 102 just after Trenton. At Southwest Harbor, turn left onto Clark Point Road. At the end of the road is the town dock across from the Coast Guard station. Parking is limited to three-hour and twelve-hour spots (no overnight). To reach the Manset ramp, take ME 102A toward Seawall Campground and turn onto Mansell Lane. Follow Mansell to its end, turn left onto Shore Road, and continue to the ramp. For overnight parking, you must make arrangements with the harbormaster; contact 207-244-7913.

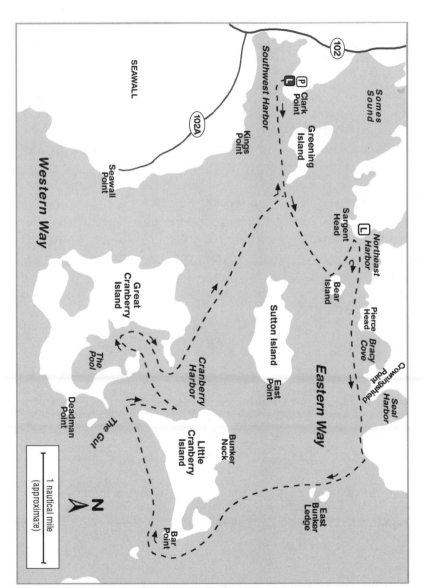

Acadia National Park

SEAWALL

Western Way

Seawall Point

Kings Point

102A

Southwest Harbor

102

Clark Point

P

L

Greening Island

Somes Sound

Northeast Harbor

L

Sargent Head

Bear Island

Pierce Head

Bracy Cove

Downingshield Point

Seal Harbor

Great Cranberry Island

The Pool

Deadman Point

The Gut

Cranberry Harbor

Sutton Island

East Point

Eastern Way

Little Cranberry Island

Bunker Neck

Bar Point

East Bunker Ledge

N

1 nautical mile (approximate)

THE BAYS AND HARBORS around Mount Desert Island provide dozens of options for dramatic sea kayak trips—so many you never have to cover the same ground twice. The backdrop is Acadia National Park's mountains, which rise abruptly from the shoreline. The 16-by-13-mile island is almost bisected by Somes Sound, the only fjord in the eastern United States.

From visual highlights alone, the trip from Southwest Harbor to Great Cranberry and Little Cranberry is one of the best Mount Desert and possibly the Maine coast has to offer. From on the water in Western Way, the view northeast includes ten of the seventeen mountains that march across Mount Desert: from left to right, Bernard, Mansell, Beech (with the fire tower), St. Sauveur, Acadia, Norumbega, Penobscot, Sargent, Pemetic, and Cadillac.

The downside of paddling here is that Acadia is the second most visited national park in the United States; more than three million tourists arrive here annually, many driving through in RVs. Especially in July and August, the congestion puts several roadblocks in the way of kayakers. Parking is limited. Tenters compete with RVs for space. The upside is that Southwest Harbor is less convenient to the popular park loop road because of Somes Sound and, therefore, less hectic than the Bar Harbor side.

The town dock at Clark Point is a good starting point. The dock has twelve-hour daytime parking and a semipaved ramp across the street from the Coast Guard station next to Beal's Lobster Pier. Public restrooms are available. Parking is limited and could prove difficult in summer. You can make approximately the same circuit with a launch from Northeast Harbor with plentiful parking at dockside for the Cranberry Isles mail boat and a shorter itinerary. The trip to Northeast Harbor, however, involves about a 12-mile drive around Somes Sound.

Paddle out of Southwest Harbor past the southern tip of Greening Island and toward the lighthouse on Bear Island, now conservation land, passing by the head of Somes Sound. In the sound, with fields stretching to the water and mountains rising up beyond, you may get the feeling you are on Lake Geneva in Switzerland watching a transported Maine sailboat fleet in action.

Next, paddle by the entrance to Northeast Harbor, where some of Mount Desert's priciest yachts moor. Paddle along the shore to the east past an unnamed cove, then Bracy Cove with a dock that belongs

The remote Baker Island's ledges are so smooth that locals used them for dancing while on picnics there.

to the Racquet Club, then the Rockefellers' house with the flag flying just before Seal Harbor, then Seal Harbor itself. Then bear south past the seals on Bunker Ledge to Little Cranberry Island. Here you will cross Eastern Way; this spot can get very busy with boat traffic in summer, so caution is needed.

The gravel beaches on the south and east of Little Cranberry feel very isolated in a special way. Look south about 23 miles to see if you can spot Mount Desert Rock. To return to Clark Point, paddle back between Great Cranberry and Little Cranberry and poke into The Pool inside Fish Point. During summer, a restaurant and gift shop are open on Great Cranberry. Islesford, where the Little Cranberry mail boat lands, in Hadlock Cove on the island's west side, is a year-round community and has a small grocery store, a dockside café (Islesford Dock), and the Islesford Historical Museum, run by the Park Service (open daily from June through September, 10:45 A.M. to 4:30 P.M.; it's free). You can land on the beach on either side of the Little Cranberry town dock, the southernmost of three docks.

In Southwest Harbor, a great breakfast spot is The Deacon Seat, and you can eat good homemade soups and salads at BYO. Beal's Lobster Pool is a reliable spot for lobster and seafood budgets but gets very crowded on summer weekends. A real find is The Boathouse at the Claremont Hotel, which serves lunch, as well as drinks at sunset. If you're dressed in Tevas and neoprene, though, you may not want to walk through the hotel lobby; go around the hotel and across the lawn to the dock.

Other Options: This trip has several variations. Venture into Somes Sound, a narrow inlet between the steep slopes of hefty Norumbega Mountain to the east side and Flying, Acadia, and Sauveur Mountains to the west side. In Valley Cove, shout loudly at the walls of St. Sauveur to hear your echo. Just beyond Valley Cove is a spot where many land their dinghies. This is also the start of a trail to the top of Acadia Mountain, from which you'll enjoy a great view of the sound.

Nearly half of Somes Sound's land is parkland, and it's a truly magical place where the mountains drop down into the sea and the top of the sound draws you in like a magnet. From the north tip of Greening Island, it's a 7-mile paddle to Somesville. Somes Sound's shortest width is at the Narrows, about 500 yards across at Fernald Point, supposedly the first spot inhabited on Mount Desert by Indians.

Another side trip is into Northeast Harbor, 1 nautical mile inland from Sargent Head in Eastern Way. As you paddle into the harbor past many snazzy yachts, the view is dominated by the large Asticou Inn on top of the hill and many large houses called "cottages" surrounding the harbor. Haul your boat up onto the dock out of the way of local fishermen, then hike up the hill, down the main street of Northeast Harbor, with expensive shops and a few cafés.

To the southeast of Little Cranberry is remote Baker Island, part of Acadia, with flat pink granite ledges and a stone public beach. Landing is on the north side, from where you can hike to the lighthouse in the island's center. The light is now lit by solar energy. Baker's famous dance floor is so called because in the last century, locals used to picnic and dance on the long, smooth granite ledges on the west side.

If you paddle in the Bass Harbor area, beware Bass Harbor Bar, which connects the cliffs at Bass Harbor Head to Great Gott Island. A strong tidal current floods west and ebbs east across the bar; in opposing strong wind and tide, the waves can get quite nasty.

The Appalachian Mountain Club sells an excellent hiking, biking, and paddling guide to Mount Desert Island called *Disocver Acadia National Park*. It includes a pull-out map and sells for $16.95. See www.outdoors.org/publications. The AMC also operates a camp at Echo Lake. For more information, see www. outdoors.org/lodging/ camps. See also "Get Out & Get Active with the AMC" at the end of this book.

Camping: Run by Acadia National Park, Seawall Campground, located on ME 102A in Manset, is open from late May to late September. A total of 213 sites are available on a first-come, first-served basis. The campground has access to an oceanfront beach at Ship Harbor, 0.5 mile away, but this is not advised as a put-in due to distance and rocky footing. Telephone 207-244-3600 or www.nps. gov/acad for more information. The Hub at the north end of Bartlett's Island in Western Bay is state owned. Lamoine State Park is on the mainland on Eastern Bay.

TRIP 6

Mount Desert

CIRCUMNAVIGATION OF BARTLETT ISLAND

Trip Mileage: 11-mile loop

Tidal Range: 10.2 feet at Pretty Marsh Harbor

Charts and Maps: NOAA Chart #13316 (Blue Hill Bay) at 1:40,000

Caution Areas: The tidal current runs through Bartlett at 2 knots and can get quite nasty in opposing wind and tide. The island's west side is wild and remote.

Access: Bartlett's Landing, open to residents of Mount Desert; Seal Cove

Getting There: To reach Bartlett's Landing from the north, take ME 198/102 to Indian Point Road and turn right. Follow this for about 6 miles; at Pretty Marsh, turn right onto Bartlett Landing Road and continue to its end. To reach Seal Cove, continue on ME 198/102 past Indian Point Road for 4 miles to the turnoff for Cape Road. Turn right and follow Cape Road to the launch spot.

W HEN THE FOG THICKENS on the south side of Mount Desert, you can often find clearer skies up by Bartlett Island in Western Bay, where the water is also warmer, according to sources. Bartlett is a broad, privately owned island set well up into Blue Hill Bay. Pretty Marsh Harbor has a paved boat-launch site known as Bartlett's Landing, which unfortunately is one of the busiest kayak-launch spots in Maine. Here several Mount Desert outfitters unload their customers in fleets of double kayaks, to follow the tide down to the take-out. You'd do well to take a page from their book: follow the tide, not just to mitigate the jumpy narrows but also to ease paddling effort throughout the circumnavigation.

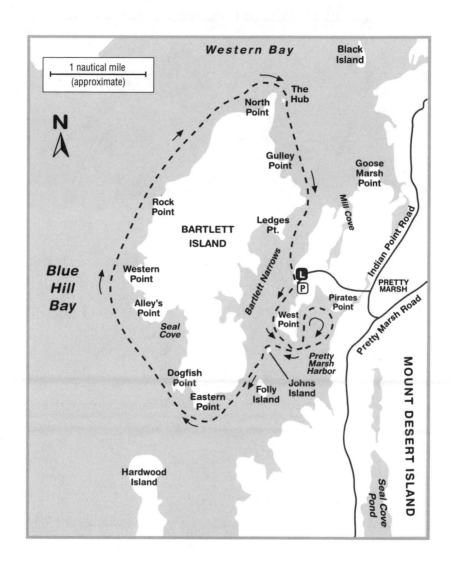

Mount Desert

The Hub is a small state-owned, steep-sided island with room for one tent.

Two-thousand–acre Bartlett Island is owned by the Rockefellers, who kindly allow landing at some areas along the remote west side. They ask that you not go into the interior, however, and respect any signs of private property. The landing is a privilege and something that could vanish at any time if overuse occurs.

The island has several gorgeous pocket sand or gravel beaches. A circumnavigation will take most of the afternoon (it took us five hours). We launched from Bartlett's Landing and decided to follow the tide south, circumnavigating clockwise. (Counterclockwise would have been better, however, as I'll explain below.) At West Point, one option is to paddle into Pretty Marsh Harbor and picnic in Acadia National Park's Pretty Marsh picnic area, which is open to the public. At West Point, paddle northeast across the harbor to the other side. Look for the gazebo and stairs down to the beach.

Since this is the start of your trip, however, you might want to get going. From West Point, paddle to Johns Island, owned by the BPL and open for day use. It is quite small. MITA members also have use of a private island in this area. From John Island, paddle southeast to Eastern Point then past the pristine Dogfish Cove. Look for ospreys perched in trees on Dogfish Point. Now keep an eye open for harbor porpoise and seals, especially when crossing Seal Cove. Follow the west shoreline around from point to point as it bends around to the northeast. The west side is wild and isolated, even lonely, except for a couple of pastures and a few boats.

Alley's Point is followed by Rock Point, which is marked by a large erratic boulder. The shore is heavily forested, with rock cliffs alternating with broad gray gravel beaches. The couple of kayakers we met were circumnavigating counterclockwise. We realized in retrospect that that direction would have been the wiser choice, because the current is fairly strong on the west side. Most focus their attention on the strong current in Bartlett Narrows and forget the larger picture.

Our major scenic point was the solitary bulge of Blue Hill off to the northwest. Long Island lies to the west. At the north end, off North Point, sits the Hub (you will be glad to finally reach it), a small, state-owned, steep-sided island with room for one tent. The beach is located on the north end and barely large enough for three boats (I'm not sure the beach is even there at high tide). Do not paddle near the Hub in May and June, during seal pupping season. Nearby Black Island is also a highly sensitive seal pupping area.

After a rest on the Hub, follow Bartlett's scenic north end, marked by long beaches, woods, and one particularly dramatic deep cove at Galley Point. It is difficult to make out the entrance to Bartlett Narrows, because the island's east end melds visually into the mainland at Goose Marsh Point. But a slight change in color at the tree tips marks the spot. The entrance is to the right of the dock at Mill Cove. Deep cliffs mark the east side of Bartlett's. Pass Ledge Point, Great Cove, pick your way around the huge barnacle-covered granite lumps exposed at low tide, then head southeast across to the put-in marked by the anchorage. You will know you're back at Bartlett's Landing by an outfitter's pod of double kayaks plying the shoreline.

The view south is past Hardwood Island, down the broad Eastern Passage of Blue Hill Bay and out to Swans Island. There is really not much protection here, and the full ocean makes its way well up into Blue Hill Bay.

After the trip, drive to Echo Lake for a freshwater dip. Owned by Acadia, Echo Lake has a swimming beach and lifeguard and is just beyond the AMC camp on Echo Lake, which would make a great base for kayak explorations of this interesting area. (See "Camping" on the next page.)

Besides a circumnavigation, another way to enjoy this area is to spot a car at one of the other public put-ins like Seal Harbor and ride with the tide. If at all possible, avoid parking at Bartlett Narrows. The chaos of both outfitters and individuals loading and unloading boats and parking well up the road in undesignated parking areas may well close down this area soon.

If you're paddling farther north, note that the passage on the east side of the Trenton Bridge dries out at low tide. You need at least an hour on either side of low tide to get through. *The Sea Kayaker's Guide to Mount Desert Island* (Down East Books, 1997) by Jennifer Alisa Paigen gives details on eleven trips in the area.

Camping: The Hub. One tentsite only, four people maximum. There's plenty of camping in Acadia National Park campgrounds; also check out the AMC's Echo Lake Camp at www.outodoors.org/lodging/camps or by calling the AMC (see "Get out & Get Active with the AMC," at the end of this book).

Penobscot Bay

STONINGTON TO HARBOR ISLAND

Trip Mileage: 14 miles round trip (one overnight)

Tidal Range: 9.8 feet at Stonington

Charts and Maps: NOAA #13313 at 1:46,500

Caution Areas: Because of its great depth, Merchant Row attracts many larger boats, ferries, motorboats, sailboats, and schooners. Keep heads-up at all times for boat traffic. The many lobstermen of Stonington work quickly even in a heavy fog, so be extra careful in fog. From Swans Island back to the Stonington area, be aware that Jericho Bay can get choppy in an afternoon southwesterly.

Access: Town ramp in Stonington. Caution: the end of the concrete ramp gets very slippery at low tide, and your feet can fly out from underneath you. Park your car to one side. Unload boats and gear quickly, then park your car elsewhere in town. Several alternatives exist. We found the neighbor's field up the hill (look for the sign) to be the most convenient; a fee is charged. You can also park at the Isle au Haut ferry terminal on Seabreeze Avenue, for a fee; the gates are locked at night. Contact 207-367-5193. Another alternative is Old Quarry Ocean Adventures in Oceanville, which offers overnight parking. A fee is charged. Contact 207-367-8977, oldquarry@direcway.com, www.oldquarry.com. The town dock next to the stonecutter statue is really no longer an alternative due to crowding and parking restrictions.

Getting There: To reach the town ramp in Stonington from US 1, take ME 15 south to ME 199 to ME 175, over Bagaduce Falls, to ME 15 at Sargentville, to Stonington. In Stonington on Main Street, turn left at the miniature houses to Bayview Avenue to the Isle au Haut ferry parking area.

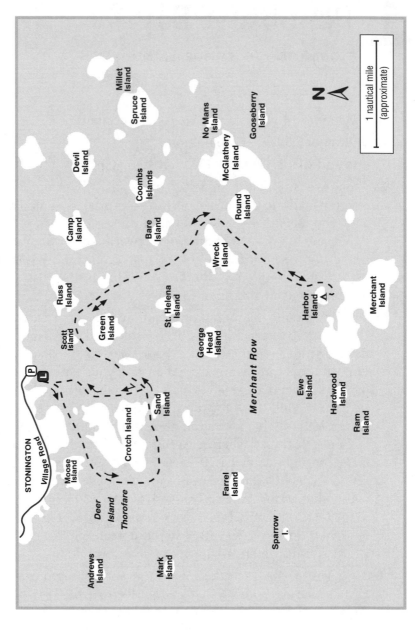

Penobscot Bay

STONINGTON
Village Road

Andrews
Island

Mark
Island

*Deer
Island
Thorofare*

Moose
Island

Crotch Island

Scott
Island

Russ
Island

Green
Island

Camp
Island

Devil
Island

Spruce
Island

Millet
Island

Coombs
Islands

Bare
Island

Sand
Island

St. Helena
Island

Farrel
Island

Sparrow
I.

George
Head
Island

Merchant Row

Ewe
Island

Hardwood
Island

Ram
Island

Wreck
Island

Round
Island

McGlathery
Island

No Mans
Island

Gooseberry
Island

Harbor
Island

Merchant
Island

N

1 nautical mile
(approximate)

Take a sharp right, then left behind the ferry building. The ramp is located between two buildings.

To reach Old Quarry Ocean Adventures in Oceanville from ME 15 (southbound), turn left at Ron's Mobil Station onto Oceanville Road, then go right onto Fire Road 22 (watch for the sign) and continue to the end of the road.

Aт тне southern end of Deer Isle off Stonington lies a collection of islands in Merchant Row, navigable by the Deer Island Thorofare. The islands are probably the best place on the entire East Coast to paddle because they are so plentiful and offer a great deal of protection; many are state owned and provide several camping options. Beyond that, all possess individual beauty, gravel beaches, dark green spruce, and clear Caribbean blue-green water. You will probably feel more like Robinson Crusoe in Merchant Row than at any other place on the New England coast.

Distances between the closely spaced islands are measured in yards, not miles. With the exception of Isle au Haut, 6 miles from Stonington, they are mostly uninhabited. Paddling choices abound—from island-hopping and picnics to landing for a hike, a long day trip to Swans Island, and an athletic circumnavigation of Isle au Haut. In short, kayaking in this area is wonderful.

To note that this area has radically changed for kayakers in the dozen years since this guidebook was first published would be an understatement. For better or worse, recommended island capacities, tent platforms, alternative campsites, camping reservations, encouragement of the use of onshore inns, new nonprofit owners, and a private shoreside campground have all left their mark on the easily accessible adventure this area once offered. Kayakers are literally loving the Deer Isle Archipelago to death—not without help from many other boat users, of course. The last edition of this book listed seven public islands to camp on; MITA now lists twenty, including both public and private islands.

With care, you can still use these islands. At less crowded times, in June or September, a good base of operation is Harbor, a large 11-acre island with meadows and spruce copses 250 yards north of Merchant Island on the south side of Merchant Row. To start the trip, launch from the Stonington public ramp by the ferry. Then follow the

Deer Island Thorofare through Stonington Harbor among lobster boats and yachts. Some islands are former granite quarries, once mined for the solid stone that fueled public works building fervor in the mid-nineteenth century. Note that some islands have freshwater quarries for swimming, one of the fringe benefits of the historic granite industry.

Paddle around the east side of Crotch Island, which is the site of Maine's only working quarry factory and where stone for John F. Kennedy's memorial in Arlington Cemetery was quarried, as was the granite for the Boston Museum of Fine Arts. Pass between Scott and Green Islands, site of another historic quarry, and continue to Bare Island, then between Wreck and Round Islands. You now face one of the widest crossings in the archipelago—it's about 1 mile across Merchant Row over to Harbor Island. It's 6.5 miles from Stonington to Harbor following this route, or about 4 miles if you paddle directly.

The best landing on Harbor Island is on a gravel beach on the south side. *Caution: Seaweed on the rocks can be slippery, and you should step in between the rocks rather than on them for security.* The island now has three separate campsites: the south meadow (with a recommended camping limit of eight people), the northeast woods (six people), and the east point (four people). Refer to the MITA guidebook for exact locations. Merchant Island, just across the cove, is privately owned, and that privacy should be honored. Island camp life in Merchant Row generally involves plucking mussels off seaweed from rocky ledges at low tide, collecting sea urchins, watching seals frolic just off the islands, and watching the sun set over the Camden Hills. In July, the island meadows are full of yellow hawkweed, yarrow, wild sweet pea, and iris.

From Harbor Island, you have several options. Nearby is state-owned Wheat Island, 1 mile southeast of Harbor and a good camping alternative (ten people is the maximum camping capacity) if Harbor is occupied. Wheat is a large wooded island with a crescent-shaped sand spit on the south side. The white shell bottom and greenish water clarity are reminiscent of Caribbean turquoise—conditions also evident on several other Merchant Row islands. Various islands owned by Island Heritage Trust and Friends of Nature allow careful day use.

Just to the south is Isle au Haut, with ferry service from Stonington. The heavily wooded, 18-square-mile island rises 565 feet out of the sea. On Isle au Haut, you can pick up supplies at

From Harbor Island, you can paddle to the remote south end of Isle au Haut.

the grocery store, see the island church, and check out vintage cars that have been kept running for twenty years or more. For an interesting account of the lives of Isle au Haut's year-round residents, read *Here on the Island* (Harper & Row, 1974) by Charles Pratt; the more recent *The Lobster Chronicles: Life on a Very Small Island* (Hyperion, 2003) by Linda Greenlaw recounts her switch from swordfishing to lobstering. She wrote her own account of the Perfect Storm in the best-selling *The Hungry Ocean* (Hyperion, 2000).

Part of Acadia National Park, Isle au Haut has a campground at Duck Harbor with five Adirondack-style shelters, open to the public by reservation only. A circumnavigation of Isle au Haut starting at Harbor Island is about 9.5 miles, a trip that may seem like a good idea at the outset but can also feel lengthy after a while.

After your trip, a great restaurant with lots of moderately priced fresh seafood is The Fisherman's Friend on School Street, which easily accommodates large groups of ravenous paddlers (reservations recommended). It's open daily 11:00 A.M. to 9:00 P.M.; the Friday Fish Fry is a bargain. Lily's Cafe on Airport Road in Stonington has great homemade dinner specials in a casual atmosphere (neoprene okay). It's open weekdays and serves dinner Wednesday through Friday.

The Deer Isle Granite Museum on Main Street gives you an idea of how the quarries operated with an 8-by-15-foot working model of quarrying operations on Crotch Island and the town of Stonington in 1900. Call 207-367-6331.

Other Options: Other state-owned islands in the area include Hell's Half Acre, located 225 yards west of Camp Island between Devil and Bold Islands. Hell's Half Acre is 2 acres of beautiful meadows, woods, and beach; obviously a misnomer. It is popular among local day-trippers and may have more visitors than you would like during the height of boating season. It's so heavily used, in fact, that it now has two MITA-built tent platforms on the west end to reduce impact. Located in the far eastern section of the Deer Island Thorofare is Little Sheep, a bald spot with a lovely gravel beach and wildflowers. It is totally exposed and not a good spot in high wind. The Maine Island Institute owns the 50-acre Russ Island, just off Deer Isle, which is available for day use for picnics and a hike up the hill for blueberry picking and the fabulous view. It gets a lot of local use. Pets are not allowed because of a year-round flock of sheep grazing on the island. Author's note: I always get lost hiking on Russ and end up thrashing through the puckerbush.

A nice, long day trip is possible from Little Sheep to Swans Island and back across Jericho Bay, with views of the Mount Desert mountains and lumpy Isle au Haut. Swans is a carefully guarded summer community; it has a public launch spot near the spot where the ferry from Bass Harbor arrives. Hen Island on the west side is owned by the state; MITA has a couple of private camping options.

A launch from Naskeag Harbor to the east of Stonington is a good start for an overnight to Little Sheep and approach to Stonington from the archipelago's less heavily used east side. Potato, Apple, Little Hog, and Sellers provide public access. Stop for a visit to the WoodenBoat School to the west on Naskeag Point just north of Babson Island, which is distinguishable by the beautiful wood boats at anchor. Center Harbor, farther west, is another public launch spot for this area. Locals enjoy the Torrey Islands in Eggemoggin Reach for picnics on the long beaches and swimming. In Blue Hill Bay, Green Island has an interesting lighthouse. You are sure to see plenty of seals.

From the east side, you can also circumnavigate Stinson Neck by carrying over the causeway; the beautiful Lazygut Islands are passed en route. Yet another option is circumnavigating Whitmore Neck and stopping at local trust-owned Polypod Island. The area's possibilities are endless.

Camping: Public islands in the Deer Isle Thorofare and Merchant Row include Harbor, Wheat, Hell's Half Acre, Hen, Weir, Steve's, and Little Sheep. Potato, Apple, Little Hog, and Sellers Islands are good for outings from Naskeag Point; Doliver, unnamed on the chart, is off the northwest tip of Isle au Haut, north of York Island. MITA offers several private options. Old Quarry Ocean Adventures Campground (see pages 77 and 79) in Oceanville caters to kayakers, with several tentsites and two launch areas into Webb Cove. Camping on the Acadia National Park portion of Isle au Haut is at Duck Harbor (open May 15 to October 15). For reservations, send requests to Acadia National Park, PO Box 177, Bar Harbor, ME 04609. Reservation request forms are accepted no earlier than April 1. Telephone requests are not accepted. For a brochure, call Acadia Headquarters in Bar Harbor at 207-288-3338.

Maine

TRIP 8

East Penobscot Bay

LITTLE DEER ISLE TO POND ISLAND

Trip Mileage: 8 miles round trip

Tidal Range: 10 feet at Little Deer Isle

Charts and Maps: NOAA #13305 (Penobscot Bay) at 1:40,000

Caution Areas: Distances between islands in East Penobscot Bay tend to be greater than those in Stonington—on average, a nautical mile—so exposed crossings are the norm. The good news is that the strong southwesterlies that come up in the afternoon will blow you back to shore.

Access: The area has two launch spots. The first is the marina at Eggemoggin Landing, located just on the right after you cross Eggemoggin Reach Bridge and next to Three Sisters restaurant. This is a safe place to leave a car overnight. Parking is available and there is a launch fee. The second launch is at the end of Eggemoggin Road on the northwest end of Little Deer Isle. Be sure to park in the middle of the traffic circle to keep summer residents happy.

Getting There: To reach Eggemoggin, follow ME 15 south down the peninsula. From ME 15 south, cross Eggemoggin Reach Bridge to reach Three Sisters restaurant and the first launch site on your right. To reach the second launch site, continue past the restaurant, turn right at the information center, and follow Eggemoggin Road all the way to the end (about 3 miles, just opposite Pumpkin Island Light).

East Penobscot Bay

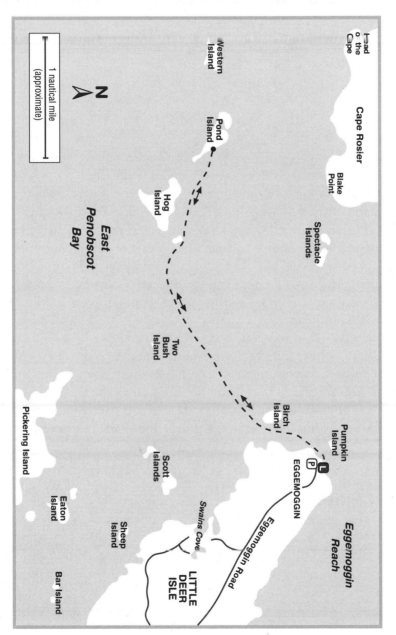

Eᴀꜱᴛ Pᴇɴᴏʙꜱᴄᴏᴛ Bᴀʏ sits quietly in a corner of the sea, tucked away from nearby Camden, Stonington, and Bar Harbor, whose busy harbors and marinas send hundreds of boats out to fish or to sail. In East Penobscot Bay, broad islands of rock granite sit by smaller gems, some made of gravel, and rocky ledges on which seals snooze away their summer afternoons.

The islands lack the smooth pink-coursed granite slabs that ring nearby Stonington's islands. Bold shores and great sweeps of beach are more dramatic than picturesque here. Despite the exposed crossings, all in all this place is paradise.

A good spot to begin exploring here is the public launch at the west end of Little Deer Isle, down Eggemoggin Road. It is located just opposite Pumpkin Island Light. From here, a good destination is Pond Island, owned by the Maine Coast Heritage Trust. Located just a mile off Cape Rosier, it sees a lot of day use from skiffs and sailboats from the nearby mainland. You can always expect company on Pond, which lies between the well-kept Hog (privately owned with a house, beach, and gardens to die for) and the Western Islands. From a long approach, the three merge visually, and it is only upon reaching Hog that the layout makes sense.

Pond looks like a backbone of an island, being beaten away at both ends. The island has long beaches on both south and north exposures and three wooded areas: one just a clump of overgrown bushes at the east end, a larger clump in the middle, and a thick spruce forest at the west end. The odd distribution of forest suggests that the interior was once all wooded but has been eroded over the years, composed as the island is of sand and gravel. (Most islands in the area are granite based.) The pond, actually tidal marsh, is located between the two clumps on the west end. Some speculate that the pond may fill in someday to become a freshwater pond, and possibly a meadow. Be sure to bring your insect repellent for the mosquitoes.

The Maine Coast Heritage Trust permits day use and camping (the site is located within the middle tree clump, marked by a sign) for two nights only; fires are allowed, but you must obtain a fire permit.

The spring and fall migrations of seabirds and waterfowl can be a sight to see here, and the island was once owned by the Audubon Society to protect sea- and shorebirds. Pond remains a nesting area for many seabirds; its northwest corner, known as John's Head, and southeast corner are closed March 15 through July 15. Please make note.

The islands of East Penobscot Bay are quiet and alluring, even in a summer rain.

Paddling in the area is a visual feast. To the south of Pond lie the broad and beautiful islands of East Penobscot Bay, all with various forms of ownership. Great Spruce Head (where nature photographer Eliot Porter did much of his Maine work) is privately owned; Butter is owned by the conservation-minded Cabot family that generously provides access for Maine Island Trail Association members. You can tell the island by the broad clearings on it; Eagle has a summer community and the historic Eagle Island Light—you may see the mail boat making its way there from Sylvester Cove. The broad, forested Bradbury Island, owned by The Nature Conservancy, is closed most of the summer due to nesting seabirds. Add the large schooners out of Camden and Rockport winging by on a fresh north wind, sails set against a cloudless sky, and the painting is complete.

If you have time, swing around to the south of Little Deer Isle. Swains Cove is picturesque, home to a few lobster boats (one reason the area is so quiet) and some sailboats. Just south of Little Deer Isle, the two Scott Islands look halved from the same cookie cutter and are both privately owned; one is inhabited and the other isn't. They offer a special place in children's fiction as the setting for Robert McCloskey's *One Morning in Maine*. It is from here that six-year-old Sal, her little sister, Jane, and their father rowed his skiff all the way to Buck's Harbor to have his motor fixed at Condon's Garage and

Salmon Farming

East Penobscot Bay's timeless islands got a jolt when a salmon farmer applied for a license to build pens and raise salmon off the Scott and Pickering Islands just off Little Deer Isle. In light of this development, Sal, of storybook fame—alias attorney Sarah McCloskey—became president of the East Penobscot Bay Environmental Alliance. She and her sister, Jane, normally keep out of the limelight. Yet both exchanged their privacy for publicity to protest placing two 15-acre high-density fish farms next to the Scott and Pickering Islands.

According to McCloskey, "The waters of Maine are for all the people to use and enjoy: fishermen, sailors, island inhabitants, visitors, marine scientists, artists. Salmon pens, as currently operated, use the waters with intensity inconsistent with existing uses. The bays are public 'commons.' A for-profit factory does not belong in the middle of this scenic area."

Salmon farming is a source of controversy along the Maine coast as the practice moves south into the more populated Midcoast. Proponents argue that it's a way to harvest food from an increasingly declining population in an industry where groundfish populations have been decimated by overfishing. Salmon farming is one of the most valuable seafood industries in New England.

Protesters cite the lack of research on salmon farming's impact on the environment. Toxins from the pesticides in the salmon's food, the outbreak and spread of disease among closely penned fish, water quality affected by concentrated fish waste, and the potential for gene pool intermingling from salmon that escape the pens and interbreed with their wild counterparts are cited as some of the problems. (Ironically, just to the north the U.S. Fish and Wildlife Service is working hard at the Craig Brook National Fish Hatchery in East Orland to return wild salmon to the Penobscot River, sending millions of fry into this and other northern Maine rivers each spring. The agency has also filed protests against the salmon aquaculturalists.)

Many of the salmon-farming issues are in court while the farmers are doing more to address water quality. For more information, contact the East Penobscot Bay Environmental Alliance, part of Friends of Blue Hill Bay, P.O. Box 1633, Blue Hill, ME 04614.

back home in time for clam chowder for lunch. Sal—whose drama revolves around losing her first tooth—will always be a young girl in summer on these islets.

After circling the Scotts, you can paddle past the Eaton Islands, named for the family that populates this area. Eaton's Lobster Pool is a popular seafood restaurant whose lobsters come from traps just outside Blastow Cove. Sheep Island, the bald bump closer to shore, is owned by The Nature Conservancy, which permits careful day use, but the steep shore prohibits access, and there are no interior trails. Ospreys nest on the ledges at the island's east end and should be avoided through mid-August.

The north cove on Pickering Island is a popular stop for yachters, with a long, quiet beach, but anyone would do well to make it around to the south side for a circumnavigation. Here bold cliffs drop into the ocean, waves slap against the sides, rough driftwood gets tossed onto pristine pocket beaches, ospreys and guillemots abound. The north and south perimeters of the islands here are like two different worlds.

Nearby Crow Island is owned by the state and is open to careful day use after August 15 due to nesting birds. Many seals haul out on the ledges (see the sidebar on page 94) to the west of Sheep, Eaton, and Pickering Islands, and you are almost certain to see seals swimming in the area.

Foraging is good here. You can pick mussels from the low-tide line on shore. If you pick them off rocks where they are hanging in a vertical position (rather than lying on the beach), they have better water filtering. Or flag down a lobster boat and negotiate for the wholesale price per pound.

For provisions, Buck's Harbor Market in Buck's Harbor has great picnic fixings, and a bulletin board. This is the best general store on the Blue Hill Peninsula. For restaurants, Eaton's Lobster Pool, Little Deer Isle, offers seafood and great sunset views from the deck. It's open daily 5:00 to 9:00 P.M.; call 207-348-2383 for reservations.

Camping: Pond Island has a two-night limit; camp only in the designated spot. Contact the Maine Coast Heritage Trust (see appendix A).

Outer Penobscot Bay

CIRCUMNAVIGATION OF VINALHAVEN
FROM CARVER'S HARBOR

Trip Mileage: 22-mile loop (three days)

Tidal Range: 9.4 feet at Vinalhaven

Charts and Maps: NOAA #13305 at 1:48,000

Caution Areas: Beware breaking waves on Folly Ledge in Carver's Harbor and mud in the passage from Winter Harbor to Mill River one and a half hours on either side of low tide. Leadbetter Narrows gets a strong current. In windy conditions, the west side is apt to get very choppy. The entrance to The Basin on the west side has a strong tidal bore.

Access: Carver's Harbor

Getting There: From Rockland, take the Vinalhaven ferry to Carver's Harbor. To reach Rockland, take I-95 to Brunswick, then ME 1 and US 1.

Vinalhaven and the surrounding Fox Islands are more remote than some other paddling areas on the Maine coast. Pristine islands far out in Penobscot Bay, a strong fishing culture, and a view of Isle au Haut 7 miles across East Penobscot Bay are the rewards.

Trip logistics focus on the Vinalhaven ferry, which crosses the 13 miles of bay from Rockland to Carver's Harbor six times a day in summer. The ride is about one hour and fifteen minutes. From Rockland, it's first come, first served. Put your car in line for the ferry and move up. You can also buy one of four car reservations available on three out of six trips. Reservations are sold starting one month in advance of the day of departure and can be made in writing or in person. In summer, reservations are usually sold out by 7:00 A.M. of the month limit. From Vinalhaven, the procedure is the same, except you get a number for your place in line the day before departure. You must write to the

Penobscot Bay

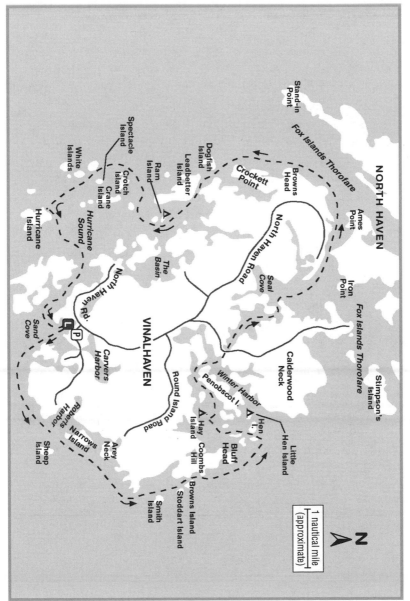

Stand-in Point

Spectacle Island

White Islands

Dogfish Island

Leadbetter Island

Ram Island

Crotch Island

Crane Island

Hurricane Island

Hurricane Sound

North Haven Rd.

The Basin

Crockett Point

Browns Head

Fox Islands Thorofare

Ames Point

NORTH HAVEN

Iron Point

Seal Cove

North Haven Road

Fox Islands Thorofare

Stimpson's Island

Calderwood Neck

VINALHAVEN

Sand Cove

Carvers Harbor

Roberts Harbor

Narrows Island

Arey Neck

Round Island Road

Winter Harbor

Penobscot I.

Hen I.

Hay Island

Coombs Hill

Little Hen Island

Bluff Head

Browns Island

Stoddart Island

Smith Island

Sheep Island

N

1 nautical mile (approximate)

Maine State Ferry Service in advance with your first and second (and possibly third, if it's a holiday) choices of dates you would like to cross and return. Ferry officials will notify you by mail of your reservations. For more information, contact the Maine State Ferry Service, www.state.me.us/mdot/opt/ferry/ferry.htm; call 800-491-4883 for general information or 207-596-2202 for the Rockland office.

Once on Vinalhaven, you will realize how island life revolves around the coming and going of the ferry. When the weather worsens, the ferry stops altogether. Islanders are often better than visitors at adapting to this flexible schedule. This kayak trip is not for someone on a tight or fixed schedule.

Note that ferries won't carry boats that are not loaded onto cars. Paddling from the west side of the mainland to these islands is not recommended except for very experienced paddlers because the stretch of open water from the mainland to Vinalhaven can range from 8 to 14 miles, depending on your launch spot. If you do get into trouble and wish to return to the mainland via ferry, I have successfully hitchhiked kayaks in someone's Whaler or on top of a friendly stranger's car, but don't count on this. More protected island-hopping access is possible through the "Northerns," the islands of East Penobscot Bay with a Deer Isle launch site. However, this involves a much greater driving distance, if you're coming from the south.

Vinalhaven is a large, wooded island. With about 1,200 year-round residents (9,000 in summer), it is one of the largest island communities and is the third largest island on the Maine coast. Vinalhaven is still very much on "island time," and after strolling down Main Street you will feel as though you have drifted back into another era.

The natural beauty of the island is remarkable. You paddle by bald, lunarlike islands on the east side with a view toward Isle au Haut. The Fox Islands Thorofare between Vinalhaven and North Haven is also very scenic. Large, indented coves and bays such as Winter Harbor and a view of Matinicus, 12 miles out in the Atlantic Ocean as seen from Carver's Harbor, are all aspects that make Vinalhaven special for sea kayaking.

The island has a lobster-fishing industry with about one hundred full-time lobstermen who work together out of the Fisherman's Coop at Carver's Harbor.

During the nineteenth century, Vinalhaven was the site of a thriving granite quarry that provided granite for the massive columns of the Cathedral of St. John the Divine in New York and the bases of the

Hurricane Island is headquarters for the Outward Bound School and is always friendly to small-boat explorers.

Brooklyn Bridge. Two of the abandoned spring-fed quarries on the island make great swimming holes.

In Vinalhaven in 1826, Maine cut the first commercially quarried granite to build the walls of a Massachusetts prison. The industry grew to the point that Vinalhaven had at least thirteen working quarries by 1880. At the industry's height, quarries operated on thirty-three islands, with schooners built on Chebeague Island in Casco Bay hauling columns, carved pediments, and paving stones south to the cities for frenzied construction of public works. Eventually, the industry was eclipsed by the invention of concrete.

Hurricane Island, another major quarry center during the 1800s and now headquarters for the Outward Bound School, is located to the southwest of Vinalhaven; thus, there is a long tradition of outdoor wilderness experience in the area, and locals don't view sea kayakers as being too intrusive. Be careful not to disturb anyone on an Outward Bound solo, marked by a blue flag. Many participants are camped on the islands around Vinalhaven. Look elsewhere for a camping spot.

Camping is allowed on one of the several state-owned islands in the area, or stay in a bed-and-breakfast or the one motel. Of the state-owned islands, on the east side are Little Hen, 150 yards west of Hen Island on the south-side entrance to Winter Harbor; and Hay, a large island in the middle of Seal Bay, about 1 mile southwest of Little Hen. On the west side is Ram, three small islands in the middle of upper Hurricane Sound. Little Thorofare, two islets connected by a bar up by North Haven, is small, exposed, and not recommended for camping. All other islands are privately owned; in particular, Vinalhaven Land Trust and Maine Coast Heritage Trust island property is not open to camping.

The recommended trip is a circumnavigation of Vinalhaven in a three-day span. The island is about 7 miles long and 5 miles wide, sliced into the ocean all around so that no point is more than a mile from the salt water. Thus, some place is protected no matter which way the wind is blowing.

Day One: Your best bet is to park in the ferry parking lot at Carver's Harbor and launch from the beach at Grimes Park to the left of the ferry. Owned by the American Legion Post, it has several picnic tables and is a good spot for a picnic while loading your boats. Public restrooms are located next to the town clerk's office.

Use the wind direction to choose the direction in which you will paddle around the island. If the wind is from the southwest, go up the east side. If it is blowing from the northeast, turn west. Typically in summer the onshore breeze starts from the southwest around 11:00 A.M. When paddling up the west side into the wind and with the tide, you're liable to encounter fairly choppy conditions. If you bring a car, you can always find a place where the wind isn't blowing. General rule: if the ferry isn't running, don't paddle!

But if all is calm, head out of Carver's Harbor and north up the east side of Vinalhaven. Pass Roberts Harbor, the beautiful Arey's Neck, and Geary's Beach. To sea, you pass several bald islands owned by The Nature Conservancy including Brimstone, a nesting area for eiders and gulls, and Smith Island.

After you have made your way up the island's east side, with a view across East Penobscot Bay to Isle au Haut, head into Winter Harbor. Right at the top of the harbor is Little Hen, a state-owned island; if you still have time, aim for Hay Island to the south of Penobscot Island. Winter Harbor is a lovely space with the same kind of rock you find in the Muscle Ridge Channel or White Islands. When sun warmed, the smooth rocks are ideal for dozing.

Day Two: At high tide, you can paddle under the bridge from Winter Harbor into Mill River (or carry over at low tide), with Calderwood

Helping Stranded Seals in Midcoast Maine

Under the Marine Mammal Protection Act of 1972, it is illegal to disturb or harass seals and other marine mammals in U.S. waters. This applies to abandoned or stranded seals found on the shoreline. While it's understandable to want to help animals in distress, it is not recommended that untrained people attempt to rescue stranded or entangled marine mammals, both because the practice is illegal and because these animals are potentially dangerous to people. If you come across a distressed marine mammal, keep your distance and restrain any pets or other people from approaching the animal, which may cause it further harm. Note the location, time, and apparent condition of the animal and contact the Marine Environmental Research Institute's (MERI) seal stranding specialist at 207-374-2135, pager 207-758-4007; MERI, 55 Main Street, Blue Hill, ME 04614; MERI@downeast.net; www.meriresearch.org.

Neck to the right. You reach the Fox Islands Thorofare and pass North Haven, teeming with yachts. *Fox* is the original name for these islands, so named by British explorers who were surprised by the many silver-gray foxes living on the islands, now long gone. The little town of North Haven has 200 year-round residents, a small grocery store, an art gallery, a small restaurant, and a landing for the North Haven ferry. Note that the tide runs east on the flood and west on the ebb. Stay close to shore to avoid midstream traffic, which is plentiful.

Paddle past Browns Head and Crockett Point and through Leadbetter Narrows, marked by the green can. Near the head of Hurricane Sound, northeast of Barton Island, sits Ram, which can be located in the BPL brochure "Your Islands on the Coast." Ram has two islets; the slightly larger eastern islet has two campsites, while the smaller western hub has one, with room for a single tent.

Day Three: Paddle down the west side of Vinalhaven through Laireys Narrows (also spelled *Lawrys*) to look at the beautiful White Islands or up Hurricane Sound. At Barton Island, not far from Ram, The Basin has a strong tidal bore and can be fun for surf practice. You can also disembark at the entrance just to watch the show. The sound has some lovely islands, including 80-acre Hurricane Island, leased by Outward Bound, which welcomes visitors. The Nature Conservancy owns the Big Garden, South Big Garden, and Big White Island, all open to day visitors after July 31, when nesting season is over. Paddle through The Reach and around Norton Point back to Carver's Harbor. Lane Island Preserve at the entrance to Carver's Harbor is owned by The Nature Conservancy and allows day use, but the floating fish gurry may put you off.

Other Options: If you paddle around the north side of North Haven, your total trip length will extend to 30 miles. A tempting crossing is the 7 miles of open ocean to Isle au Haut, but this is not advisable in less-than-perfect conditions.

Back on the mainland, Camden State Park is a great place for an overnight. The hot showers (bring your quarters) are sublime, and a drive up Mount Battie for a view of all the Penobscot Bay islands is definitely worth the entrance fee. Mount Battie has some hiking trails with more views.

North of Camden, from Lincolnville, it is about a 3-mile paddle to Warren Island State Park, just south of Isleboro. The 130-acre park is the only island park in the state devoted exclusively to boats. Warren has two Adirondack shelters and several walk-in tentsites, some waterside. It also has picnic tables, all on the east side; privies; fresh water; and a hiking trail. You are encompassed by Spruce, Seven Hundred Acre, and Islesboro Islands, which contribute to the "water-park" feel. You can reserve a spot ahead of time by contacting the Bureau of Parks and Lands at www.state.me.us/doc/parks/programs or calling 800-332-1501 within Maine and 207-287-3824 out of state. Or you can paddle in on a first-come, first-served basis. The ranger's cabin is located in the middle of the island. The 3-mile crossing over West Penobscot Bay can be rough, with gnarly seas and much large-boat traffic. The alternative is to take the Islesboro Ferry over to Islesboro (a much larger vessel than the one that goes to Vinalhaven, so it's less problematic) and paddle the short distance to Warren. Still, you must cartop your kayak, and nonresident parking in Islesboro is limited. For ferry information, see appendix A.

Ducktrap Sea Kayak on Lincolnville Beach, near the spot where the Islesboro Ferry departs, offers tours and rentals. It's found at RR 3315, Lincolnville Beach, ME 04849; 207-236-8608.

Camping: Bureau of Parks and Lands islands of Little Hen, Hay, and Ram around Vinalhaven.

TRIP 10

Muscle Ridge Islands

Trip Mileage: 8-mile loop

Tidal Range: 9.3 feet at Tenants Harbor

Charts and Maps: NOAA #13305 (Penobscot Bay) at 1:40,000

Caution Areas: The tide can run upwards of 2 knots through the Muscle Ridge Channel; it also runs swiftly through the islands, especially the guts. The outer sides of the islands are very exposed in strong south winds. Watch out for breaking waves on the many ledges in the area in heavy weather.

Access: Lobster Buoy Campsite at Waterman Beach, South Thomaston. You can launch from the tentsite beach or in the designated launch area.

Getting There: To reach the Lobster Buoy from US 1, take ME 131 south, turn left onto Westbrook Street, and continue to South Thomaston. Head left onto Spruce Head Road, taking the first left at a sign for the campground, then turning left again into the campground.

THREE THINGS YOU should know about the Muscle Ridge Islands. One: The island group's name refers to the Old English spelling for indigenous colonies of blue mussels—not to what you'll need to paddle out to these islands (you may see it spelled differently on different maps). Two: The islands are spellbinding in their beauty but somewhat intimidating because once you've paddled the 2 nautical miles out there, there is nothing beyond them but open ocean. Three: Limited public access requires you to be prepared to stay in your boat for long stretches. (MITA members are privileged to use at least two private islands.)

Muscle Ridge Islands

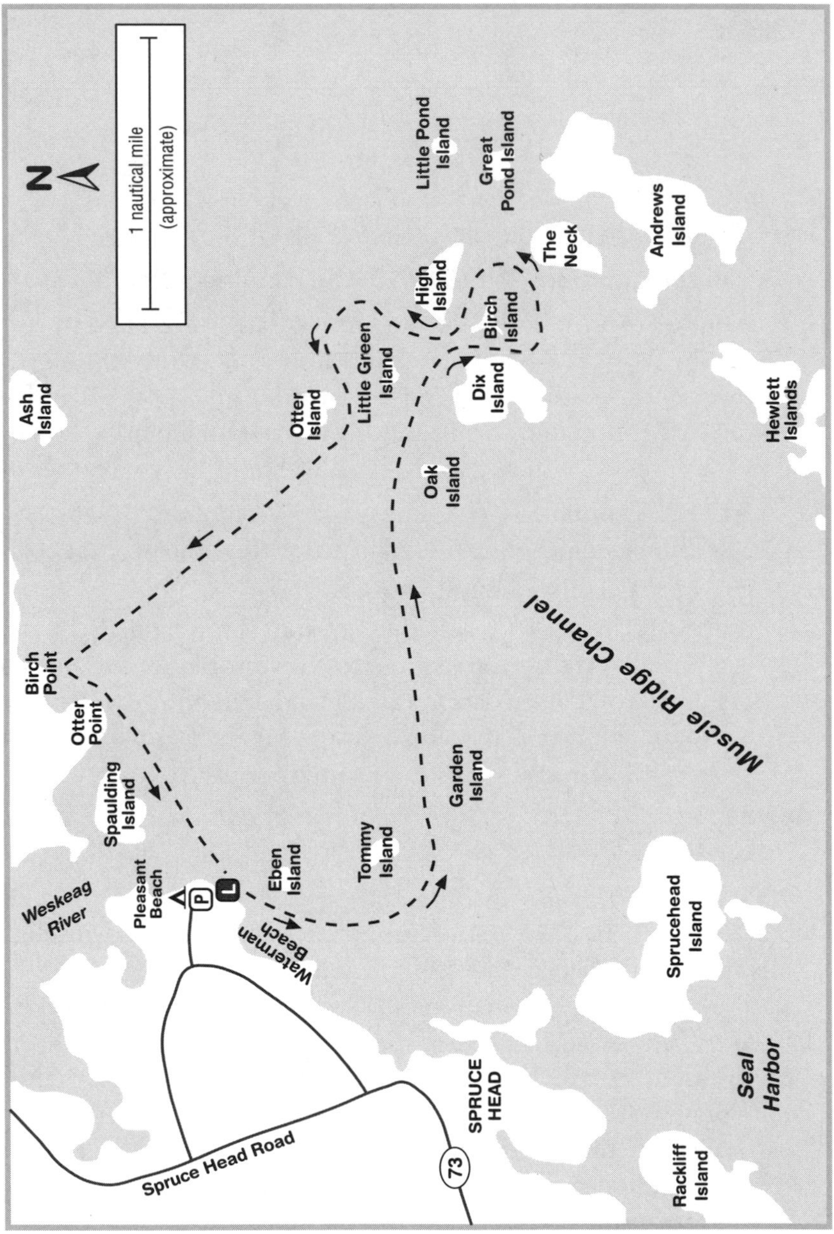

N

1 nautical mile
(approximate)

Ash Island

Birch Point

Otter Point

Spaulding Island

Weskeag River

Pleasant Beach

Waterman Beach

Eben Island

Tommy Island

Otter Island

Little Green Island

High Island

Dix Island

Birch Island

The Neck

Little Pond Island

Great Pond Island

Andrews Island

Hewlett Islands

Oak Island

Garden Island

Muscle Ridge Channel

Spruchead Island

Seal Harbor

Rackliff Island

SPRUCE HEAD

Spruce Head Road

73

Many have found that staying and launching from the commercial Lobster Buoy Campsite on Waterman Beach at South Thomaston is the best way to time a trip during fair weather. The campground is primarily geared to RVs, but it reserves a small tenting area on the beach, at the campground's southern end, from which you can launch.

Muscle Ridge Channel is known for its ledges and shallow water, which makes lobstering prolific. You will be dodging many lobster buoys and boats on your way out. The ledges, however, do not deter many sailboats from traveling here, although sailors have a very narrow channel to steer through. The ledges are also one of the major haul-out and whelping areas for seals in Maine and should be avoided during pupping season in May and June.

After a launch from Waterman Beach, paddle past Tommy Island, about 0.5 nautical mile out, then past Garden Ledge (identified by a day marker)—watch for seals. From here, paddle toward Otter Ledge, marked by another day marker; at Red Nun #10, bear east past Oak toward Little Green Island. It's about a 2-nautical-mile crossing. Not many of the islands are inhabited, so you will have the place to yourself along with large cruising sailboats that use Dix for anchorage. Putter around Dix, which used to be a major granite-quarrying site. Surrounded by Dix, High, Pond, and Andrews Islands is pretty little Birch Island, with several protected sandy pocket beaches. After exploring, head back to Otter Island.

Note that the currents run very swiftly through the islands, and if you need to stop and stretch for any reason, you may find your kayak scooting away as you try to disembark. Paddle past Otter and cross back to the mainland. The trip back can be difficult in a following sea. Fisherman Island lies distinctly to the northeast. Ash Island is barely distinguishable from Ash Point. Back on the mainland, you can stop at Birch Point Beach, the sand beach between Birch and Otter Points. The beach is managed by Camden State Park, open 9:00 A.M. to sunset (privies available). It may be difficult to land in a strong southwesterly. Watch out for swimmers. MITA also has private island-use permission in the area.

Pull up to Waterman Beach, confer with other campers, and watch the sunset.

If you are feeling particularly strong, an alternative is to cross from Waterman Beach to Dix, then make your way south down the islands, past the Clam Ledges, Andrews Island, Hewett, Flag, Pleasant, and Graffam. The guts between the islands are pretty passageways from one fir-studded paradise to another, but the water can run swiftly between them. Cross from Graffam to Sprucehead Island, then make your way along the shore back to Waterman Beach (about a 10-mile trip depending on how much wiggling you do around the islands). You can also continue your trip to Tenants Harbor (see Trip 11, next page).

Camping: Lobster Buoy Campsite. Most of the waterside campsites are for tenters (with picnic tables and fire rings) in this predominantly RV campground. Privies, shower, camp store. The owners are kayak friendly. Stop in at the camp store for latest news about or mishaps of your fellow kayakers. A fee is charged (cash only). Contact Lobster Buoy Campsite, 280 Waterman Beach Road, South Thomaston, ME 04858; 207-594-7546. See page 97 for directions.

TRIP 11

Wheeler Bay

TENANTS HARBOR TO SPRUCEHEAD ISLAND

Trip Mileage: 11.5-mile loop

Tidal Range: 9.3 feet at Tenants Harbor

Charts and Maps: NOAA #13301 at 1:40,000

Caution Areas: The islands are exposed to the full fetch of the Atlantic, so you will feel any storm effects from the south whenever you're out of the protection of coves. Note that if you head south along the peninsula, toward the exposed Mosquito Head, you are facing cliffs (which will send off refracting waves) and no landing for nearly 2.5 miles. This is one of the most challenging spots on the Maine Island Trail.

Access: The public ramp at Tenants Harbor. Launch from the roomy gravel beach; there's parking in the upper lot. Another launch, at Spruce Head Island on the causeway, is possible but only during the three hours on either side of high tide.

Getting There: To reach the public ramp off US 1 coming from the south, turn right at Thomaston onto ME 131, then continue 9 miles south to Tenants Harbor. Look for concrete ramp next to the Cod End restaurant.

Tenants Harbor is a pretty little town located right on ME 131 on the road down to Port Clyde, where the ferry leaves for Monhegan. The harborside is picturesque, with the Cod End lobster pound's deck overlooking the beach and promising a lobster feast upon return. Along the way you're bound to see seals, ospreys, and, in September, rafts of guillemots in winter plumage.

Start off down the long, narrow Tenants Harbor, a balance of well-kept lobster boats and sailboats, all with great names. Pass several lobster pounds to the north. At Red Nun #2, turn north into Long Cove,

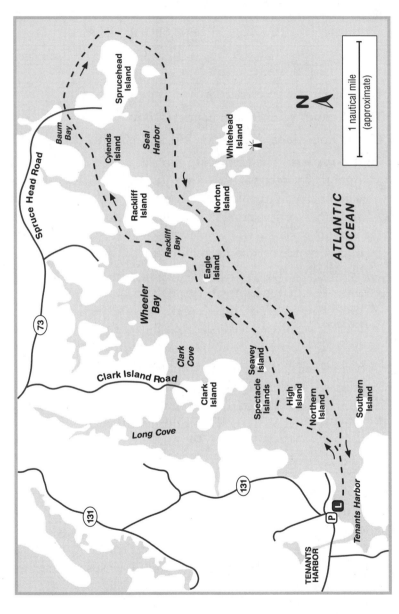

Wheeler Bay

ATLANTIC OCEAN

Sprucehead Island

Baum Bay

Cylends Island

Seal Harbor

Whitehead Island

Rackliff Island

Norton Island

Spruce Head Road

Rackliff Bay

Eagle Island

Wheeler Bay

73

Clark Cove

Clark Island Road

Seavey Island

Clark Island

Spectacle Islands

High Island

Northern Island

Southern Island

Long Cove

131

131

TENANTS HARBOR

Tenants Harbor

P L

1 nautical mile
(approximate)

N

where more commercial fisheries can be seen. At Green Can #1, pass out of Long Cove between High and Spectacle Islands. Choose island passages carefully, because at low tide several are impassable with rock and stone.

Unfortunately, there are no public islands in this area, although MITA members have access and overnight privileges to one private island. Pass south of Seavey Island, then cut straight across to Elwell Island and Wheeler Bay, a little more than a mile. Aim just north of Green Can #3. Elwell is easy to find because it's the only long piece of land in the bay with no buildings on it. The view out to sea is spectacular from the south end of the island. Four miles out is Two Bush Light with its flashing red light, managed by USFWS for nesting seabirds; 6 miles out is Metinic Island.

The next part of your trip passes north of Rackliff Island. This is possible by portaging through the large culvert at the causeway at low tide. You can also portage your kayak across the road. If it's still low tide on the other side, wait a while until the tide comes in.

To the south is Seal Harbor. At the head of the harbor is the beautiful Cylends, privately owned. Beyond Baum Bay is the bridge to Sprucehead Island. It has a harbor with many fine yachts, a scenic shoreline, and at its eastern tip one of the most beautiful pocket beaches I have seen in Maine. It's coldwater paradise. To the northeast lie the Muscle Ridge Islands.

Sprucehead's harbor is full of lobster boats. Now paddle back to Tenants Harbor. Head for the gap between the pointed-fir-studded Norton and Rackliff Islands. These two islands, along with Whitehead, look like one mass. You can tell the island break by a slight color change in the line of treetops. If the weather is settled, you can paddle out around Whitehead; a lighthouse here has been key to mariners reaching the Muscle Ridge Channel for nearly 200 years.

Then it's a straight shot past Eagle and over to Seavey and so back into Tenants Harbor. The entrance is marked by the lighthouse on Southern Island. You have a better view of the outer islands this way. Don't forget to stop at Cod End and sit on the deck with that lobster feast you promised yourself at the trip's start. Tenants Harbor was where author Sarah Orne Jewett spent her summers, so you may find resonance here from her book *The Country of the Pointed Firs*, published in 1896.

Camping: None.

TRIP 12

Muscongus Bay

BROAD COVE MARINE TO FRIENDSHIP VIA CROW ISLAND

Trip Mileage: 11 miles round trip (one overnight) (Broad Cove to Crow Island, 1 mile; Crow Island to Friendship, 4.5 miles)

Tidal Range: 9.5 feet at Waldoboro

Charts and Maps: NOAA #13301 at 1:45,400

Caution Areas: The stronger the wind, the higher the beam seas you will negotiate when paddling in an east–west direction. If you travel south to Pemaquid Point (an Indian name for "long finger") at the southwest corner of Muscongus Bay, it's best to round the point in settled conditions in early morning or late evening, according to MITA. If headed east, try to hit the flooding tide into Muscongus Bay. Swells striking the ledges create clapotis; quieter water is normally found 100 yards or so offshore.

Access: Broad Cove Marine (207-529-5186), Medomak. A daily fee is charged per car, but the peace of mind is worth it; there have been reports of car vandalism at Dutch Neck (likewise at Medomak and Keene Neck).

Getting There: To reach the marina from Waldoboro, take ME 32 south for about 7 miles, then turn left onto Medomak Road at the Bremen town office and fire department. It's about 2 miles to the marina (look for the post office on the left) at the end of this road. Unload by the beach, then park in upper lot.

M USCONGUS BAY is the perfect getaway for two reasons: it is well protected and is not on the way to anywhere else. What this means for sea kayakers is a handsome bay that sees little use from many craft other than lobster boats. The pretty 2-acre Crow Island,

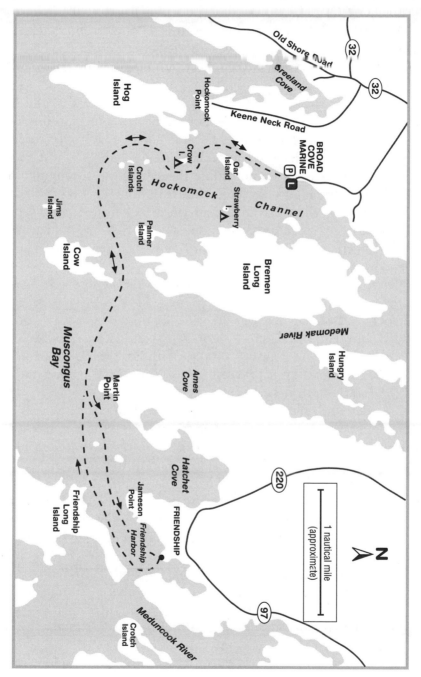

Muscongus Bay

distinguishable by the one tall spruce growing higher than the rest, can be reached from Broad Cove through the protected water of Hockomock Channel.

The bay is quiet because from Pemaquid Point, yachters tend to bypass Muscongus Bay on their way to the better-known Bar Harbor waters. Another reason for bypass, however, is the thousands of lobster buoys here. According to Philip W. Conkling in *Islands in Time*, Muscongus Bay is "lobster heaven" because the waters of the St. George and Medomak Rivers bring rich, suspended nutrients into the bay, whose shallowness means the water temperature is several degrees higher than it is in the Gulf of Maine. The flush of fresh water from the rivers does not dilute the salt of the sea enough to affect the lobsters. It also has the optimum bottom for lobster breeding. *Muscongus* is the Abenaki Indian word for "fishing place," but probably refers to smelt rather than lobster. So rich was the bay, the great Indian chieftain Samoset went to Louds Island every summer to fish and hunt.

One fellow kayaker has remarked on what he thought made Muscongus distinct from other large bays in Maine—a particular shade of blue. Looking out over the wide bay dotted by widely spaced islands, both large and small—Louds, Thief, Cow, Wreck, and Harbor—encircled by a spruce coastline with little visible settlement and hidden harbors (even Friendship is folded into a harbor out of view), the color blue does take on a particular shade.

At sunset, the lobster pots light up like bobbing fireworks in evening light. According to Conkling, some of the most industrious lobstermen, the "crushers," have 1,200 traps in this area, requiring a tremendous amount of work. A lobsterman needs to visit a trap at least every other day or the lobsters will begin to cannibalize each other.

The islands, both large and small, march across the bay in an extended northeast-to-southwest line, remnants of drowned glaciers, and open up to the Atlantic, like actors on stage left, stage right, with potentially heavy beam seas as the stage floor. It is truly a unique area to paddle, with mainland always close by, but not so close as to feel intrusive. Unfortunately, Muscongus Bay is another area that kayakers paddle in a lot, and MITA has done much to protect islands from overuse. Crow in particular is a beautiful little island, situated at the top of Hockomock Bay, so you get wide water views of the ocean but have a nice protected feel. It's a gem of an island for camping, with good landing spots and a 360-degree view of the bay.

An AMC group enjoys a picnic on Crow Island.

Unfortunately, due to its popularity, erosion, human waste, and trampling have all made this island unrecognizable to some who have paddled here for a decade or more. Fortunately, island adopters and volunteers are helping restore its character, and it is on the mend. If Crow (twelve people maximum) is full, go to nearby Strawberry. Crow has two camping sites at the interior north end with established trails. Give wide berth to nesting ospreys.

A good paddle plan is to put in at Broad Cove Marine, paddle down to Crow, set up, then explore. Todd Wildlife Sanctuary on nearby Hog Island is run by the National Audubon Society. Audubon welcomes visitors to hike the nature trail but asks that you keep your boat away from the dock. Stop in at the office to sign in and get a trail map. Hockomock Nature Trail on Keene Neck also provides good opportunities for bird watching. Pull up at the boathouse, set your boat to the side, and walk up the hill to the visitor center. The passage between Keene Neck and Oar Island is a scenic one but not passable at low tide.

The Maine Audubon Camp at Hog Island now offers several sea-kayak-related naturalist programs. Contact www.maineaudubon.org or The Audubon Camps in Maine, Maine Audubon, 20 Gilsland Farm Road, Falmouth, ME 04105; camps@maineaudubon.org; 888-325-5261 (camp registrar and camp information only).

Friendship Sloops

Friendship has some pleasure craft, notably something called the Friendship Catboat, but only a few Friendship Sloops, which is surprising for the craft that has made this Muscongus Bay town famous in the boating world.

Here is what the Friendship Sloop Society has to say about this boat developed in Muscongus Bay:

> The Friendship Sloop has no real birth, but was gradually developed around 1880 from the fishing and lobstering needs of the men of Muscongus Bay on the Maine coast. It is certain some of these fishermen had seen a Gloucester fishing boat, and being impressed with lines, had incorporated some of its features into their own hull designs. These men did not build a "class boat" where every hull is the same length. From existing records we find that the original builders constructed sloops varying in length of 21'–50'. Probably the average length would be about 30'–40'. The basic design was scaled up or down depending on length, and followed a pre-set formula. They all had an elliptical stern, and most of them a clipper bow, and were gaffed rigged. The pre-set formula included such measurements

For dinner, you can paddle to Round Pond to one of the local seafood restaurants or to the dock next to the wrecked schooner in Greenland Cove. Chances are good that you will find some lobsters for sale, and it is a ten-minute paddle back to camp for almost immediate cooking.

The next day, make the trip to Friendship, a working town on the east side of the bay. To get there, paddle south to the Crotch Islands (watch for bald eagles), then pass between Bremen Long Island and Cow Island (note the channel markers, Green Cans #3 and #1). It's a 1-mile crossing of the Medomak River to Martin Point. Pass by the scenic Hatchet Cove on the left and continue to Jameson Point and into Friendship Harbor. Friendship has a town landing at the east end of the piers with dock access only, across from Garrison Island. It's best as: the beam equaled one third the overall length, and the length of the mast should equal the length overall plus half the draft, etc.

Boat shops dotted the coastline of Bremen, Bremen Long Island, Morse Island, Cushing, Thomaston, and Friendship. In 1903 there were 22 sloops being built on the shores of Bremen Long Island alone. Many of the men went into the woods to cut their own wood, and hauled it to the sawmill with horses. The island builders floated their sawed planks (25'–36') suspended over two dories to get it to their offshore boat houses. Each builder had some little secret innovation which in his estimation made his model better than the others.

The annual Friendship Sloop Regatta used to take place here but due to popularity has now moved to Rockland, usually in mid-July. Friendship Sloop numbers are pretty much limited to the existing sloops, with very few being built to replace those that deteriorate. The most popular part of the regatta is the parade where the boats sail by the waterfront, their identity announced, and each one given a cannon salute! For more information, visit the website at www.fss.org. After the Rockland event, many of the boats sail on to Friendship for Friendship Days.

just to stretch your legs and move on, because Friendship is a busy fishing town and not necessarily gracious to those not working by boat. Besides, amenities such as restaurants or other attractions are few. Friendship does have a well-stocked grocery store, however, if you need to replenish your camping supplies. Keep heads-up for lobster boats when paddling through the harbor. From here you can return to Crow or go directly back to your Broad Cove Marine put-in.

Several other day trips from Crow Island include: Round Pond (3.5 miles), paddling along Louds Island; Thief Island (3.5 miles); New Harbor, just south of Pemaquid Point and near the Rachel Carson Salt Pond Preserve (9 miles). You could also spot a car at Port Clyde and paddle the 10 miles from Crow passing to the north of Friendship, Caldwell, and Hooper Islands.

Many ospreys live around Greenland Cove. The National Audubon Society and Cornell Laboratory of Ornithology through Dr. Steve Kress have successfully established an Atlantic puffin colony on Eastern Egg Rock with imported chicks from Newfoundland. Do not even think of paddling here—it's 8 miles out to exposed sea anyway. Commercial boat trips out of Boothbay Harbor or New Harbor provide puffin viewing for the public.

Other Options: Several state-owned islands provide camping alternatives to Crow. Thief Island is located farther out; Round Pond is the better launch spot for Thief. On the Maine Island Trail, Thief gets a lot of day and overnight use. It has a nice meadow on its northwest corner, where there is camping for twelve people. The south end campsite can accommodate four people. Launching or landing can be difficult at high tide. Don't dismantle the established fire ring. Just southwest is Killick Stone Island (private), known for the shores lined with split rock used as anchors in former centuries. Little Marsh, also called Thrumcap, is a tiny island off the southern tip of Marsh Island, to the east of Loud, a good port in the storm with room for one tent. MITA members have access to several private islands in the area, which helps relieve congestion on the state-owned islands.

The islands of western Muscongus Bay are incredibly beautiful but will await description in a future guidebook.

Camping: Crow, Strawberry, Thief, Little Marsh, and Havener Ledge Islands.

TRIP 13

Fort Popham to Fort Island

VIA BOOTHBAY HARBOR

Trip Mileage: 43 miles round trip (three days)

Tidal Range: 8.0 feet at Phippsburg; 8.7 feet at Boothbay Harbor

Charts and Maps: NOAA #13293 at 1:46,000 and 1:44,400

Caution Areas: Volumes of water sweep in and out of the mouth of the Kennebec River in a constricted area. Thus conditions here can be powerfully adverse; especially in an opposing wind and tide, you will get standing waves. The tide is also powerful enough to make it impossible to paddle against. In 1991 a young woman lost her life when her kayak got swept out to sea by the powerful outgoing tide. It is best to cross the mouth of the river early in the morning before the winds have come up, close to slack on an incoming tide. It is worth the patience to wait out conditions until they are favorable. If weather is settled, you may also consider the crossing, but the incoming tide is always advisable. Currents run fast, on average of 2 to 4 knots, but with reports of upwards of 6 knots. The currents are confused by bending around headlands and islands. Goose Rock Passage from the Sasanoa to the Sheepscot River can get fierce tidal rips; the north and west sides of Fort Island have very strong currents at the Narrows and Back Narrows.

Access: Fort Popham or Morse Cove

Getting There: To reach Fort Popham from US 1 at Bath, take ME 209 south to its end. The dock launch is in Atkins Bay, across the street from the fort parking lot. To reach Morse Cove from ME 209, turn left on Fiddlers Reach Road and follow it 1.1 miles to its end. Unload and park in the upper parking lot.

Fort Popham to Fort Island

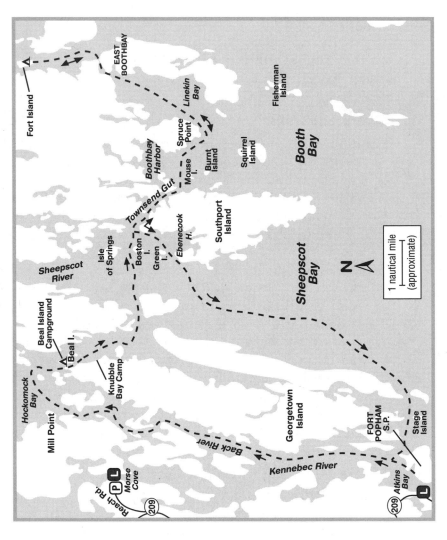

A TRIP FROM POPHAM BEACH to Fort Island is a three-day tidewater journey through three rivers, across the mouth of the Kennebec River, and around an exposed peninsula in open ocean. This trip is for experienced paddlers only. Highlights include the barren landscape around Popham Beach, the haunting Sequin Light, long sand beaches, the quiet beauty of the Back River and Hockomock Bay, and schooners gallantly sailing out of Boothbay Harbor.

Many seals swim at the mouth of Kennebec, at the ledges across from Bay Point and along Popham Beach, possibly waiting for handouts from the many fishermen.

The timing of the trip to the tides is key. The trip starts at Fort Popham at the mouth of the Kennebec River, from where you travel up the Kennebec, veer off to the Back River, then Hockomock Bay, with an overnight at AMC's Beal Island Campground. On day two, you paddle through Goose Rock Passage across the Sheepscot River and through Townsend Gut to East Boothbay via Boothbay Harbor and Linekin Bay, to Fort Island on the Damariscotta River, with an overnight on Fort. The total distance of that leg is 24 miles. The return trip of 19 miles is back to Fort Popham around the south tip of Georgetown Island on open sea.

The launch is from Atkins Bay, which on the Saturday morning of Memorial Day weekend can be a quiet affair—but just the opposite on the holiday Monday. Over the weekend, people have had the chance to put their boats in the water.

There is no longer overnight parking at Fort Popham, so you will have to move your car. One option is to unload boats and gear, then park at the Morse Cove public launch in Phippsburg. However, this requires a 12-mile car shuttle. Another option is to inquire about overnight fee parking at Stonehouse Manor, located just down the road. (Call owners Tim and Jane Dennis at 207-389-1141.) You can launch from Atkins Bay from the small public pier on the point's west side or from a small part of the rocky shore here (hand-carry only). A beach on the west side of the bay is also usable and can be found straight ahead off ME 209 down Fort Baldwin Road.

Day One: Paddling out of Atkins Bay, you will encounter some rips, the intensity depending on time of tidal flow and wind. Once you cross to the north side of the river and beyond Bay Point, the water settles down. The best time to launch is at slack water with the tide beginning to come in so you can ride the tide swiftly up the Kennebec. With the wind at your back, you'll fly. Perkins Island, a state-owned island available for camping with an abandoned lighthouse on the west side, can be reached within an hour (about 3 miles from the mouth of the Kennebec). The landing on Perkins is halfway down the east side, with a trail into the interior's established campsite. Beware fierce mosquitoes in the woods. One kayaker, however, has reported that she thinks it is one of the nicest islands on the Maine Island Trail. So much depends on daily conditions: weather, wind, and bugs. Note the pyramid bell tower, restored by hardy MITA volunteers and state funds in 2000.

Your compass will read northeast even as you might think you are heading straight north up the Kennebec River. Just beyond Phippsburg, marked by a white church steeple, bear right (east) into the Back River. The Back River is magnificent and unspoiled, with marshes, tall cliffs, just a scattering of houses, and faint sounds from US 1. Red-winged blackbirds, blue herons, ospreys, and cormorants under a gently falling spring rain can enhance the experience.

The Back opens into the sublime Hockomock Bay, indicated by a red marker. It's hard to distinguish mainland from island and harder still to believe that you are still on the ocean and not a freshwater lake. Bear right (east) to the north end of Beal Island. The official campsite is on the south beach. You will know it by the stairs that lead up the bluff to a conifer forest and meadow beyond for camping. Blue herons and ospreys are evident, and pink lady's slippers bloom in late May. The mosquitoes, however, can be quite voracious in season.

Day Two: Head south down Knubble Bay to Robinhood Cove, a quick trip when wind and tide are in your favor, past a collection of large yachts at Robinhood Marina on Georgetown Island. The yachts all hang in different directions from colliding currents and eddies in the cove. Next, head through Goose Neck Passage. You will need to read the buoys to determine the location of this passage, aptly named with a narrowing that produces stiff current and tide rips, best paddled an hour before or after slack when they are less severe.

As in any river situation, if a strong wind and tide are opposing one another, the crossing of the Sheepscot can be rough, but it is only about 1 mile if you can hold course. A good place to cross is from Whitman Island to the Isle of Springs. Pass by the green marker with the osprey nest, then pass between Spectacle and Boston Islands to enter Townsend Gut.

In Townsend Gut, you will pass excursion boats and a procession of other pleasure craft. Eddies on the north shore will help you through. Please stay close to shore to let boats pass. Leave Mouse Island to the right (south) and Boothbay Harbor to the left (north) and head for Spruce Point, but watch for boats coming in and out of Boothbay. The paddle up Linekin Bay isn't very interesting, surrounded as it is by hundreds of houses in a big body of water, but it is protected. At the end of Linekin is the Murray Hill boat ramp. Carry your boat over the road to the pond, paddle a few hundred yards to the culvert, then be prepared to carry again.

The access to the culvert from the pond is a sharp, rocky little drop of a couple of feet with another drop of a foot or so from the culvert into the Damariscotta River. It is possible to pass through the culvert when enough of the drops are flooded yet the tide is not so high as to make the culvert impassable.

In any event, Lobsterman's Wharf at East Boothbay is a fine restaurant at which to wait for optimum passage. You may have to proceed with another portage across the road to the Damariscotta River. This maneuver is touchy because of the posted private property around the culvert.

Once you're launched in the Damariscotta River, paddle north to Fort Island. Note that the currents around Fort are very swift, and you may have to lean into eddy lines. The eastern shore of the river has a big eddy that you can use until you're ready to ferry over to the island. A lovely cove on the southeast side at Fort Point has a suitable landing and camping spot. Downriver from Fort, you have a beautiful view of just a slice of open ocean between Rutherford Island and Linekin Neck. Some kayakers make the beautiful Fort Island their destination, using it as base camp for several appealing day trips from the area. It is also popular with large groups like the Boy Scouts, so if you're in search of solitude, look elsewhere.

Fort Island, managed by Parks and Recreation, was once the site of Fort Webber, built during the war of 1812 against the British. Upon careful examination, you can still see the ramparts and cellar hole of the old blockhouse. The island is about 20 acres in size, with a large camping area, a privy, a spring, and an established fire ring at the southeast corner at Fort Point. The island's narrowness allows you to walk easily from west to east to view the respective sunset and sunrise.

AMC's official campsite on Beal Island is on the south beach.

Day Three: Retrace your route down the Damariscotta River to East Boothbay and paddle and portage back out to Linekin Bay. Paddle through the Townsend Gut, but this time bear left (south) at Cameron Point, down Ebenecook Harbor, passing between Green Island and Dogfish Head. Cross the Sheepscot River at an angle to Five Islands. Then head down Sheepscot Bay, past Harmon Harbor, to Griffith Head. The paddling now is past long, sandy beaches of Reid State Park, which can get quite tedious, even though it is exhilarating to be on the open sea. Round the coast back to the mouth of the Kennebec, where your view to the south is of Sequin Light.

A passageway between Stage Island and Kennebec Point, not visible at low tide, negates the need to paddle around the south tip of Stage. Cross the riptides to Fort Popham. Watch for big motorboats kicking up a wake as they enter and exit the Kennebec on summer weekends. The best advice is to make your crossing in a group for higher visibility and to paddle hard. *Important:* read "Caution Areas."

The current around the fort is particularly strong, but once you're past that current and into Atkins Bay, you are back in calm water. If the current is overwhelming, you may want to consider a portage across the narrow neck leading out to the fort from the Kennebec into Atkins Bay.

After this excursion, a cold drink or a lobster at Spinney's Restaurant, located next to Popham Beach, is in order, as well as a dip in Phippsburg's freshwater pond. The best put-in spot for swimming is at the Parker Head Road bridge. The cold water is fresh even though it is connected to this tidewater section of the Kennebec River.

Other Options: To see Bath, take the alternate route up the Kennebec, bypassing the Back River, then head down the Sasanoa River. This makes for a longer trip; you'll also need to time your paddling around the current at the Sasanoa Upper Hell Gate.

Camping: Beal Island and Fort Island. For more information about AMC's Beal Island Campground, go to www.outdoors.org/lodging/camps or see "Get Out & Get Active with the AMC" at the back of this book.

Knubble Bay

KNUBBLE BAY CAMP TO MAINE MARITIME MUSEUM, BATH

Trip Mileage: 12 miles round trip

Tidal Range: Tides change at different times in the tidal rivers, so make necessary adjustments. Strong winds can alter the time of high and low tide by as much as one hour.

Charts and Maps: NOAA #13293 at 1:46,000; the Appalachian Mountain Club route map for Beal Island and Knubble Bay Camp.

Caution Areas: The Sasanoa River is subject to severe tide rips at Little and Lower Hell Gates, adjacent to Beal Island, at Upper Hell Gate, and at Goose Rock Passage. The rips continue for several hours on each half of the tide cycle. The currents subside for about an hour on each side of slack water, when they are navigable. The best advice is to give yourself leeway and wait out the tide until the turbulence is at a level you feel you can handle; otherwise, only experienced kayakers and canoeists should run these waters. They should not be run in the fog. The Lower Hell Gate is to the east of Beal Island. The Side Gate, the passage to the east of Lower Hell Gate, avoids the Lower Hell Gate. A small tidal flow, known as the Little Hell Gate, is located to the west of the island.

Access: The Appalachian Mountain Club's Knubble Bay Camp. Kayaks and canoes can be carried to the pebble beach by the gully stairs next to the storage rack. This access is wheelchair accessible.

Getting There: Follow US 1 through Bath and across the Kennebec River Bridge. Just beyond the bridge, turn right onto ME 127 and proceed 5.8 miles to a paved road intersecting from the left. This is Robinhood Road and is

Knubble Bay

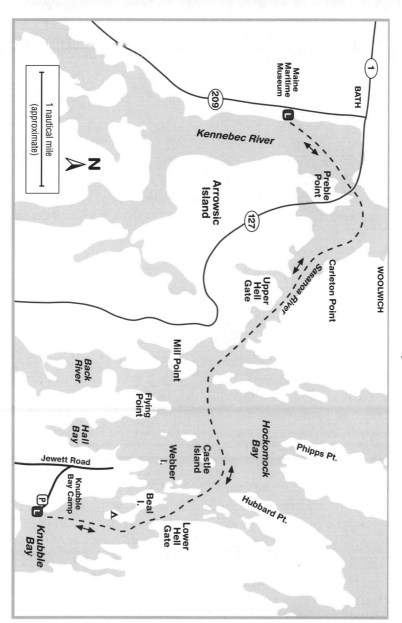

Maine Maritime Museum

BATH

1

209

Kennebec River

Preble Point

WOOLWICH

Arrowsic Island

127

Sasanoa River

Carleton Point

Upper Hell Gate

Mill Point

Back River

Flying Point

Hall Bay

Jewett Road

Knubble Bay Camp

P L

Knubble Bay

Hockomock Bay

Castle Island

Webber I.

Beal I.

Phipps Pt.

Hubbard Pt.

Lower Hell Gate

N

1 nautical mile
(approximate)

marked by a sign reading Robinhood Marine Service, Inc.—
Cape Dory Trawlers. Go 1 mile and turn left onto Webber
Road at the large white Robinhood Meeting House (it looks
like a church). Follow Webber Road 1.2 miles to the first
right turn. Note the AMC marker on the Residents sign-
post. Follow this road (Jewett Road) to the end at Knubble
Bay Camp (KBC), about 0.6 mile, turning right at each fork.
The road gets more rutted the closer you get to Knubble
Bay Camp.

THE POSSIBILITIES FOR sea kayaking and tidewater canoeing are
limitless from Knubble Bay, literally a turntable of rivers giving access
to commanding bays, lonely islands, secluded coves, and busy coastal
towns.

Knubble Bay Camp, located near Georgetown, and Beal Island
Campground on Beal Island, a twenty-minute paddle from Knubble
Bay Camp, are owned and managed by the Appalachian Mountain
Club. Beal Island, 64 acres of wooded land covered in pines, cedars, a
few oaks, and alders, is about 0.25 mile north up Knubble Bay from
Knubble Bay Camp and is accessible in all tide levels. The island has
a rustic campground and a permanent fire permit in place for the season. Dedicated volunteers on fall and spring work parties keep the
island in great shape, including solid stairs down to the beach and
posts to tie your kayak to.

Tidal-river kayaking depends much more on the flow of tides for
travel than does open-sea kayaking. If you use the tides correctly,
they can ferry you swiftly over long distances. You must pay close
attention to rips and currents in narrow channels. One paddler has
reported that he and his wife paddled for twenty minutes in their
canoe against the tide in the Lower Hell Gate while the light tower
remained steadfastly to their right. They finally had to give up and
wait out the tide. If you head north of Beal Island to Bath or
Wiscasset, you should time your trip around high or low slack water,
when the currents subside.

The trip to Bath and the Maine Maritime Museum and back is 12
miles. The best timing is to flood up, ebb back, and plan to go
through the Sasanoa Upper Hell Gate at slack tide. The trip starts at
Knubble Bay Camp or Beal Island.

Knubble Bay is a turntable of rivers giving access to secluded coves.

Head north up Knubble Bay through the Lower Hell Gate on the east side of Beal Island. If you are in a large group, space yourselves when going around the buoy to avoid knocking into each other. Prepare to paddle brace if necessary. The trip continues into the roomy, tree-ringed Hockomock Bay, past Castle Island and Hockomock Point. Then enter the Sasanoa River to the west, its entrance marked by Red Nun #20 and a string of green cans. It is advisable to bring binoculars with you when paddling this area to identify nuns and cans from a distance. Just beyond is the Upper Hell Gate (see "Caution Areas"). Pull over to the beach on Arrowsic Island on the south side of the river to scope out conditions, and be prepared to stay put until they are favorable. Sometimes, you may barely notice that you are passing through. As one Knubble Bay Camp veteran noted, "It's always different whenever you come through here."

Paddle through Hanson Bay, past Preble Point, and enter the Kennebec River under the Woolwich Bridge, a passage between Preble and Sasanoa Points with some current running, then cross the Kennebec, pass the naval shipyard, to the Maine Maritime Museum, recognizable by tall masts and 1 nautical mile south of the Bath Bridge. Kayakers are welcome. Pull into the dock, then carry your boat ashore. The grounds of the former Percy & Small Shipyard include a rebuilt schooner, a boat shop of Maine's historic small boats, a lobster-fishing exhibit, boatbuilding shop, yachters' building, and children's play area.

You can easily spend a couple of hours here, including a picnic on the shaded lawn. (Maine Maritime Museum, 243 Washington Street, Bath, ME 04530; 207-443-1316; www.bathmaine.com. Open every day, 9:30 A.M. to 5:00 P.M., except major holidays. Admission fee.)

On the way back, wait at the Upper Hell Gate for a favorable tide, watching motorboats dive through the holes created by the currents or canoeists running the rapids repeatedly. For variety on the return trip to Knubble Bay Camp, you may want to go through the Little Hell Gate, to the west of the island, which can have a strong current. Stick to the middle. Then head south down Knubble Bay to Knubble Bay Camp or Beal Island. Beal's great asset is the hiking option when wind and tide keep you on shore. Beal is a figure-eight-shaped island, and the crossover of the eight is where people tend to get lost on the trail. Stay left to follow the perimeter trail for a full 2 miles around. The trail is kept clear thanks to fall and spring work crews. May is a lovely time to hike here, with blooming wildflowers of pink lady's slippers, Canadian mayflower, and the fringed polygala. A colonial-era settlement, Beal Island has two old well sites (the water is not drinkable), lilac groves, a graveyard, and the foundations of the last inhabited house on the island. Some speculate that the family left in the 1870s or 1880s after their son fell off the bridge connecting Beal to Georgetown Island. Probably the presence of Lower Hell Gate and Little Hell Gate on either side of the island made this a difficult island to access for farmers. The AMC bought Beal Island in 1969 after its members had been using it for several years for tidewater canoeing.

Other Options: The AMC provides a map (available from the registrar, and nearly a collector's item) with descriptions of sixteen routes and trips in the area, noting the best tide and conditions. A similar map, with more detail, is posted on the equipment shed at Knubble Bay Camp. One such trip is to Robinhood Cove, which has a few lovely islands and the five-masted schooner hull *Mary Barretts Bones*. It is 3 miles round trip from Beal Island or Knubble Bay.

At Georgetown, lower Robinhood Cove divides into two forks by the road. The fork to the right (west) has a mild tidal flow and ends in a quiet backwater. The fork to the left (east) has a strong tidal rip at the narrows and could require a portage. Here, in spring and fall during 12-foot tides, you can take a trip called "Alfred's Dilemma" by continuing on that east fork and passing over marshes to the ocean via Little River or Sagadahoc Bay (5.5 miles one way). Another trip is to

Fort Island via Boothbay Harbor. See Trip 13, "Fort Popham to Fort Island," for a description of that route.

Still another favorite trip is to the beautiful Five Islands (8 miles round trip), where you can stock up on ice cream and cold drinks. Five Islands are located on the west side of the Sheepscot River, out Goose Rock Passage. Go through the passage around slack, but already there will be some good water kicking up between Lowe and Soldier Points, marked by a navigation light to warn you of the false entrance into the Little Sheepscot. Goose Rock Passage gets no fewer than four navigational devices: one light, two red cans, and a green can. Paddle into the Little Sheepscot River, to the west of Macmahan Island, and through the passage at the island's south end, past Turnip Island, and so on down to the lovely Five Islands. You can pull up at the public dock. On the return trip, paddle to the east of Macmahan Island. Cross over from Northeast Point to Brooke Point by Green Can #1 and make your way along the south tip of Westport Island, far preferable to the south side of the river. You can use the eddies of the small coves to make your way against the current. The current at Nedwick Point is particularly strong, but finally eases up at Round Cove Point. From here, you can paddle directly across to the knubble of Knubble Bay and so back to Campbell Cove and your car at Knubble Bay Camp.

If you're headed toward the Sasanoa River but decide not to run the Hell Gate, you can pinball from island to island around Hockomock Bay, or go around Flying Point down the Back River. A good turnaround spot is the bridge to Georgetown Island. Note that the no-name island from the Back River into Hall Bay is marsh and not passable in any tide. In Hall Bay, Erratic is a pretty little pine-covered island suitable for one tenting party only and barely landable at low tide. It is named for the erratic bolder in the island's center, left by a receding glacier. MITA members have access to two private islands in Hockomock Bay.

Camping: Knubble Bay Camp consists of a newly built cottage above the water with bunk space for twelve; tentsites; kitchen with propane stove, oven, and refrigerator; woodstove; well with hand pump; solar electric lights, electricity, an outhouse, and a terrific porch overlooking Knubble Bay. Parking is available for about twelve cars. The cottage is rented exclusively to one party. Camping here is only allowed to people who have rented the cottage or are windblown and can't get over to Beal in the late afternoon. In either case, no fires of any kind are allowed. Knubble Bay Camp is usually booked for the summer well in advance.

Beal Island Campground is situated in a large meadow above the south beach of Beal Island and has an outhouse at the west side of the meadow, a freshwater well (*not* for drinking), and a 2-mile perimeter trail. The beach has a good cooking area with some driftwood set up as a buffet table and a permanent fire ring. Weekends at Beal are fully booked early in spring. Sunday through Thursday nights can usually be booked a few weeks or even days in advance. Fires are allowed only on the beach.

All camping fees are made payable to the registrar with reservations, preferably two weeks in advance. Aluminum canoes with paddles and life jackets are available for rental at Knubble Bay Camp by contacting the registrar: Dave Wilson, 40 Lake Ridge Drive, Sidney, ME 04330; 207-547-4477 or hompawilson@adelphia.net. Note that you can join an AMC trip to take advantange of the facilities.

TRIP 15

Sebascodegan Island

BETHEL POINT TO QUAHOG BAY

Trip Mileage: 8 miles round trip (alternate 18-mile loop)

Tidal Range: 8.9 feet at Cundy's Harbor

Charts and Maps: NOAA #13290 at 1:44,400

Caution Areas: Southern peninsulas are very exposed and can get a lot of wave action in high winds, from all directions. Submerged ledges can be tricky. The tide and current rush through Ewin Narrows and Gurnet Strait.

Access: Bethel Point, at a small, all-tide paved boat ramp on Hen Cove, but parking is by permit only. Instead, unload, then park your car in the Bethel Point Boat Yard, a short walk up the street for $5 a day or $30 for a week ($50 a month, for those who really come back a lot). Contact the Bethel Point Boatyard, 207-725-8145. A privy is available. Other launch spots include Great Island Boat Yard and Sawyer Park.

Getting There: To reach Bethel Point from Brunswick, go south on ME 24 for about 4 miles, then turn left onto Cundys Harbor Road (when you start seeing the tourist signs). Follow the road for about 4.5 miles; about a mile beyond the sign for Dingle Island Road (on the left), turn right onto Bethel Point Road. Follow this road 1.5 miles to the town landing.

In northern Casco Bay, long, ragged peninsulas stretch to open ocean, punctuated by a few large islands and ledges. The paddling here is one of contrasts, intimate in the narrow upper bays, coves, sounds, or harbors as if on an inland lake, and exposed at the ends, with open ocean and possibly large swells or breaking waves

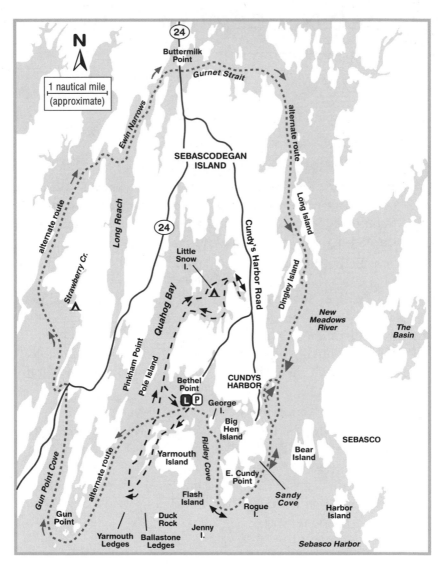

Sebascodegan Island

building on strong southwest breezes across the Atlantic's long fetch.

South of Brunswick lies Sebascodegan Island, meaning "almost through" to the Native Americans who named it. From west to east, narrow strips of land and water march north–south: Middle Bay, Harpswell Neck, Harpswell Sound, Orr's and Bailey Islands, Quahog Bay, Sebascodegan Island, and the New Meadows River to the east. It is a delightful place to paddle. Generally, tides and currents are not a factor except when they constrict through narrow passages like Ewin Narrows or Gurnet Strait. Gurnet Strait requires special attention, because it has a 90-foot-deep hole surrounded by shallows of 6 feet or less, which means a huge water-level difference. The current is said to reach up to 8 knots.

Bethel Point is a lovely place to launch into the waters here to explore Little Snow Island up in Quahog Bay. Cross over to Yarmouth Island, paddle south in a narrow unnamed passage between Yarmouth and Little Yarmouth, and round the south end of Little Yarmouth. Travel north up Quahog Bay, following the mainland to the east, past Pole Island to the west. The mainland is heavily forested with pine and birch and no settlement, in contrast to the western peninsula, which is full of houses and marinas. Bear east to Snow Island, with a house on it. Little Snow is located just to the west, recognizable by an osprey nest and probably people walking on it. You may also see the blue-and-white BPL sign or other kayakers. Little Snow is a low-lying island with a salt marsh meadow and clumps of sea lavender the size of bushes. It has three tentsites, the middle one rarely used because of nesting ospreys. The northwest campsite has a nice bench. Fires are only allowed with a state permit. The island is unfortunately well worn, due to heavy use.

Many sailboats anchor in this deepwater bay, which is protected from wind in all directions. The coves to the west along the bay are interesting to explore. Some—like the nameless cove due west of Little Snow—are almost like fjords with steep rock cliffs, while others are rimmed in marsh and more open. It's best to try to follow the flow tide up and ebb tide down, but the tidal current is not a real factor. Return to Bethel Point.

Warning: the outer peninsula's submerged rocks hidden under rockweed make grounding out easy, leading to the loss of fiberglass layers. It is difficult to judge where the rocks are. On a windy day with breaking waves, you should paddle well out from the submerged reefs at the end of the peninsulas. The area is full of ledges, all named, including Sloop, Cedar, Jenny, Little Bull, Yarmouth, Blacksnake, and Ballastone, and all with some sort of history—not always a positive one, to be sure. The area has shallow water, 2 feet, quite far out.

Another option is to paddle from Bethel Point east to Cundys Harbor, down Ridley Cove, around West and East Cundy Point, and south following the west side of Sebascodegan. This trip is more exposed than the trip into Quahog Bay. Here is the itinerary: Launch from Bethel Point and paddle past George Island to West Cundy Point. Here you get a full view of the islands out to sea. Jenny Island is the nearer clump, located about 0.5 mile from Cundy Point. Jenny Island is owned by the U.S. Fish and Wildlife Service, and National Audubon manages a tern restoration project here, including the federally endangered roseate tern. Duck Rock lies to the west. Privately owned Ragged Island to the southwest is the largest island and is where the poet Edna St. Vincent Millay spent summers.

Continuing around Cundy Point, you will be quite exposed. Paddle past Rogue Island, Sandy Cove, Fort Point, then west into Cundys Harbor. If you're interested in seafood or a snack, pull into the dock at Hawkes Lobster Pound. The public landing is farther north. Cundys Harbor is a working harbor, with many lobster boats moored and docks full of No Trespassing signs. It also has a trawler or two. Fishing is serious here, and sailboats are scarce.

Across the New Meadows River just north of Green Can #5 is the entrance to The Basin; in the middle lies state-owned Basin Island. To the south is Small Point, with imposing granite cliffs, and one of the riskier places on the Maine Island Trail due to exposure and minimal landing sites. Also tucked into Cape Small Peninsula is Sebasco Estates and, farther south, the Hermit Island Campground, which welcomes kayakers (reservations are required for shore sites June through Labor Day).

More than a dozen of these islands, ledges, or rocks are owned by the USFWS and are key sites for nesting sea- and wading birds. Most are closed through the end of July. Wildlife viewing is abundant; you're sure to see ospreys, great blue herons, seals, and many kinds of terns.

One more ambitious option is a circumnavigation of Sebascodegan Island with fun but tricky logistics. The total mileage is 18 nautical miles, and it's best to go through Gurnet Strait at slack tide, finding camping spots on MITA islands. It's nearly 6 nautical miles from Bethel Point to Strawberry Creek and 12 miles from Strawberry Creek back to Bethel Point, so the mileage is a little lopsided. In planning the trip, study the map carefully to see which narrow passages you can paddle through and which are landlocked.

Other attractions: Brunswick is a college town, home to Bowdoin College, one of the oldest in the United States. It has a wide variety of inexpensive eateries, including Thai, Italian, Mexican, and Chinese.

Peary-MacMillan Arctic Museum, located in Hubbard Hall at Bowdoin College, has a well-displayed collection of artifacts, including an Inuit sealskin kayak that two Bowdoin alumni, Robert Edwin Peary and Donald Baxter MacMillan, collected on their trips to the North Pole. Peary was the first man to reach the North Pole and used to live on Eagle Island, now a historic site off Harpswell Neck. Hours for the Peary-MacMillan Museum are Tuesday through Saturday 10:00 A.M. to 5:00 P.M., Sunday 2:00 to 5:00 P.M.; it's closed Mondays and holidays. Free admission.

Camping: Little Snow, Strawberry Creek, and Basin Islands.

Casco Bay

FALMOUTH FORESIDE TO JEWELL ISLAND

Trip Mileage: 14 miles round trip (one overnight)

Tidal Range: 9 feet at Portland

Charts and Maps: NOAA #13290 at 1:44,400

Caution Areas: Waves can build up at the southern tip of Cliff Island and continue a long way out. Disturbed water lies between Cliff and Jewell Islands at the north tip of Jewell. If conditions get too nasty and you have to get back to Portland, the Casco Bay Lines ferry, which lands on several islands, will take hand-carried kayaks.

Access: Falmouth town landing—an all-tide paved ramp—in Falmouth Foreside. Overnight parking is limited to four spaces across the street from the Town Landing Market. Nonresidential parking is also limited. For a day trip, you can launch and park (no overnight) from East End Beach.

Getting There: To reach Falmouth Foreside from I-95, take the exit marked Falmouth Foreside, then ME 88 north. Just past the Portland Yacht Club is the Town Landing Market. Turn right down Town Landing Road to Falmouth town landing. To reach East End Beach from the Casco Bay Ferry Terminal, drive north on Fore Street; soon after the road makes a sharp left, look for a turnoff into the parking area for the Eastern Promenade. Park in the upper lot. A fee is charged.

J EWELL ISLAND is easy to reach from the mainland, and the sense of accessible wilderness in a large urban setting is still a great lure. Over the years, however, it has gotten more and more popular with weekend boaters and has now developed a reputation as party central

Casco Bay

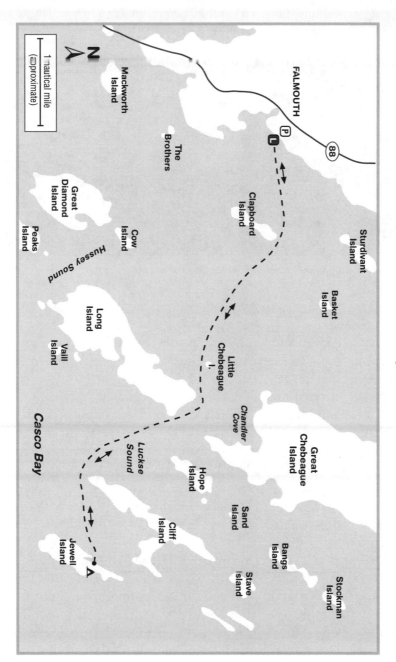

FALMOUTH

88

P L

Mackworth Island

The Brothers

Clapboard Island

Sturdivant Island

Basket Island

Great Diamond Island

Cow Island

Hussey Sound

Peaks Island

Long Island

Vaill Island

Little Chebeague

Chandler Cove

Great Chebeague Island

Luckse Sound

Hope Island

Sand Island

Cliff Island

Bangs Island

Stockman Island

Jewell Island

Stave Island

Casco Bay

1 nautical mile
(approximate)

N

Off the north end of Jewell Island, the water can get rough.

come Friday. As many as thirty boats congregate in "Cocktail Cove" on the northwest side on weekends. Fortunately, MITA and BPL have stepped in and continue to work hard to preserve the island and manage its public use. Jewell has a full-time caretaker in summer; his campsite is located at the north end. In 1992, MITA, the BPL, local lobstermen, and the Rotary Club joined forces build privies (now four) and fire rings. The fire rings are located at established campsites, and fires are not allowed outside those areas. Campsites are located along the west and south shores; there is also a campsite just north of the Punch Bowl. It's best to visit in the off-season when you can enjoy pleasing views overlooking the broad Atlantic in relative peace. A circumnavigation of the island makes a lively trip, with rock gardens and cliffs and a wide view out to the Atlantic on the southeast coast.

If you are tied in by weather, you can hike the perimeter trail along high bluffs overlooking the Atlantic, past World War II defense towers. The trip makes a good weekend outing in the off-season, when parking is not a problem at Falmouth Foreside. In normal conditions, it takes about two hours and fifteen minutes to reach Jewell. A good route is to paddle between Little Chebeague and Long Island, two of the largest islands in Casco Bay. At higher tide levels, it is possible to pass between Little and Great Chebeague. East of Little Chebeague, paddle through the two wrecked schooners placed there to deter German submarines, past the houses along Long Island (including an unusual gray octagonal house on the point), past Hope Island, to the south end of Cliff Island (where waves refracting off the cape can get quite big), and on to Jewell. If water is too rough north of Cliff, you may want to reroute to Crow Island.

On your way back, you may want to divert to Inner Green Island. From here in October, you can see Mount Washington covered in snow.

Other Options: A state historic site, Eagle Island is slightly more than 2 miles from Jewell, accessible only by private boat. The island has a protected beach on the north side for landing. Guides are on hand, and a trail leads around the island (about a twenty-minute hike).

North Pole explorer Admiral Robert E. Peary lived here for seven years following his seventh and final trip to the Arctic. His wife was on Eagle when she heard the news that Peary had reached the North Pole. Because of the subsequent controversy surrounding the North Pole discovery, Peary retreated here, according to a caretaker on the island. He supposedly kept his sled dogs across the way on Upper Flag Island (a practice common in Greenland in summer when they are not being used) and would yell at them to quiet down when they got too noisy.

The simple but grand house is open in summer for a $2 fee and has exhibits and photos from Peary's expedition. The porch view over the Atlantic could easily lure even the most satisfied explorer back out into the great unknown.

If you have time after paddling, visit the Gilsand Farm Sanctuary in Falmouth Foreside, located at 118 US 1; it is headquarters for the Maine Audubon Society and has walking trails, an education center, and programs. Contact 207-781-2330; www.maineaudubon.org.

Camping: Jewell Island.

TRIP 17

Casco Bay

**PORTLAND HARBOR AROUND ORRS ISLAND
TO STRAWBERRY CREEK**

Trip Mileage: 35 miles round trip (four days)

Tidal Range: 9 feet at Portland

Charts and Maps: NOAA #13290 at 1:44,400

Caution Areas: You must cross a major shipping lane into Portland to access the islands. The lane goes from Portland Head Light north to Spring Point, then around the north tip of South Portland into the Fore River. In Portland, pick up the brochure "Big Ships, Little Boats," which delineates the major shipping channel. Here is what the brochure warns: "Tankers berth at various oil and cargo terminals from Spring Point up the Fore River to the Veterans Bridge. While waiting for a berth, these ships may anchor between House Island and Munjoy Hill. They may veer unexpectedly under the influence of wind, current or an assisting tug. Great care should be taken when operating in their vicinity." Bailey-to-Orrs Island Bridge has a tidal rip at certain tide levels. Also see Trip 16, "Falmouth Foreside to Jewell Island."

Access: Overnight parking at public launch areas in Portland is nonexistent. The best bet is to launch from East End Beach and seek overnight parking in one of the nearby commercial parking lots, or at the Casco Bay Ferry Terminal (fee). Or you can launch from a ramp at Bug Light Park in South Portland. Day use only (sunrise to sunset); again, a fee is charged. Call Port Harbor Marine (207-767-3254) to see about overnight parking. When launching from Bug Point Light or Port Harbor Marine, you cross a major shipping lane. It might be wise to paddle around the corner to Spring Point Light, then sprint across the shipping channel (0.5 nautical mile) to House or Cushing Islands.

Getting There: Follow I-295 to Exit 8. At Washington Ave., turn left onto Eastern Promenade and follow it 0.75 mile to East End Beach. If you're launching from Bug Light Park in South Portland, take Exit 6A off I-95 and continue to I-295, then take Exit 4 to ME 1. Turn left onto Broadway. Take Broadway nearly all the way out to the point. Turn left onto Pickett, then right onto Madison.

———

THIS IS A LEISURELY four-day trip starting in busy Portland Harbor and traveling up to quiet Harpswell Sound and back, stopping on state islands. Overnight trips in the Casco Bay area cannot be treated as casually as they once were because the residents have become far stricter about nonresident parking, especially overnight. It is sometimes possible, however, to find parking with a local store, gas station, restaurant, or marina by offering to pay. Naturally this will require some research and local knowledge, but it will afford you peace of mind. Barring that, use the popular launch spots in the off-season, early June or after Labor Day.

Casco Bay surrounding Portland is a great place to paddle because it provides easy access to uninhabited islands without going very far Down East. Because Portland is one of the busiest shipping ports in New England, however, be prepared to give wide berth to intimidating, five-story oil tankers delivering most of the state's oil, fishing vessels, and barges. Also add ferry boats, tour boats, and fleets of racing yachts to the list of craft to reckon with.

Some sea kayakers consider such dodging a challenge. Others might want to opt for a launch farther north in the bay such as at Falmouth Foreside, Cousins Island, or Yarmouth out of shipping channels. Once out of Portland Harbor, you will be rewarded. Just a few miles out are deserted gems such as state-owned Crow, Jewell, and Little Chebeague, where you can camp, hike, swim, and explore in pristine privacy. In June and July, however, note that many Casco Bay islands harbor the browntail moth caterpillar, which builds its web at the end of tree branches and in some people can cause rashes and even respiratory problems.

On the way, you can retreat to one of the many other islands for protection from wave and wind. Casco Bay Islands used to be called the Calendar Isles because there was seemingly an island for every day

Casco Bay

Upper Goose Island

Lower Goose Island

Whaleboat Island

Harpswell Neck

Harpswell Sound

Orrs Island

Bailey Isl.

SOUTH HARPSWELL

Potts Harbor

Upper Flag I. Haskell I.

Great Mark I.

Eagle Island

Casco Bay

Great Chebeague Island

Crow Island

Bangs I.

Ministerial

Steve I. I.

Hope I.

Cliff Island

Jewell Island

Little Chebeague I.

Chandler Cove

Luckse Sound

Long Island

Cow I.

Great Diamond Island

Peaks Island

Clapboard Island

FALMOUTH FORESIDE

Little Diamond I.

House I.

SOUTH PORTLAND

PORTLAND

FALMOUTH

295

1

N

1 nautical mile (approximate)

of the year. More scientific counts have turned up 222 islands, including those connected by bridges such as Orrs and Bailey, according to Philip Conkling in *Islands in Time* (Down East Books, 1985).

The views are always interesting. Several lighthouses guard the bay, including Spring Point Ledge Light, connected to the mainland by a jetty, and Portland Head Light high on a bluff, both still active. The bay also has several forts strategically built to protect Portland Harbor during various wars.

At Casco Bay's north end, in the direction of the tall, gray towers of the Cousins Island power plant, is the quieter Harpswell Sound area. Here you'll find protected paddling in sounds between the long fingers trailing down into the ocean forming coves, bays, and the New Meadows River. You can paddle around Harpswell Neck, Orrs, Bailey's Islands, and Sebascodegan (Great) Island (see Trip 15). A few state-owned islands are located up in the bays where there are fewer houses, making them ideal camping spots. The 20-acre meadow at Clark Cove on the east side of Harpswell Neck is a good picnic spot.

Crossings in Casco Bay and the Harpswell Sound area are typically never more than a mile, which makes for comfortable paddling. In strong winds, however, conditions can become extreme, with refracting waves off big headlands; even as close as you are to landfall, you should never be lulled into a false sense of security. The outer islands receive the full force of the sea.

Day One: The first day's paddle is from Portland Harbor down the passage between Peaks Island and the Diamond Islands headed east. Peaks Island is the most populated island in Casco Bay with 1,000 year-round residents; four times that in summer. Stop in at the beach of the friendly Maine Island Kayak Co., run by Tom and June Bergh. It is located just to the north of the ferry terminal (watch out for the ferry, which goes back and forth to Portland almost every hour). MICKO offers half-day to multiday tours of Casco Bay and sponsors the Round-the-Peaks-Island Race, usually at the end of June. You will probably see its clients out and about.

Paddle along the inside of Long Island. Stop on Little Chebeague for a rest stop. Then paddle across Chandler Cove and continue north through the passage between Great Chebeague and Hope Islands to Crow Island, just to the east of Great Chebeague. Crow is your camping spot for the night. In normal conditions, this trip takes about three hours.

Crow is a cozy island, recognizable from the sea by the wooden cottage, which has been repaired, and if weather gets dicey you can camp inside. The island is very popular in summer, so don't expect to have it to yourself. Crow has a protected cove and good landing on the northeast side, along with a site for two tents above a gravel pocket beach. The cottage is surrounded by ripe raspberry bushes in mid-August. Fishermen and their families from Chebeague often picnic here, and their traditional use of the island deserves respect. The Casco Bay caretaker regularly visits here.

Day Two: The route goes from Crow Island to the north end of Bangs Island, to the north end of Stockman, following the inside, from Stockman to the south tip of Whaleboat (0.75 mile), from Whaleboat to Basin Point at Potts Harbor (1 mile). BPL-owned Bar is a small, grassy island just east of Ash Point and makes a good place to stretch your legs; day use only.

The route then crosses Potts Harbor to Potts Point, heads north across Merriconeag Sound to the Orrs–Bailey Islands Bridge, a unique cribwork bridge in which granite panels mounted on top of each other are spaced to let the tide run through. At slack tide, the current here in Wills Gut is benign, but the daily tidal rip under the bridge can reach 4 knots, accounting for the bridge's unique construction. Continue north past the lovely Lowell Cove, then up Gun Point Cove along Orrs Island, which is lined with summer houses, private beaches, and docks. Cross under the ME 24 bridge where the sound narrows again but at certain tides presents no problems. A mainland site at Clark Cove in Harpswell Sound, run by the Parks and Recreation Department, is a good picnic spot available for day use only.

The small 1-acre island at the mouth of Strawberry Creek Island (unnamed on the chart) is marked by a blue-and-white BPL sign. The heavily wooded island is hard to distinguish from the mainland. At low tide, it is completely surrounded by mussel flats and marsh grass except for access on the south tip, where an open, grassy area accommodates one tent. The north end accommodates one tent, and a spot halfway up the west side, two tents. Not many people use the island, so there's a good chance you will have it to yourself.

From the campsite, you can see the bridge across Ewin Narrows. Other suitable camping options include the BPL-owned Little Snow Island, located at the south end of the exceptionally pretty Quahog Bay (see Trip 15).

Day Three: The route goes from Strawberry Creek up Harpswell and Merriconeag Sounds back to Potts Harbor, south through the passage between Jewell and Cliff Islands, then through Chandler Cove to Little Chebeague. Be sure to poke into the lovely coves with rock walls and deep shade along Haskell Island. A hamburger/ice cream stop at Dolphin Marina at Basin Point and a hose shower from the marina dock are both welcome after three camping days. Head south to Jewell, passing by a succession of Upper Flag and Eagle Islands with Little Birch, Ministerial, and Bates Island to the right. Little Birch, owned by Maine's Department of Inland Fisheries and Wildlife, allows careful day use after nesting season, July 31. Pass between Jewell and Cliff. The water can be quite wild in this passage, refracting off Cliff and stirred by stiff breezes. A cove to the left at Jewell usually has several sailboats moored. Head south through Luckse Sound, past the north tip of Long Island, through the two wrecked schooners to Little Chebeague.

Little Chebeague, an Indian word for "island of many springs," has camping in the grassy field off the trail leading in from the eastern side of the southeast-facing beach. The thoroughfare is very busy during the day but quiet at night. There is a hiking trail through the interior, as well as a privy. Large shell deposits in a cliff may have been Indian shell middens. The larger islands in Casco Bay were all important Indian encampments in summer, used for fishing, berry collecting, and drying shellfish. The Indians reached the islands by birch-bark canoe. Little Chebeague gets a lot of use in summer, and the Casco Bay caretaker visits from Memorial Day through Labor Day. The island also has several historic sites, now marked by interpretive signs.

Day Four: It is now a short paddle back to East End Beach. A fine sandy beach on the north side of Long Island has good swimming. Head back between the Diamonds and Whaleback, the same way you came. Fort Gorges (pronounced *gorge*) on Hog Island Ledge near the Spring Point Ledge Light is worth a visit. Accessible only by boat, city owned, and free, the fort sits virtually in the middle of the water with a landing spot on a gravel beach near the front door. Begun in 1858, the fort was never used, outdated by the invention of rifled cannon capable of destroying granite forts. It was one of three major forts built to protect Portland Harbor and was named in the memory of Sir Ferdinando Gorges, a seventeenth-century English settler. The fort has great 360-degree views of the entire Casco Bay from the third-tier ramparts, but careful going is required through overgrown bushes.

When in Portland, if it's a weekday, stop in at the MITA office at 41A Union Wharf (207-761-8225; www.mita.org), located down from the ferry in the Old Port.

Other Options: Other access spots in the Harpswell Sound area include Lookout Point (from I-95, take ME 123 south from Brunswick for about 8 miles, then turn right), and Dolphin Marina at Basin Point in Potts Harbor, which charges a small fee and offers overnight parking (continue south on ME 123 to the end). Recompense Shore Campground (207-865-9307), located just north of Wolf Neck on a little bay, is a good jumping-off spot for exploring islands in Western Casco Bay. It is part of Wolfe's Neck Farm, a private, nonprofit organization. From Freeport, at L.L. Bean, turn left onto Bow Street, turn right onto Wolfe Neck Road, then left onto Burnett Road. The campsite is on the left.

Camping: Crow, Strawberry Creek, and Little Chebeague Islands.

TRIP 18

York River

WIGGLY BRIDGE TO SMELT BROOK

Trip Mileage: 9 miles round trip

Tidal Range: 8.6 feet at York Harbor

Charts and Maps: NOAA chart #13283 at 1:20,000 for York Harbor. Farther upriver, you will need a USGS map.

Caution Areas: Strong currents at York Harbor. The tidal flow under the Wiggly Bridge runs too swiftly to paddle against. Avoid oncoming motorboat traffic under the Sewall Bridge.

Access: York Harbor town docks (two launch points)

Getting There: York Harbor is located about 5 miles north of Kittery Point, Maine. To reach the Wiggly Bridge, take Exit 4—"The Yorks"—off I-95, then turn right onto US 1, left at US 1A, and right onto ME 103, Lilac Lane. You'll find diagonal parking at a lot on the left across from the Wiggly Bridge. Keep going on this road and you will reach the two launch points at the town docks.

———

T HE YORK RIVER'S fast current runs you swiftly past some of the most interesting spots in New England history, as well as some great nature preserves. This scenic river in southern Maine is well worth a detour from coastal paddling. Start at the Wiggly Bridge in York Harbor and let the current and tide take you up to the juncture of the York River and Smelt Brook, then back. Enhance your trip by getting a copy of the York Rivers Association's brochure, "Boating on the York River and York Harbor," with a map that points out the interesting spots (York Rivers Association, P.O. Box 1106, York Harbor, ME 03911-1106; 207-363-2708; www.yorkrivers.org).

Park your car on Lilac Lane and carry your boat across the busy road to the jetty that leads to the Wiggly Bridge, a narrow suspension

York River

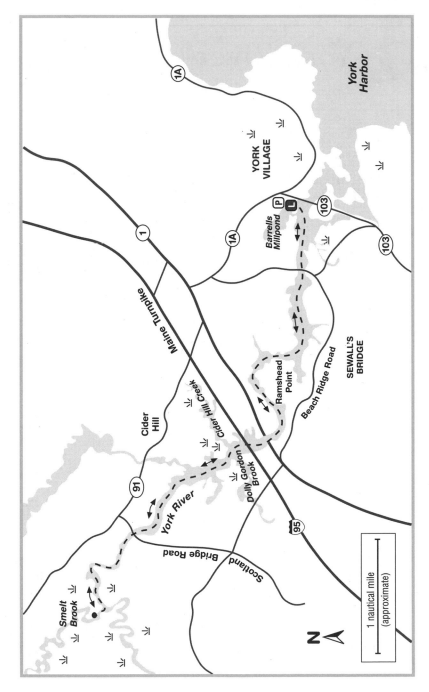

bridge that spans Barrells Mill Pond. Here in summer, families gather with inner tubes, beach chairs, dogs, and coolers while the kids jump into the water from the bridge. At the bottom two-thirds of the tide, the current runs too swiftly to paddle against.

Hand your boat down over the walkway. Depending on the tide and whether you can paddle under the bridge, launch on the river or the pond side. To the left, it is 2.0 miles down to York Harbor. To the right, upriver, it's a little more than 4.5 miles to Smelt Brook.

As you paddle north, shortly upriver is a small shack decked out with colorful buoys. Next door is the John Hancock Warehouse, named for the famous American patriot who signed the Declaration of Independence. Hancock became part owner of the warehouse in 1780 and, being the patriot he was, used the spot to store traded merchandise he did not want taxed by the British government. The out-of-the-way warehouse tucked just inside the York River is one of several along the New England coast that served a similar purpose. Next to the warehouse is the Marshall store, built in 1870 and served by the schooner trade, New England's early trucks. Both are now preserved as historic sites.

Just upriver is the Sewall Bridge, with another bit of interesting history. Built in 1754 by Samuel Sewall, it replaced the ferry service that operated across the river here. Much of the bridge's original design has been preserved as a National Engineering Landmark. Note the standing waves at full ebb tide. One bay, marked as the channel with a 5 MPH warning sign, by no means channels all the motorboat traffic, which uses all the bays. Stay alert for oncoming traffic.

The river has an inland freshwater sense to it, yet you have only to look down at the rockweed flowing in the emerald water to be reminded that it's tidal. The best approach to paddling here is to go up with the flow and return on the ebb. (If need be, you can make your journey the other way and start at the Scotland Bridge, which has a public launch ramp. You can also use side eddies if you're going countercurrent.)

To the left, beyond the Sewall Bridge, is a rambling dark red colonial-era house. The main house was built in the 1730s and was situated to access river traffic, including schooners and wherries. It was owned by summer resident Elizabeth Perkins, who turned it over to the Old York Historical Society in the 1950s. Just upriver from the house is the wooden Indian statue, placed by Perkins in tribute to the original inhabitants of the area and to signal the start and end to

The trip starts near the Wiggly Bridge.

York's summer social season. The statue still stands from June through Columbus Day.

Across the river is the York Country Club's golfing green. Back on the other (west) side, you can catch shade from the tall pine trees at midday on this stretch. In September, kingfishers drop with a chatter from the tall trees, patrolling the river for fish. Just before the US 1 bridge is the "River House" estate, built by the daughter of American millionaire B. F. Goodrich and now part of Bowdoin College.

Next you pass under the US 1 and I-95 bridges. Between them on the right you can picnic at The Grant House in Goodrich Park. The loud noise quickly subsides, and on the other side residential development mixes with the pastoral and some deep indents such as Cider Hill and Bass Cove Creeks. You will share the river with several other kayakers—many docks have well-stocked kayak racks—and fishermen, all making some effort to work with the tidal current. You may see a York Rivers Association volunteer paddling by, picking up garbage.

The next landmark is the Scotland Bridge, a put-in for those paddling the river's upper reaches. After the Scotland Bridge, the river changes character entirely and meanders through wide marshland that stretches to forest and field. Look for the large yellow barn and farmhouse on top of the hill on the east side. Head for the distant pine grove that marks the divergence of the York River (to the left, or west) from Smelt Brook. The York continues to the left in a narrow corridor of marsh and wanders up in several bows, eventually turning into a creek and then York Pond.

We chose the Smelt Brook juncture as our turnaround, because at last we were feeling the tide against us. The point is about 4.5 miles from the start at the Wiggly Bridge, so it makes a nice afternoon outing of about 3.5 hours and a total 9-mile round trip.

Fly back with the tide to the Wiggly Bridge, pull your kayaks over to the small beach on the river side, and take a swim. If you still have time, paddle down to the harbor and back. Pass the handsome Sayward Wheeler House, built by a wealthy West Indies trader in 1718 and preserved by SPNEA (Society for the Preservation of New England Antiquities), then check out the mix of lobster and pleasure boats.

At all costs, avoid driving along York Beach, just to the north, in the height of summer. It is very crowded.

Camping: None.

Gerrish and Cutts Islands

CIRCUMNAVIGATIONS

Trip Mileage: 8-mile loop

Tidal Range: 8.1 feet at Portsmouth

Charts and Maps: NOAA #13283 at 1:22,700

Caution Areas: Surf breaks across the entrance to Brave Boat Harbor in even moderate wind. The outer coast is exposed, with waves breaking on the many reefs.

Access: Frisbee Wharf at Kittery Point. Year-round parking is for residents only (you need the local dump sticker), but free parking is allowed at Mitchell School just down the street.

Getting There: From I-95, take ME 103 to Kittery and follow it east to Kittery Point. Turn at the sign for Cap'n Simeon's Galley at Frisbee Market on the right, and pass the restaurant to reach the launch ramp.

A CIRCUMNAVIGATION of Gerrish and Cutts Islands from Kittery Point shows you the contrast between protected paddling in salt marsh and creek and open-ocean paddling. The trip is tide dependent. A good place to start is at the public launch in Pepperell Cove at Cap'n Simeon's Galley at Frisbee Point. If you're going clockwise, start at the top of the outgoing tide in order to get through Brave Boat Harbor before low tide.

The view from Frisbee Point is beautiful. It looks toward the low, long, bald head of Fishing Island and the powerful Whaleback Light marking the Whaleback Reef and beyond to the Atlantic. The harbor is enveloped by sparsely settled Gerrish and New Castle Islands, marked by the Coast Guard lighthouse with a green beacon.

Pepperell Cove has become a very busy launch area for all kinds of boats, so it is best to park to one side, unload as quickly as possible, then move out of the way to the parking area. Paddle between Phillips

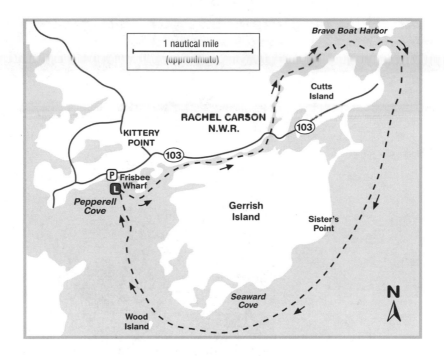

Gerrish and Cutts Islands

and Gooseberry Island, then head up Chauncy Creek, to the northeast. After entering the creek, head for the anchorage or road. A deeply indented cove (no name) straight ahead can be misleading. Paddle up Chauncy Creek, past charming waterside houses and the Chauncy Creek Lobster Pound. Note that the creek completely empties at low tide and is impassable, so time your circumnavigation accordingly. Pass under the Pocahantas Bridge. A little farther on, you will arrive at the culvert that passes under Seapoint Road bridge to the north at Cutts Island. Paddle under here—you will need to get up a good head of speed and bend at the waist to avoid the top if you're paddling near high tide. It is impossible to get through on a low tide.

Now you are in the Rachel Carson National Wildlife Refuge, a beautiful protected marsh with little settlement. The channel narrows and winds quite a bit, so it is good to have a lot of water when paddling through. Leaned turns are the most useful. We saw three bluebirds in the area one early-October day. The channel winds through here for a little more than a mile. Most remarkable is how clear the water is for a marsh. That is because it isn't fed by fresh water carrying silt.

The winner of the Gerrish Island Race, an annual event, takes a break after the race on Fishing Island.

You come to the pilings of the old railroad crossing. This is your first look at open-ocean conditions at the entry to Brave Boat Harbor. If in doubt, paddle to the jetty at the south end, get out of your boat, and climb up to better see what conditions are. The main thing to keep in mind on inspection is that the outer passage is full of reefs, with sea salt spray crashing upward, but you can paddle through and around the reefs with a fair degree of safety even if the water is a bit squirrely. When we last paddled through, winds had been from the northeast at 15 mph for most of the morning but died down to 10 in the afternoon. The seas were still busy, however, with wind waves on top of swells. We decided to paddle the outside passage, and stayed well clear of the reefs even if it meant paddling well off of shore. In an afternoon sun it is hard to judge whether the inside passage is clear or not.

The circumnavigation is the route of the annual Gerrish Island Race, which takes place in fall, and more than once swells from hurricanes have caused intimidating crashing surf on the reefs but safe passage in between. Those brave souls who choose the inside passage tend to win the race.

The coast is bold and beautiful, with few houses and two long beaches, Seapoint and Crescent, as you make your way around, a little more than 3 miles.

Fort Foster, identified by picnic tables, is a town park and a good spot to picnic. With any swells, the best landing is around the point. It also has a couple of World War II bunkers and observation towers used for spotting German submarines. If you are caught in a lightning storm, stay out of the bunkers. Several years ago, some paddlers were killed when using bunkers for protection; the lightning hit the iron bars inside the concrete.

At the southwest tip, you have a full view of the Wood Island Light and Lifesaving Station and across the Piscataqua River to Portsmouth, New Hampshire. Fort McClary sits on Kittery Point to the west, recognizable by the hexagonal-shaped blockhouse built in 1846 and site of two colonial-era forts used to prevent Massachusetts ships from being taxed by New Hampshire's Tories. It is now a seasonal state park.

As you round the island, paddle under the pilings—at low tide you will need to negotiate the rocks and rockweed—head for the low-lying mound of Fishing Island, then for the anchorage, and you are back at Pepperell Cove. Relax and enjoy viewing many handsome sailboats.

Every September, the 6-mile Gerrish Island rowing race follows that route (it starts at the Cutts Island Bridge), with a finish and clambake on Fishing Island, and is always a lot of fun. You can also do this trip in reverse, depending on wind and tide.

Camping: None.

New Hampshire

Historic Waters

WHILE SHORT COMPARED with other New England states, New Hampshire's 18-mile shoreline includes dynamic Portsmouth Harbor at the mouth of the Piscataqua River, through which all the state's coastal commerce has funneled for more than 350 years. The harbor is a fascinating place to paddle.

The tidal coastline measures 131 miles, with inviting rivers and bays, most notably the 17 square miles of Great and Little Bays, about 12 miles from the mouth of the Piscataqua, bordering Durham.

Other key paddling spots include the Piscataqua River from Dover Point to South Berwick; the many rivers of the fan of the Piscataqua estuary, including the Cocheco, Salmon Falls, and Bellamy; and the Isles of Shoals, 10 miles across open ocean from Portsmouth.

Physiography

The New Hampshire coast starts from the Piscataqua River at Portsmouth with a shoreline of commercial wharves, rocky coast, and marshland interspersed with islands. The state public beaches start below rocky Odiorne Point. These 10 miles include Rye, North Hampton, Hampton, and Seabrook. Behind the beaches lie embayments with well-developed tidal mud flats and marsh systems.

The beaches are inhospitable to landings due to dumping surf, although Rye Harbor, which is protected by rock jetties, and roomy Hampton Harbor, which is backed by more than 1,000 acres of marsh, have sheltered public town landings. Note that Hampton Harbor is dominated by the two domes of the Seabrook nuclear power plant.

The shoreline is interspersed with rocky outcrops of primarily unconsolidated glacial material, which provides the sand and silt material for nourishment of the beach areas.

Camping Considerations

The New Hampshire coast is intensely settled, with no public camping spots. It is best to contact private owners of rural land and islands for camping permission.

Access, Launching, and Parking

The New Hampshire coast has nineteen sites that provide public boat access to the water, but only four nonbeach sites—Hilton Park at Dover Point, Odiorne Point State Park in Rye, Peirce's Island in Portsmouth, and Jackson's Landing in Durham—have substantial parking. Since the state is a prime fishing and duck-hunting area, some state ramps are maintained for use by sportsmen. The New Hampshire Coastal Program produces a coastal access map. Contact the Seacoast Office, New Hampshire Coastal Program, 152 Court Street, Portsmouth, NH 03801; 603-431-9366; www.seacoastnh.com. All the state ramps charge fees.

The best access in the Portsmouth area is Odiorne Point State Park or Peirce's Island boat ramp just beyond Strawbery Banke. Down the coast, Seabrook, Hampton, and Rye have town ramps in their harbors.

The Great Bay estuary has about a dozen launch spots that belong to river towns such as Durham, Newmarket, and Newfields. The Department of Fish and Game maintains the ramp at Adams Point in Great Bay for duck hunters, which is useful to small boaters when duck-hunting season is not in progress, as well as the ramp at Sandy Point just below the Sandy Point Discovery Center.

Aside from beaches, coastal recreation or nature areas are somewhat limited, some of the notable exceptions being Odiorne Point Park, the coastal forts, Hilton Park, the New Hampshire Audubon Sanctuary along the Bellamy River in Dover, and the Rachel Carson Preserve at Brave Boat Harbor in Kittery, Maine (just over the state line).

Coastal Wildlife

The marshes and ponds behind New Hampshire's barrier beaches are habitats for many species of migratory waterfowl, with black ducks and mallards present year-round. These areas are also resting spots for ducks, geese, and shorebirds migrating during fall and spring. Hampton Harbor and marshes, the state's largest salt marsh, is the richest area for birdlife on the coast, with such rare birds as common terns, willets, and seaside sparrows. Foragers such as herons, egrets, and ibises also use the marshes. For more information, visit www.nhaudubon.org.

Great Bay is a major wintering area for waterfowl. It is also a primary winter habitat for bald eagles, which stay here when the lakes and rivers freeze to the north, seeking the food sources of the open water, along with the high perches and dense conifer forests to get protection from the weather. A few common terns nest on islands; six pairs of ospreys have been producing young for several years. An enthusiastic group of local volunteers runs Project Osprey, monitoring all nests in the area and building new nesting platforms. An inventory in Great Bay lists 281 species of birds, including endangered or threatened species—the bald eagle, osprey, marsh hawk, common tern, common loon, pied-billed grebe, northern harrier, sedge wren, and Henslow sparrow. Meanwhile, ospreys use the banks of the Piscataqua as far as South Berwick during migration. Overall, Great Bay protects twenty-three species of threatened or endangered animals and plants.

Harbor seals are often seen in winter, including those that hitch a ride on the ice blocks upriver on the Piscataqua. Thirty-two species of finfish have been identified.

On the Isles of Shoals, roseate tern breeding pairs are growing in numbers, with twenty-five reported in 2002. Common terns are also increasing, and 2002 saw the first breeding of an arctic tern pair in more than fifty years. These islands without terns for so many years are now home to one of the largest tern colonies in the Gulf of Maine, according to New Hampshire Audubon.

Living Off the Wild

The coastal water quality has been considered Class A, and digging clams and shellfish for human consumption is problem-free unless a red-tide warning is in effect. Taking soft-shell clams is strictly recreational, but licenses are only issued to state residents.

Along the coast and in the estuaries, recreational fishermen catch smelt, flounder, cod, haddock, striped bass, and bluefish.

TRIP 20

New Castle Island

CIRCUMNAVIGATION

Trip Mileage: 5.75-mile loop

Tidal Range: 8.1 feet at Portsmouth Harbor

Charts and Maps: NOAA #13283 at 1:22,700

Caution Areas: There is a strong current under Goat Island Bridge and to the south of Seavey and Clark Islands. Swells sometimes occur at Little Harbor jetty. There is also a swift current under Blunts Island Bridge.

   The current culminates at Dover Point, where the water rushing to fill Great Bay can reach upwards of 6 knots, equal to some of the strongest currents on the Atlantic Coast. The Piscataqua's current is a lot more benign going north of Dover Point. A trip from Dover Point to South Berwick is recommended when the harbor is ripped up from strong southerly winds.

   It is illegal to land at the naval base on Seavey Island. The Back Channel behind Seavey has strong currents.

Access: Peirce's Landing has ample parking and a large launch beach area, with a separate concrete ramp for motorboats, making it an ideal launch, especially for kayak groups. There is a fee to launch, which includes parking. Other launch spots include Odiorne Point State Park; Great Island Common on New Castle, which charges a fee to nonresidents and has ample parking; and the New Castle town ramp.

Getting There: From I-95, take Exit 7 (Historic District) to Market Street (past the Albacore Submarine), to Bow Street, to Marcy Street (follow signs for NH 1B), past Strawbery Banke Museum on the right. Look for signs for Peirce's Island and turn left just past Prescott Park to Peirce's Landing.

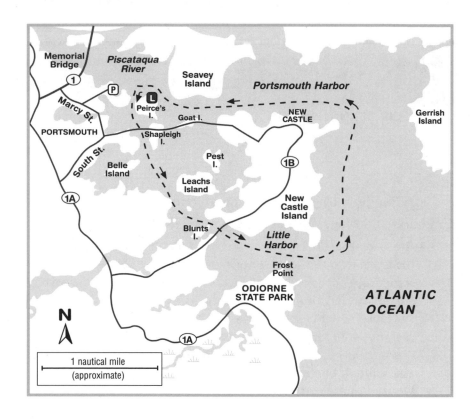

New Castle Island

NEW CASTLE is not only one of New England's oldest settlements, but also the only town in New Hampshire completely contained on an island. It is an interesting paddle because of the busy working waterfront, historic houses, forts, lighthouses, parks, beaches, hotels, and yacht clubs. You can also picnic on the public beach at Frost Point.

The Piscataqua River is the second fastest navigable river in the United States, after the Columbia River in Oregon, and reaches upwards of 4 knots. When paddling around Portsmouth Harbor, at the river's mouth, you are certain to have a fast ride. The waters are calmer on the inside of New Castle Island and a circumnavigation is well worth the trip, taking the river's strong currents into account.

Start at Peirce's Island Boat Ramp, just south of Strawbery Banke in Portsmouth's historic district. The view looks as it might have in the eighteenth century, with old fish houses, wharves, the graceful

Wentworth-Gardner House built in 1760 at water's edge, and the slim North Church tower in the distance. Many kayakers launch from Peirce's, but Portsmouth Harbor has so many different boating activities that the boating community seems to have readily accepted kayakers.

Start on the ebb tide on New Castle Island's west side, or interior waterway, and ride the tide down. Most of the area behind New Castle empties at low tide, but a narrow channel (unnamed) makes the area navigable.

Paddle south, under the bridge that connects the mainland to Shapleigh Island, then over to Frame Point, on which sits the Wentworth-Coolidge Mansion, a forty-room, rambling, mustard-yellow house. Royal Governor Benning Wentworth lived here during the colonial era, his fortune made from a ship-mast-building business. The mansion is just one of Portsmouth's grand early houses, built with the wealth of the eighteenth-century shipbuilding industry, which prospered through use of the seemingly unlimited resources of New Hampshire's forests. The mansion's lilacs are said to be the first planted in America. A side excursion is possible into Sagamore Creek, where the channel ends about 1 mile up at a bridge.

Paddle into Little Harbor under the Blunts Island Bridge. From Little Harbor, picnicking and hiking are possible on the sandy beach at Frost Point, part of Odiorne Point State Park.

Odiorne is the site of one of Portsmouth's first permanent settlements. In 1623, colonists built a fort on the rocky promontory there. The land has gone through a succession of use since then: large coastal farms, summer estates, then Fort Dearborn during World War II; it eventually reverted to public property (much to the bitterness of the former landowners) when it became a state park in 1960. The upside is that the coastline is undeveloped. If you continue down this coast, you will reach Jenness Beach and Rye Harbor, a good surfing spot.

From Little Harbor, high-tide excursions can be made into Witch Creek and Fairhill Swamp. The Odiorne Point state ramp in Witch Creek just to the south of Little Harbor is an excellent launch spot, with a paved ramp and lots of parking (for a fee).

Little Harbor is dominated by the grand nineteenth-century Wentworth-by-the-Sea Hotel, long abandoned by owners who gave up on its heating bills. It first opened in 1874. After years of neglect, the Marriott Hotel chain renovated and reopened the behemoth in

Lilly paddles by the Wentworth-Coolidge Mansion.

2003 by building onto both wings beyond the cupolas. Paddle by the hotel's marina and golf course (watch out for flying golf balls), which have been well maintained for many years.

Paddle south out of Little Harbor, past the jetties on either side, and sweep east into the mouth of the Piscataqua River, past Jaffrey's Light, then head up the east side of New Castle Island, characterized by rocky reefs and grand houses. The view is sweeping, south to Odiorne Point, home to the Seacoast Science Center; 10 miles east to the Isles of Shoals (sparkling white on a clear day); northeast to Whaleback Reef Light and Wood Island, and beyond to Gerrish Island and Kittery Point in Maine.

Whaleback Reef Light was built in the late 1800s, the third lighthouse on that site (it took lighthouse engineers several years to get offshore marine construction right), and is made of 5-foot-thick granite blocks, which did not crumble, unlike other building materials tried. In the no-name storm of 1998, later named the Perfect Storm, waves broke over the top of the 60-foot-high lighthouse. Next to the reef is the old Wood Island Lifesaving Station, with its distinct red roof, now restored.

Nautical charts show the New Hampshire–Maine border going down the Piscataqua River's middle. The border has an interesting history. In 2000, New Hampshire disputed the border, claiming that the river boundary ran along the Maine shore and that the entire river and all of Portsmouth Harbor belonged to New Hampshire. Maine countered by claiming that King George II made the boundary determination in 1740 and that a 1977 case of a lobstering-rights dispute ("the Lobster Wars") supported that historic claim. The courts granted Maine's petition to dismiss the complaint, and the midriver boundary stands.

A good plan is to paddle to Little Harbor, wait for slack, then go with the flow as you come up the notoriously current-driven Piscataqua River, following the tide times for Portsmouth Harbor. However, the official tide times for Portsmouth Harbor are overridden by the river's strong flow. If you find yourself paddling against the tide, the paddle will require effort but is not overly difficult. Take advantage of back eddies when you're not blocked by docks. The tide runs up to 1.5 knots at ebb, less at flow.

At the river's mouth, during World War II, the navy strung a submarine net across the harbor. Paddle north about a mile to Fort Point and Portsmouth Harbor Light, the only mainland lighthouse on New Hampshire's 18-mile seacoast (see the sidebar on page 160).

Pass by Salamander Point. At Lighted Can #5, make a sharp turn left or west and follow Castle Island's north shore. You pass by the Portsmouth Yacht Club, the second oldest yacht club in the United States after New York. Note how within the anchorage, sailboats are pointed in every direction. That gives you some idea of the countereddies caused by the river's swift current.

Across the river in Maine is Pepperell Cove at Kittery Point, filled with sailboats. On the point is the Civil War–era Fort McClary. Next is Spruce Creek, which a bridge crosses, then the back channel behind Seavey Island, then a sailboat anchorage where the navy used to sound-test submarines for quietness.

On Seavey Island is the historic Portsmouth Naval Shipyard, where people have been building ships since the 1600s. In the colonial era, workers builts a few Royal Navy ships here, but they soon moved into building boats for the American Revolutionaries, including three warships. (Captain John Paul Jones was one of Portsmouth's early residents.) Swift waters, a good supply of timber upriver, and skilled labor all led to the establishment of a federal shipyard here in 1800. The workers continued to build ships from the War of 1812 to the Vietnam War—they built the last submarine here in 1969—and now overhaul nuclear-powered submarines, which you may see

Portsmouth Harbor Light

This lighthouse's history reflects that of early New England. Portsmouth Harbor Light was the tenth lighthouse built in the colonies, and like many lighthouses on the New England coast, originated as a simple lantern on a mast. It was located at what was then Fort William and Mary and maintained originally in 1771 by British soldiers, who levied a tax on the local shipping merchants to pay for it. After the Revolution, the fortifications became Fort Constitution, and in the 1780s officials built a more permanent wood lighthouse tower, which was then replaced in 1804 by an 80-foot-high octagonal structure.

After officials built Whaleback Light in 1831, they decided the Portsmouth Harbor Light was not as important and eventually reduced its height to 55 feet. Officials once again changed the light in 1877 when they replaced it with a new 48-foot cast-iron lighthouse, a rare type in New England at that time; some disparagingly likened the structure to a fat stovepipe.

Still, it is a fine example of the low-maintenance, fire-resistant brick-lined cast-iron lighthouse developed by the Lighthouse Board. Details like the Italianate hoodmolds above the arched windows and the iron balustrade make it historically special.

In 1946, Elson Small became keeper of Portsmouth Harbor Light. His wife, Connie, described the view from the top of the tower in her book *The Lighthouse Keeper's Wife:* "I looked down forty feet to the little white scallops of incoming tide washing over the rocks, caressing each one lovingly . . . We could look up the Piscataqua River to Portsmouth, with its gleaming white belfry of North Church, a landmark for sailors, silhouetted against the sky . . . At the center of the harbor was Whaleback Lighthouse, and ten miles out to sea from that was the lighthouse on White Island, part of the Isles of Shoals. Both sent their beams across the water."

The Coast Guard electrified Portsmouth Harbor Light in 1934 and automated it in 1960. The 1877 fourth-order Fresnel lens remains in place, covered by a green acrylic cylinder. Before the cylinder was installed in 1941, the light was produced by a green bulb. The lighthouse remains an active aid to navigation, is lit green

Portsmouth Harbor Light was the tenth lighthouse built in the colonies.

at night, and is part of the Fort Constitution Historic Site, adjacent to an active Coast Guard station.

In 1998, in the interest of environmental safety, the Coast Guard removed all the lead from both the inside and outside and repainted it, and in 2000 the Coast Guard leased the lighthouse to the American Lighthouse Foundation of Wells, Maine. The Friends of Portsmouth Harbor Lighthouse are now charged with its care.

For more information on this and other lighthouses, contact:

Friends of Portsmouth Harbor Lighthouse
P.O. Box 5092
Portsmouth, NH 03802-5092
603-431-9155
e-mail: keeper@lighthouse.cc

American Lighthouse Foundation
P.O. Box 889
Wells, ME 04090
207-646-0245
e-mail: alf@lighthousefoundation.org

docked at the shipyard underneath scaffolding. The submarines operate for thirty years but midlife need to be refitted with nuclear fuel, at a cost of about $100,000 per sub a year (it takes three years to rehaul). Portsmouth is one of four remaining working government shipyards in the United States.

At Henderson Point on Seavey Island, the large castle structure, called "The Rock" or "The Castle," is a former naval prison, and notoriously nasty for cramped quarters, bad living conditions, and no escape (prisoners were deterred by the strong currents).

Until the early 1900s, Henderson's Point stuck out about 400 feet in the river, while the mainland stuck out on the other side. As a result, most major ship traffic couldn't make the turn here because of the constricted current (the sharp bend was called "Pull-and-be-damned Point") and went through the back channel. In 1905, government officials dynamited Henderson's Point; since then the river has been passable for larger traffic.

When you are nearly back at Memorial Bridge (the large green iron suspension bridge) and see the picnic tables and pavilion, turn left into the marina. Watch out for standing waves at midtide by the green can at the north tip of Peirce's. There is clear passage to the north of the docked boats. Paddle past Prescott Park and the Sheafe Wearehouse, the oldest warehouse in Portsmouth and relocated to this spot, and the gundalow replica parked at the dock here. In the colonial era, the bargelike gundalow with a sail brought timber down the rivers to the shipyards. Both take you back to a few earlier centuries. Come around to the left, underneath the footbridge, and you are back at Peirce's Island. When paddling this section of the river, be sure to stay out of the main channel because of large-boat traffic and strong currents.

Portsmouth is full of restaurants, many in historic buildings overlooking the river with decks and umbrellas. We keep returning to The Portsmouth Brewery, 56 Market Street, a lively spot with an in-house microbrewery, fast service, and a large menu.

If you want to find out more about all the sights you are seeing, try the narrated Portsmouth Harbor Cruises, at Ceres Street. For a deeper look into the history, read the intriguing *Cross-Grained & Wily Waters: A Guide to the Piscataqua Maritime Region*, edited by W. Jeffrey Bolster.

Camping: None.

TRIP 21

Isles of Shoals

A TOUR OF APPLEDORE, DUCK, SMUTTYNOSE, AND LUNGING ISLANDS

Trip Mileage: 4 miles round trip

Tidal Range: 8.5 feet at Gosport Harbor

Charts and Maps: NOAA #13274

Caution Areas: Crossing from Appledore to Duck Island is exposed and can be a rough ride due to numerous ledges. The east side of Appledore has cliffs and open water.

Access and Getting There: *Ninth Wave* (see the text on page 167)

T HE ISLES OF SHOALS, 10 miles off the New Hampshire coast, is one of New England's more ambitious sea kayak trips. It's a 7.5-mile open-water paddle from Rye Harbor; 10 miles from Portsmouth. Logistics and timing are key. One way to enjoy the isles without the long-crossing commitment is to take advantage of one of the commercial operations that piggyback kayakers onto their regular tourist runs out to the Shoals.

The Isles of Shoals consist of nine islands, four in New Hampshire and five in Maine. They are Appledore, Star, Seavey, Cedar, Smuttynose, Duck, White, Lunging, and Malaga. Far from being barren and windswept, the Victorian-era vacation retreat is well maintained, the result of ongoing and vigilant conservation efforts.

As early as the mid-sixteenth century, during the reign of Elizabeth I in England, European fishermen set up a fishing outpost here, hauling in hundreds of pounds of cod and drying it on racks, called flakes, to be sent back to Europe to feed the Catholic population. Captain John Smith mapped the Shoals in 1614 and named them for himself, but the name didn't stick. At one point, the isles had a population of 600 people, fishing the rich grounds around them and processing fish.

Isles of Shoals

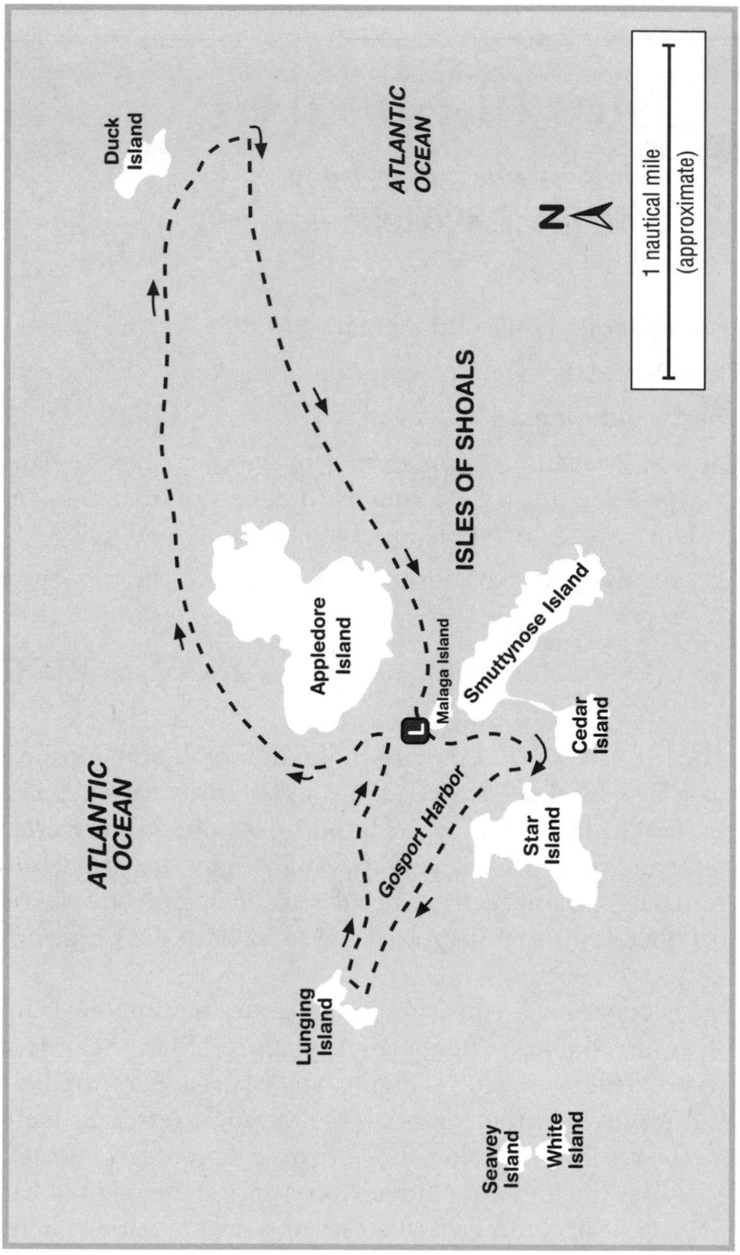

Duck Island

ATLANTIC
OCEAN

ISLES OF SHOALS

Appledore
Island

Malaga Island

Smuttynose Island

Cedar
Island

Gosport Harbor

Star
Island

ATLANTIC
OCEAN

Lunging
Island

Seavey
Island

White
Island

N

1 nautical mile
(approximate)

The inhabitants built sheds, taverns, a meetinghouse, and even a school to support their year-round residency, although the numbers of people varied from island to island and from year to year. Eventually, the fishing business went bust and the inhabitants became destitute, despite the good intentions of religious organizations, which sent missionaries and goods to help out.

In 1848, when Thomas Laighton opened the Appledore House on Appledore Island, the Shoals had began to prosper again. That was during the age of the great hotels, when city dwellers would flee and spend entire summers on vacation. Another hotel, the Oceanic, arose on Star. That burned to the ground and was rebuilt and is the structure you see today. It is now owned by the Unitarian Universalist Church, which continues to have summer conferences here and owns most of Appledore as well. The Star Island Corporation, as it is called, leases the land to the Shoals Marine Laboratory, a joint venture of Cornell University and the University of New Hampshire for marine science students.

A day's itinerary includes paddling around Appledore, largest of the isles, then a mile open crossing to Duck Island, then back to Smuttynose Island and Haley's Cottage for lunch, a paddle around Gosport Harbor, then out to Lunging Island and back.

Cross over to Appledore and paddle along the west shore. Along the south end you pass well-maintained buildings used by the Shoals Marine Laboratory. Along the west shore are some fun rock gardens to poke in and out of if the tide is right. The water, well beyond the mainland, is clear, and the scenery is spectacular. Midway up the west shore, pull into the pocket beach. From here you can follow a path up to Celia Thaxter's famous garden.

Poet and writer Celia Thaxter, daughter of innkeeper Thomas Laighton, grew up here when the Isles of Shoals was one of the most popular and fashionable summer communities in New England. She drew many literary and artist types to the island, including Childe Hassam, the American impressionist painter. She wrote about growing up on Appledore in her book *Among the Isles of Shoals*. Visiting the island and her famous garden on Appledore is by special permission from the Shoals Marine Laboratory. Officially, the garden is open to visitors only on Wednesdays from the end of June through the end of August. The garden is at its peak from July through mid-August. Contact the Shoals Marine Lab by calling 607-254-2900, or 607-255-3717 for Garden Tours. Thaxter's garden was, in fact, an annual

It's fun to poke around in Appledore Island's rock gardens.

garden that changed from year to year. The Portsmouth Garden Club faithfully follows the plans and illustrations Thaxter had for the garden and searches out some of the older seed varieties.

From the north tip of Appledore, it's a mile crossing to Duck Island. Apparently, the navy had done practice bombing here in World War II (Appledore has a lookout tower from the war years, when the navy was ever vigilant about the proximity of German submarines). As a result, the ocean bottom contours are uneven, and a brisk breeze makes for a bumpy ride. On the ledges, you might see gray seals. Watch for breaking surf. Now head back to Appledore.

The east side of Appledore consists of high cliffs and no-landing zones. Cross over to Smuttymose, staying to the west. Paddle around Malaga Island and into the shallow Haley Cove. Here you can pull your boat up onto ledges or directly onto the grass. At Haley's Cottage, the Park Service provides a picnic table. The small, restored cape is where the Smuttynose rangers sleep in summer to be present for the groups of tourists who come borne on various recreational boats out of Portsmouth. The lawn in front of the Haley House is a popular spot for yachters to walk their dogs.

Look for the stone remains of the Hontvet House, site of the infamous Smuttynose murders in 1873—subject of Anita Shreve's novel

The Weight of Water (Back Bay Books, 1998). Follow the path to the Spanish graves and the Haley cemetery.

Back in your boat, you can putter around Gosport Harbor. Then paddle over to Lunging, which has a broad beach.

For an up-to-date weather report from the Isles of Shoals automated weather station at the lighthouse on White Island, go to www.ndbc.noaa.gov/ and entire "iosn3" in the Station ID field.

To hitch a ride out to the Isles of Shoals, contact Adventure Learning, 67 Bear Hill, Merrimac, MA 01860; 800-649-9728; www.adventure-learning.com. It runs several trips out here in summer, using its own kayaks, on a roomy catamaran called the *Ninth Wave*.

Camping: None.

TRIP 22

Great Bay

ADAMS POINT TO EXETER

Trip Mileage: 10.5 miles one way

Tidal Range: 8.1 feet at Portsmouth Harbor

Charts and Maps: NOAA #13285 at 1:20,000

Caution Areas: Water flushing in and out of Great Bay into Little Bay at the narrow Furber Strait can cause some major tidal rips, particularly in conditions of strong opposing wind and tide.

Access: Adams Point; Exeter town ramp

Getting There: To reach the Adams Point launch, take I-95, then US 4 west, to NH 108 (Durham/Newmarket exit). Take NH 108 south. Make sharp left turn at the Durham Historical Association. Then turn left at Durham Point Road, at the old Town Pound marked by stone wall. Follow Durham Point Road 3.7 miles to the entrance to Adams Point, at the chain fence with signs for Adams Point Road and Jackson Estuarine Laboratory. Follow the road 0.85 mile to a concrete launch ramp just beyond the first parking area on the left. Overflow parking is up the hill at Jackson Estuarine Laboratory.

To reach the Exeter town ramp from the south on NH 108, go into Exeter Center and drive straight onto Water Street, leaving the rotunda to the left. Watch for a blue boat-launch sign and turn right at the Exeter Boat House. The paved ramp is straight ahead, with parking spaces to the right.

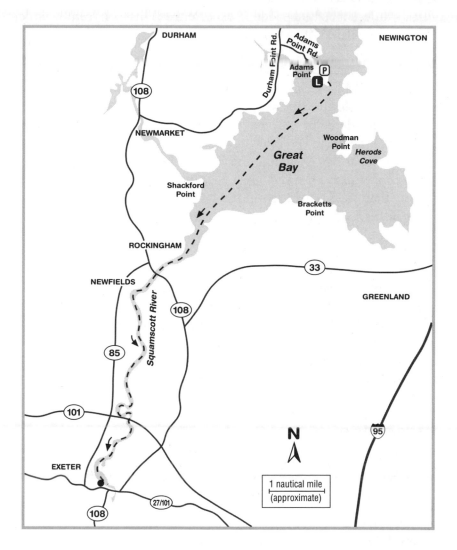

Great Bay

GREAT BAY, surrounded by rural countryside, provides an entirely different coastal paddling experience. This wonderfully undeveloped place has a 360-degree view of low-lying land dotted with oak woods, farms, fields, scattered houses, stone walls, and a few small islands.

About 12 miles from open ocean, Great Bay is one of the most recessed estuaries in the country. It is big and shallow, about 5 by 2 miles, and bordered by the cities and towns of Portsmouth to the east, Durham to the north, and Newmarket to the west. Seven major rivers flow into Great Bay, including the Salmon Falls and Cocheco Rivers, which converge to form the upper Piscataqua River, and the Bellamy, Oyster, Lamprey, Squamscott, and Winnicut. Just to the north of Great Bay is Little Bay, another large estuary, which also feeds Great Bay.

Great Bay is unique on the Northeast Coast. Not until you reach the Chesapeake do you find a similar profile. The flow of fresh water from the seven rivers and ocean access from the Piscataqua create a rich mix of fresh and salt water that supports hundreds of species of plants and animals. Because of its warm water, this rich estuary has one of the few large populations of oysters north of Cape Cod (they're harvested recreationally); it also has a fish population of smelt, coho salmon, striped bass, and bluefish. Great Bay became a National Estuarine Research Reserve in 1989, federally funded for special estuarine research—one of twenty-five in the country, including Waquoit and Buzzards Bays on Cape Cod.

Paddling can be tricky because a huge portion of Great Bay (60 percent) empties at low tide, but you can follow the channel through the dry bottom and shallows. A small channel from the Winnicut and large ones from the Squamscott and Lamprey Rivers join in the center of the bay to form a main channel that connects to Little Bay at Adams Point. When the tide is going out and the mud banks are growing up around the sides, you get the feeling that you are in a giant bathtub after the drain plug has been pulled, and you will swirl uncontrollably before coming to rest on the bottom, so great and vast is the water's movement. The extensive mud flats keep boat traffic to a minimum, a bonus for sea kayakers.

Because the bay is so wide and shallow (on average, 8 feet deep), wave action and wind can be a factor. A sound plan is to paddle into the bay, then into one of several rivers to get out of the wind. All rivers

Great Bay is one of the most recessed estuaries in the country.

conveniently end in dams, so you needn't wander lost into the countryside. The Squamscott makes a good trip to Exeter because of its rural nature, but other possibilities include the Oyster River to Durham, the Bellamy River to Dover, or the Lamprey River to Newmarket.

The reserve has 800 acres of key land and water areas representing the range of different environments around the estuary, including salt marsh, bluffs, rocky shores, woodlands, and open fields. Bird species number nearly 300 and include bald eagle, osprey, marsh hawk, common tern, and common loon. Overwintering migrants include the Canada goose, greater scaup, mallard, black duck, common goldeneye, red-breasted merganser, and bufflehead. At the Wilcox Point shoreline, the estuary is host to about twenty bald eagles, one of the largest winter population of bald eagles in New England. You can find out more at the reserve's education center at Sandy Point Discovery Center on Depot Road in Stratham. From Exit 3B off I-95, the Depot Road turn is 5 miles west on NH 33. From Exeter, Depot Road is 4 miles east on NH 33. The New Hampshire Department of Fish and Game maintains a boat launch here; it also has an interpretive center, a nineteenth-century gundalow replica, a boardwalk and wood-chip trail for the handicapped, short trails through the wooded uplands, and 2,000 feet of mud flats.

The 1,800-acre Great Bay National Wildlife Refuge is located on the eastern shore in Newington on the former Pease Air Force Base, including 6 miles of undeveloped shoreline. The 2-mile Ferry Way Trail loops down to Great Bay. (Take Exit 1 off Spaulding Turnpike to Pease International Tradeport, then follow Great Bay Refuge signs.)

The best access spot for exploring Great Bay is at Adams Point, run by the Fish and Game Department (free, with parking available), with a paved ramp. Durham Point Road to Adams Point winds through the hills and woods of New Hampshire, and it is easy to think you have taken a wrong turn somewhere, even though you see the bay at various points through the woods. The shallow-water launch site keeps the big powerboats away. The launch gets busy during duck-hunting season, however. At Furber Strait, the current runs strong and conditions get rough in opposing wind and tide. It is best to pass through Furber two hours on either side of high tide.

Adams Point is named for the minister from the same family that gave the United States two presidents; large crowds gathered Sunday mornings to hear his sermons. Later he bought a large portion of farmland here. A short interpretive trail winds around the point, past the old stone walls, and gives various views of the bay.

From Adams Point, paddle past the Jackson Estuarine Lab, through Furber Strait, and past the two privately owned Footman Islands, then follow the shoreline as close as the mud flats allow. Head straight up the bay, past the mouth of the Lamprey River (which leads to Newmarket) to the Squamscott, recognizable by the low-lying checkerboard pattern of the railroad bridge in Stratham. The Squamscott, which becomes the Exeter River at Exeter when it is no longer tidal, is scenic and undeveloped with the distinct Oxbow Cut. You will pass Chapman's landing in Stratham on the left, then pass picturesque Newfields on the right with the pretty river houses and the dock marking the public landing in that river town; then you will follow extensive marsh to the right and scarce houses in the conifer woods with docks to the left. Pass under the busy Rt. 101 bridge, past the sewer treatment holding tanks, then paddle into Exeter, following the tall church steeple. Take out at the town dock, marked by the handsome Exeter Academy boathouse and just beyond the falls of the Exeter River that become the Squamscott. The launch area is a scenic one, with the falls and several old houses next to converted brick factories. It's a good idea to spot a car in Exeter.

You can take variations on this trip using the put-ins at other towns. From Newmarket Town Landing on the Lamprey River (from NH 108 traveling south, in Newmarket, turn left at the church onto Water Street and look for the old-fashioned sign for the Lamprey River Boat Launch and Park): 7 miles one way. From Chapman's Landing on NH 108 in Stratham (from NH 108 traveling south, cross the bridge over the Squamscott River; the ramp is on the left): 4 miles one way. From the Newfields Town Landing (south on NH 108 to NH 85, then take the first right after NH 87 onto Swamscott Road at a church; follow Swamscott to its end at a River Road sign, going straight; parking is behind the industrial building up from the launch): 3.5 miles one way. From the Sandy Point Discovery Center located on Great Bay in Stratham (see above for directions): 5.5 miles one way.

Other Options: The New Hampshire Coastal Access Map has a good map for Great Bay launch sites and land access. Other Great Bay access sites include Cedar Point Cove on the Bellamy River, an active sailboarding spot; Jackson's Landing on the Oyster River in Durham (you need to launch one and a half hours on either side of the tide); and Fox Point, owned by the town of Newington (tidal current in here, however, can be quite severe).

At the Sandy Point Discovery Center, be sure to check out the long, flat-decked gundalow with its short and heavy rudder. The early colonists used Great Bay for its many resources—timber, salt marsh hay, fish, lumber—and took advantage of the tides to move their heavy loads around with little effort. They developed the simple, flat-bottomed gundalow with its huge boom and one sail. By the mid-nineteenth century, you could have seen ninety gundalows plying the waters of Great Bay and involved in various businesses—transporting lumber from the sawmills located along the tidal rivers to the ship-building yards along the Piscataqua River, or blue marine clay bricks made from clay gathered along the shores, or cotton for the mills. The bay saw the last gundalow in the 1950s, the end of an era for this workhorse of the shallows and the tides. The speed and efficiency of the Boston & Maine Railroad—whose tracks you still see around the bay—replaced the gundalow.

Camping: None.

TRIP 23

Piscataqua
and Salmon Falls River

DOVER POINT TO SOUTH BERWICK

Trip Mileage: 14 miles round trip

Tidal Range: 8.1 feet at Portsmouth

Charts and Maps: NOAA #13285 at 1:20,000

Caution Areas: The current under the bridge at Dover Point reaches 6 knots. The best advice is to consult *Eldridge Tide and Pilot Book* for Portsmouth tides in order to be going with the tide under the bridge.

Access: Hilton Park has a paved launch ramp and free parking, picnic tables, barbecues, restrooms, and a water fountain.

Getting There: To reach Hilton Park, take I-95 to US 4/Spaulding Turnpike. In about 5 miles, you will cross the Piscataqua River. Just over the bridge at Exit 5, turn right into Hilton Park.

THIS IS A SCENIC TRIP up the historic yet built-up Piscataqua and is a good alternative if Portsmouth Harbor is too rough from a southerly wind. Beyond Dover Point as the river heads north, the tidal flow is weaker, and you need not be too concerned about timing your trip with the tide.

The river's greatest point of velocity is under the Dover Point Bridge, where the waters of Great and Little Bays and several rivers flood into the Piscataqua. The current under the bridge reaches 6 knots, one of the strongest flows on the East Coast. That is because the water is filling and draining the huge expanse of Great Bay—and also because Great Bay is higher than the Piscataqua, so when the current starts running, it does so with additional force.

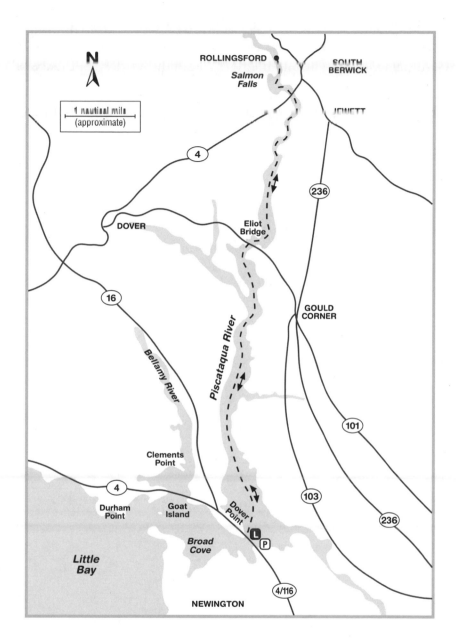

Piscataqua and Salmon Falls River

The launch is at Hilton Park just north of the Dover Point Bridge. Signs all around Hilton Park declare, Dangerous Currents; No Swimming. Head north up the river to South Berwick, a distance of about 7 miles. After about 4 miles, the river splits into the Cocheco River (left) and the Salmon Falls River (right). Very large, new houses with inviting walkways and docks and various flotillas of canoes, kayaks, and wood dories line the river. The best section is Salmon Falls, with the 250-acre historic tract of Vaughn Woods crossed by nature trails. Hamilton House is an impressive Georgian mansion with lovely grounds on the river. Farmland with clover and cows gives a sense of ruralness. In South Berwick, as with all rivers in the area, your passage ends abruptly at a dam.

In winter, seals like to drift down the river on ice slabs and make the sharp turn to the left (west) under the bridge at Dover Point. They tend to abandon their craft, however, before going under the bridge. Then they resume their posts on the other side—a wise move but not one that should be practiced by kayakers. A great restaurant on the bay at Dover Point is Newicks, which serves inexpensive seafood, and the dress code is "come as you are."

Camping: None.

Massachusetts

Accessible Remoteness

THE FIFTEEN HUNDRED MILES of the Massachusetts coast have large and satisfying sweeps of open land—some public, some private—that give sea kayaking a flavor of remoteness yet accessibility despite the built-up shoreline of the Massachusetts megalopolis. These spots shine as alluring sea kayak treks: Plum Island, Cape Ann, the Boston Harbor Islands, Monomoy, and the Elizabeth Islands.

Variety along the coast is plentiful, drawing many kayakers from other parts of New England. The Massachusetts coast can be divided roughly into seven sections. The upper North Shore is made up of the long barrier beaches of Salisbury, Plum Island (8 miles), Crane, and Wingaersheek, as well as rocky, historic Cape Ann, famous for granite quarries; the lower North Shore from Gloucester to Nahant is a rocky coast interspersed with pocket beaches, islands, and the broad indentation of Salem Sound; Boston Harbor, enveloped by the jutting peninsulas of Winthrop and Hull, is historic, commercial, busy, and dramatic, with wild islands joined in a unique urban public park system; the South Shore, roughly from Cohasset to Plymouth, has long sandy beaches indented by key harbors and broad Plymouth Bay.

Cape Cod too has various sections. Cape Cod Bay is encircled by the long arm of the Cape up to the fingertips of Provincetown. Nantucket Sound, which borders the south end of the Cape from Chatham to Woods Hole, has unique glacial indentations that provide protected paddling in shallow bays. Buzzards Bay, an elongated horseshoe, opens into Rhode Island Sound between Cuttyhunk Island and Horseneck Beach.

Closer scrutiny yields more variety: barren rocky islands on the North Shore such as the Salvages and Norman's Woe, both inspiration for famous poems; 50,000 acres of broad salt marsh and tidal estuary guarded by barrier beach; commercial fishing cities such as Gloucester and New Bedford; the small lobstering towns of Rockport and Marshfield; 50 square miles of Boston Harbor with thirty islands and much-documented history; eighty coastal towns.

Look closer still: the surf breaking over Plum Island Sound shoals, Thacher Island Light off Rockport, the smooth slope of World's End in Hingham, the current running swiftly between North and South Monomoy, Hadley Harbor at Naushon Island—all publicly accessible, and all great sea kayaking destinations.

Physiography

From the New Hampshire border, the Massachusetts coastline consists of 12 miles of barrier beach broken by the Merrimack River and Plum Island Sound, then more barrier beach followed by the Essex River. Next is rocky Cape Ann, intersected by the Annisquam River to the north at Annisquam and the south at Gloucester.

Gloucester is the oldest seaport in the nation and one of the world's leading fishing ports, but the fortunes at the 200-boat fishing fleet are shifting with new restrictions on George's Bank. One of the highlights here is the annual Blessing of the Fleet, held on the last weekend in June.

From the south of Cape Ann, you are in the waters of Massachusetts Bay. The coast, intersected by a few sand beaches, is rugged and rocky with deep waters and outlying islands. From this vantage point, the skyscrapers of Boston's financial district lie on the horizon.

The harbors of Manchester, Beverly, Salem, and Marblehead are all boating centers. Salem is rich in maritime history, with annals and mementos that can be seen at the Peabody Museum, formerly headquarters for the East India Trading Company. Marblehead is one of the East Coast's major yachting centers, with thousands of sailboats going in and out of Marblehead Harbor.

Continuing south, you'll find Nahant's rocky coves, Revere Beach, then the windswept, barren outer islands of Boston Harbor. Below, the harbors of Cohasset, Scituate, Marshfield, Duxbury, and Plymouth indent the sandy coastline.

The giant sand dunes and shoal waters of Cape Cod begin as you reach Cape Cod Bay south of Plymouth. Cape Cod's large bent arm has 300 miles of sandy beaches, desolate and wild on the Atlantic side. Windswept dunes front salt marshes, pine and scrub-oak forests, cranberry bogs, ponds, and lakes. Small gray-shingled Cape Cod houses press against newer and larger houses lining the shore, and quahog rakers wade in the bays.

The Cape Cod Canal, built in 1914, travels from Sandwich to Bourne and the fast-moving water and shoals of Buzzards Bay, known for its chop. On the busy west side is Sippican Neck and Marion's sleek yachts, followed by South Dartmouth, then the industrial city of New Bedford, and so on down to Westport Point and the mouth of the double-pronged Westport River at the Rhode Island border.

Camping Considerations

The experience of the Maine coast, where you can island-hop on public land for days or weeks on end, is not part of the Massachusetts sea kayaking experience. Camping on the shoreline is limited due to a privately owned coastal zone, and sea kayaking is, therefore, most suited to day trips.

Some great camping spots that provide fine sea kayak outings do exist, however. State-owned Washburn Island in Waquoit Bay is the only place on Cape Cod with camping on the water, and gives access to a quiet bay with lots of shellfishing or beautiful barrier beach on Nantucket Sound. On Cape Ann, Thacher Island, run by a nonprofit association in Rockport, is just a short paddle from Loblolly Cove. Five Boston Harbor Islands, maintained by the state, allow camping not far from the financial district. Horseneck and Salisbury Beaches both have state camping areas just off the asphalt but near the beach. Audubon Society members have camping access to the Wellfleet Audubon Sanctuary on the quiet end of the Cape. None of these options precludes making arrangements with individuals or various conservation organizations for camping privileges, however. A full list of public campgrounds in Massachusetts is available from the Department of Conservation and Recreation (see appendix A).

Trip Planning

While travel up or down the full length of the Maine coast is infinitely possible, if fairly ambitious, paddling the entire Massachusetts shoreline is problematic. Overnight and launch spots are limited. With preparation anything is possible, however. Several people have now paddled the entire East Coast, New England, or the Gulf of Maine with successful access of this state's coastline, mostly through private arrangements.

If you're unfamiliar with paddling in the state, you have several options. Clubs offer a variety of informal trips, races, outings, meetings, and newsletters with trip reports, which are all good ways to touch base with local waters and paddlers. The Boston Sea Kayak Club and the North Shore Paddlers Network, two of the most active clubs, have regularly scheduled trips, as does the Southeastern Chapter of the Appalachian Mountain Club (see appendix A). Conservation organizations such as Mass Audubon and the Cape Cod

Museum of Natural History offer ecologically oriented trips to both members and nonmembers. And finally, the many outfitters in the state are a good way to get started (see appendix A).

The Cape is a good place to paddle in fall, with its mild temperatures and warm water. The water of Buzzards Bay is generally 10 degrees warmer than the Atlantic. Probably the worst place for car traffic in the state, however, is Cape Cod during summer. The best time to go to the Cape (if you have a choice) is a weekday. Saturday morning is usually not too bad, because most people have arrived on Friday night. A Saturday-night return is navigable, but a Sunday-night return can be a nightmare, with cars backed up the Bourne Bridge for hours (don't even try on Memorial Day weekend unless the weather is bad). Usually, if you're off the Cape by 2:00 P.M. on Sunday, you're safe.

Ocean beaches usually have surf, in contrast to the calmer beaches on Cape Cod Bay. In 1961, the Cape Cod National Seashore became an area protected by the National Park Service. While some kayakers have paddled the length of the Cape's outer arm of some 35 miles, others have avoided it simply because of boredom: nothing but long miles of beach to look at.

Martha's Vineyard and Nantucket are accessible in summer by ferries from Woods Hole, New Bedford, Hyannis, and Boston. From Woods Hole, the Steamship Authority (508-540-2022) Martha's Vineyard ferry goes to Vineyard Haven and takes kayaks for a fee. Extra ferries are added to Oak Bluffs in summer. The passenger-only ferry from Falmouth to Martha's Vineyard, the *Island Queen* (508-548-4800), will take boats when the ferry isn't too crowded.

Access, Launching, and Parking

The coast has about 110 launch sites, most municipally owned, some state run, but because of the coast's suburban nature, parking is a major problem. Boaters are often sent scurrying down side streets looking for a spot without a No Parking sign. Also, the launch areas are not always well marked. The state ramps tend to have more parking places and may charge a fee, but are open to out-of-towners.

The Cape has the highest concentration of official launch sites in the state. Falmouth, for example, has eleven harbors and ten public beaches. But many towns on the Cape restrict launching from their wharves to residents with town stickers, with a few exceptions. (This is the situation in most of the rest of the state as well.) Off-season

(Labor Day to Memorial Day), these ramps are open to anyone. Most beaches on the Cape are town owned, and a parking fee of $5 to $8 is usually charged for nonresidents.

State agencies have information on coastal access. The Public Access Board (PAB), part of the Massachusetts Division of Fisheries, Wildlife, and Environmental Law Enforcement, publishes *Public Access to the Waters of Massachusetts.* The full-color, 150-page guide describes the location and facilities at more than 200 state-funded boat ramps in both the marine and fresh waters of the state. It provides maps for ninety of the most popular sites; the smaller cartop sites (good for kayakers) are shown on the general index map for each geographic area. The guide also includes information about sportfishing piers, fishing in fresh and marine waters, boating law, rights of access, and boating and fishing programs in the Department of Fisheries, Wildlife, and Environmental Law Enforcement. You can buy the book directly for $5 from the PAB office (1440 Soldiers Field Road, near the intersection of Market Street and Western Avenue in Brighton) during business hours, or you can order it through the mail by sending a check for $8 payable to the Commonwealth of Massachusetts: Public Access Board, to 1440 Soldiers Field Road, Brighton, MA 02135; 617-727-1843. You can also see the sites posted on PAB's website: www.state.ma.us/dfwele/PAB/Pab_table2.htm.

The Massachusetts Coastal Zone Management office (MCZM) has produced two guides: *The Boston Harbor Access Guide* (updated in 2003) and *Getting There: A Recreational Guide to the South Shore Waterfront from Hingham to Plymouth.* They list more than one hundred municipally and state-owned parks and public beaches along Boston Harbor, Massachusetts Bay, and Cape Cod Bay. MCZM also produces (through Applied Geographics, Inc., Boston) an online coastal access atlas (www.appgeo.com/resources.asp—then click on Coastal Access Atlas). That atlas shows launch spots for greater Boston Harbor and the North Shore (volume I) and land ownership by federal, state, municipal, and nonprofit bodies.

The legal question of who owns beachfront property is still a point of controversy. According to ordinances established in Massachusetts Bay Colony in 1641 and 1647, beachfront property between the high- and low-water marks, called the intertidal or wet-sand area, belonged to the upland landowner subject to "public rights of fishing, fowling, and navigation." The colony established the law to encourage the building of wharves on the "intertidal flats." In 1974, the state's supreme judicial court ruled that simply strolling on such areas constituted a violation of the landowner's rights, but precisely what the public can do legally about this wet sand area is still unclear, especially in regard to newer recreational activities such as surf casting or birding. For example, does bird watching come under the heading of "fowling" or does that use apply solely to hunting birds? Walking, sitting, and swimming are simply not allowed. The Massachusetts courts have ruled, however, that the right to navigate can be broadly interpreted as "the right to conduct any activity involving the movement of a boat, vessel, float, or other watercraft, as well as the transport of people and materials and related loading and unloading activity." Bottom line: In order to keep the peace, kayakers should be careful not to infringe upon the rights of private property owners; the reverse is also true—private property owners can't discourage the use of the intertidal zone for the public's rights of fishing, fowling, and navigation. Maine and Massachusetts are the only states where ownership is allowed down to the low-water mark.

Access to Conservation Lands

Several conservation organizations have protected areas within the coastal paddling zone. The Trustees of Reservations is a private, non-profit conservation organization started in 1891 by landscape architect Charles Eliot to preserve the Massachusetts landscape. As Eliot said, "The time is coming when it will be hard to find within a day's journey of our large cities a single spot capable of stirring the soul of man to speak in poetry." The Trustees organization puts out a property guide to the eighty-nine reservations it administers, helpful for Crane Beach area in Ipswich and Essex, World's End in Hingham, the Misery Islands in Salem Sound, Crowninshield (also known as Brown) Island in Marblehead, the Charles River, and places on Martha's Vineyard and Nantucket. Except for Crane Beach, admission to these areas is free to members. On the Concord River, the Trustees is rebuilding the historic boathouse and landing at the Old Manse in Concord—worth a detour, as Michelin would say.

On Boston's North Shore, contact the Essex County Greenbelt Association for permission to use islands and areas administered by that conservation organization. The Massachusetts Audubon Society has several shoreside sanctuaries. On the Cape, Wellfleet Bay has family tenting available to members.

Coastal Wildlife

Prime habitats for migratory waterfowl and nesting birds include the National Wildlife Refuges of Parker River on Plum Island and Monomoy off Chatham. Beach officials have roped off areas for nesting piping plovers and terns. Efforts in Massachusetts to protect the piping plover, on the federal endangered list, have surpassed those in any other state; since 1987, the statewide population has increased from 126 pairs to more than 500. Protection of the plover habitat has resulted in increased numbers for the black skimmer, American oystercatcher, laughing gull, and willet, all rare in the state. Off-road vehicle use, erosion-control measures, and increased human disturbance continue to be a threat to nesting coastal birds such as the plover.

The Merrimack River is a major site for wintering bald eagles, and the Westport River boasts the highest concentration of ospreys in the state. In winter, you can frequently see harbor seals that have migrated south.

No licenses are required for saltwater fishing. For shellfish, contact local town halls; a fee is usually charged.

TRIP 24

Merrimack River

**CASHMAN PARK TO AMESBURY
AND THE MOUTH OF THE MERRIMACK RIVER**

Trip Mileage: 12.5 miles round trip

Tidal Range: 7.8 feet at Newburyport

Charts and Maps: NOAA #13274 at 1:42,000

Caution Areas: The mouth of the Merrimack River has a fiercely strong ebb current, which is very difficult to paddle against. Shoals just outside the jetty and on the south side create large rolling waves, some breaking. Every year, fishermen lose their lives here or capsize and are rescued because of strong current and waves. "The place is to be treated with profound respect but not with terror," said Duncan and Ware in *A Cruising Guide*. A portage over Salisbury or Plum Island beach to avoid the channel at the mouth has been done by sea kayakers. Strong current flows around Black Rocks.

Access: Cashman Park; Black Rock Creek at Salisbury State Beach Reservation

Getting There: To reach Cashman Park, take MA 1 north to Newburyport. At the riverfront, turn left under the bridge onto Merrimac Street. (Don't cross the river.) Go past the first sign for Cashman Park on the right. Look for a brown sign for the public boat ramp. Turn right onto Sally Snyder Way; the concrete ramp is straight ahead. Parking is free. An alternative launch is at Black Rock Creek at Salisbury State Beach Reservation. In Salisbury, from MA 1, take MA 1A (also called Beach Road) east toward the beach, bear right onto State Reservation Road, follow to its end in a camping area, then bear left out to the concrete launch. This site is very crowded, but you can find a place to park (fee) between trailers.

Merrimack River

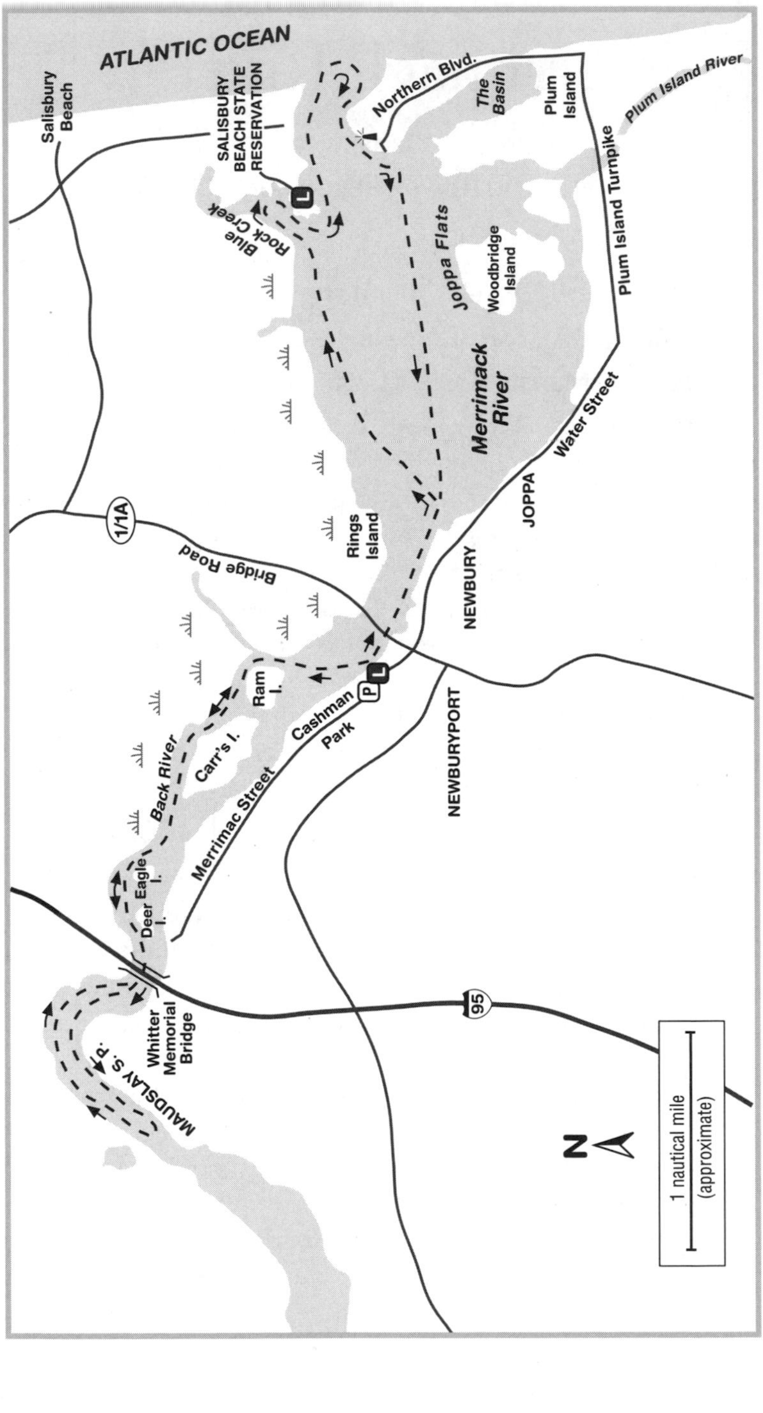

ATLANTIC OCEAN

Salisbury Beach

SALISBURY BEACH STATE RESERVATION

Northern Blvd.

The Basin

Plum Island

Plum Island Turnpike

Plum Island River

Blue Rock Creek

Joppa Flats

Woodbridge Island

Merrimack River

Water Street

1/1A

Bridge Road

Rings Island

JOPPA

NEWBURY

Back River

Ram I.

Carr's I.

Cashman Park

Merrimac Street

NEWBURYPORT

P

Deer Eagle I.

Whittier Memorial Bridge

MAUDSLAY S. P.

95

N

1 nautical mile (approximate)

THE MOUTH of the Merrimack at Newburyport is a strong and exciting place. The 115-mile river flows through most of New Hampshire, including Manchester and the Massachusetts mill towns of Haverhill, Lowell, and Lawrence, then meets the sea at two stone jetties between Plum Island and Salisbury Beach. With a name derived from the Indian word *merruasqumack*, the river starts at the confluence of the Pemigewasset (which starts at Proflie Lake in Franconia) and Winnipesaukee Rivers (starting from the lake of that same name). The mouth has some exhilarating paddling for the sea kayaker provided necessary precautions are taken for timing the trip with a fair tide.

The area is superior for bird watching because it borders the Parker River National Wildlife Refuge, a primary flyway for migrating birds. On a late-April day, you may spot brant ducks and snow geese, both of which live in the Arctic during summer. In winter, bald eagles nest around Carr's Island and Maudslay State Park, which has a protected habitat for wintering eagles. The river is also home to wintering ducks, including mergansers, goldeneyes, and mallards; a host of cormorants perch under the Swing Bridge.

This trip includes a paddle as far up as Amesbury and as far down as the mouth of the river. The public launch spot at Cashman Park has a paved ramp and parking for sixty cars. Turn right (east) to head downriver, passing under the green MA 1 bridge and Newburyport's dockside brick warehouses, marinas, restaurants, and the old granite Customs House, now a maritime museum. The river widens into a broad tidal estuary as it pushes into long, flat marshes behind Plum Island and Salisbury Beach. Much of that shallow estuary is Joppa Flats, half of which dries out completely at low tide. Joppa Flats provides a major resting and feeding area for migrating birds returning from their Arctic breeding grounds. The deep channel to the north side of the river is well marked and has a strong current.

From the estuary, Newburyport's low profile is visible: waterfront houses, white church steeples, and water towers. Beyond the city's contour are tall mounds including Old Town Hill to the south, a glacial drumlin once used for farmland by colonial settlers and now property of the Trustees of Reservations. (A short hike to the top gives you a good view of the Merrimack River and the Isles of Shoals.)

To the east of Newburyport lie the marshes and barrier beach of Plum Island, joined by a road starkly marked by power lines as it traverses marshland. At the bridge across the Plum Island River is a

A group from ConnYak paddles to Maudslay State Park for a lunch stop.

handy, if low-tide-mud-bath, put-in spot, which gives you access to the estuary through the marsh within a mile.

Plum Island's north tip is thickly settled with summer cottages, some rickety, some splendidly remodeled with decks and turrets. Newburyport Harbor makes a long dent into that settled part of Plum Island, whose northeast tip is occupied by the old white, wooden Coast Guard station. A light mounted on the station is said to flash when waves of 2 feet or more break over the bar at the river's entrance.

A shallow bar at the mouth of the Merrimack has been created by silt deposited just outside the arms of the jetties through which the river empties into the Atlantic. This bar serves to create some large rolling waves within the jetties, causing motorboats to leap entirely into the air.

The best bet is to head up the north side in the channel when going with the tide. Waves break over shoals on the south side, which provide good surfing, and back eddies on the south side allow a passage when you're paddling against the tide. If conditions are really rough, you can portage across the peninsula on the south side near the Coast Guard station to quieter water at Newburyport Harbor.

It is nearly impossible to paddle against an ebb tide at the mouth because all of the Merrimack, gathering speed since New Hampshire, rushes through that narrow channel with the additional force of all the water in the broad tidal estuary. Add an east wind, and conditions are very treacherous.

Once in open ocean, if you turn left (north), you head up Salisbury Beach, which turns into Hampton Beach at the New Hampshire border. From the beach inside the breakwater, you can see the dome of Seabrook nuclear power plant in New Hampshire. If you turn right (south), you follow Plum Island.

The jetty is a favorite spot for surf casters, so beware lines. In late spring, as many as fifteen seals can be spotted at once, leaping about the reefs on the north side of the river near the large fluorescent orange triangular marker. The current also runs hard up the channel, so it's best to plan your trip around a fair tide.

On return, paddle past your put-in at Cashman Park upriver to Amesbury. At this section, the Merrimack is a slower, broad river that meanders and alternately narrows and widens; it's divided by four islands. The river is a corridor of the wild and the settled. If you follow the channel behind Carr's and Ram Islands, on the river's northern banks you will see pasture, marshland, rock outcroppings, cedar trees, pines, and birches, part of the Parker River National Wildlife Refuge.

If you paddle along the south side, you pass Newburyport's outskirts, with marinas, small manufacturing plants, houses, cabins, and duck blinds. Continuing upriver, you will pass under two bridges connecting Newburyport to Amesbury: first the older Chain Bridge, which lands on Deer Island in the middle of the river, and then the Whittier Bridge on which I-95 crosses the river.

In Amesbury, 8 miles from the river's mouth, are quaint New England houses on the water's edge, along with the Lowell Boat Yard, which has been making dories on-site since 1793. At the start, Lowell specialized in building a type of surf dory seaworthy enough to withstand the often treacherous conditions at the mouth of the Merrimack so fishermen could get out to their work. The craft had rounded sides, a flat bottom, and a "tombstone" transom; according to some historians, it's said to have been the precursor of the Banks or Gloucester dory, later mass-produced for nesting on fishing schooners.

Across the river is the beautiful 450-acre Maudslay State Park. Paddle by at the end of May when a sea of lavender Carolina rhododendrons tumble down to river's edge past flowering white dogwood, the remaining gardens of the former Moseley estate. In June, the native mountain laurel bloom.

The Merrimack has long been a recipient of the industrial wastes from the factory cities of Manchester, New Hampshire, Haverhill, Lowell, and Lawrence, as well as sewer overflows. It was once considered one of the most polluted rivers in the United States. If you fell in, you were sent to the hospital. The river has become much cleaner over the years in large part due to the passage of the federal Clean Water Act in 1972 and the efforts of the Merrimack River Watershed Council. It now even serves as a drinking water source for several towns. Contact that agency (see appendix A) for maps, pamphlets, information, and sea kayak trips on the river and its tributaries. For sections higher up on the Merrimack, consult the *AMC River Guide: Massachussetts, Connecticut, and Rhode Island, 2nd edition* (AMC Books, 2000).

An alternative is to launch from Salisbury Beach, traveling up to Maudslay State Park and back. In Newburyport, a good postpaddle spot is The Grog, which offers a wide-ranging menu, including Mexican food, in an informal setting. Another option is the Black Cow Tap and Grill, which serves pub food on an inviting deck right on the river. It also has a children's menu.

Camping: Salisbury Beach State Reservation, Beach Road, off MA 1, Salisbury (see the directions above), has 481 campsites; 508-462-4481. RV and campers abound in mid-season.

TRIP 25

Plum Island

CIRCUMNAVIGATION

Trip Mileage: 19-mile loop

Tidal Range: 7.8 feet at Newburyport

Charts and Maps: NOAA #13274 at 1:42,000

Caution Areas: The mouth of the Merrimack River (see Trip 24, "Merrimack River"). Rips can occur under the Plum Island River Bridge and at the mouth of Plum Island Sound.

Access: Pavilion Beach, Ipswich

Getting There: To reach Pavilion Beach from MA 128, take MA 1A to MA 133 into Ipswich. Go straight at the town green onto County Road, which will lead into Jeffrey's Neck Road. Follow that road all the way to its end.

A POPULAR SEA KAYAK TRIP is a circumnavigation of Plum Island, about a 19-mile excursion. The trip combines paddling up one side of Plum Island along ocean beach, passing through the mouth of the Merrimack River, and winding down the other side through the Plum Island River and into Plum Island Sound.

Plum Island is an 8-mile–long barrier beach with 4,650 acres of dune protecting the marshland, which is a refuge for waterfowl along the Atlantic flyway. More than 300 species have been sighted, especially during spring and fall shorebird migrations. Large flocks of waterfowl are present in fall and early spring. Peak migration is from March 1 to June 7 and from August 1 to October 31.

The direction you choose for a circumnavigation will depend on optimum wind and tide conditions: the bottom line is that you should be going with the tide through the mouth of the Merrimack River. Also, it helps to go with the tide through the Plum Island River.

The Plum Island River diminishes to a trickle at low tide, and you may find yourself wandering into channels that go nowhere. When

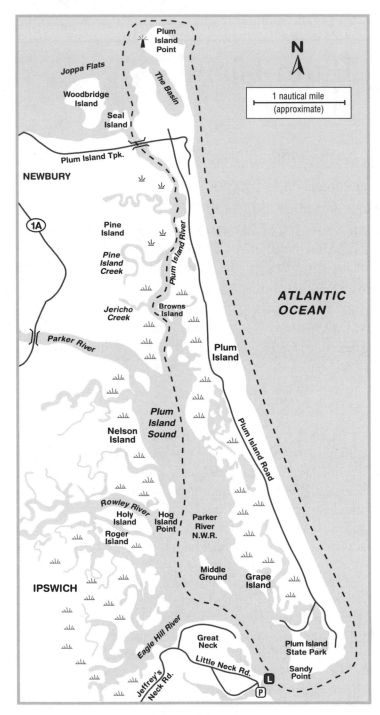

Plum Island

paddling north up the Plum Island River, if in doubt, bear right (east); that generally works to keep you headed in the right direction.

Just to the north of the Plum Island River Bridge is a rock jetty exposed at low tide, but beware rocks at midtide, and pass to the west side. At low tide, also bear west of Seal Island for a passable channel.

If the mouth of the Merrimack is too ripped up, you can portage across the beach either to the north (Salisbury Beach) or to the south (Plum Island Beach), depending on which direction you are paddling. Stamina is required to paddle Plum Island's long shore of sand dune, which can get monotonous after a while. Some oar-weary rowers once nicknamed Plum Island the "eighth continent."

The shore drops off sharply, creating a dumping surf off the beach, so landing is almost impossible. Wildlife refuge officials do not allow landing and will warn you away via jeep-mounted loudspeakers. You can alight, however, on the 1.75-mile municipal beach on the north end of Plum Island, clearly marked by summer cottages before the refuge begins, and on the south tip at Sandy Point Reservation, administered by the state.

Be aware that the trip will inevitably take longer than expected. After the trip, visit Mass Audubon's newly built Joppa Flats Education Center (P.O. Box 1558, Newburyport, MA 01950; 978-462-9998; joppaflats@massaudubon.org) for viewing the newly restored 2-acre salt marsh and for birding information and programs, at the site of the former Sportsmen's Lodge. To get there from I-95, take Exit 57 (MA 113, West Newbury/Newburyport). At the end of the ramp, take MA 113 east about 4 miles to Rolfe's Lane. At the traffic light, turn left (north), note the sign for Plum Island/Parker River Refuge, drive to the end of Rolfe's Lane, and turn right. The sanctuary is 0.6 mile up on the left, across the street from the airport. It's open daily dawn to dusk, and conducts birding tours every Wednesday morning year-round, except in July.

On the back side, you will be paddling through hundreds of acres of marshland. In the late 1990s, Mass Audubon spearheaded a project to protect thousands of acres of marsh behind barrier beaches from Salisbury to West Gloucester in what is known as the Great Marsh, the largest span of marsh north of Long Island. The Great Marsh encompasses 17,000 acres and includes the Parker River National Wildlife Refuge, Parker River, Ipswich River, and the Essex Bay Estuary. Officials hope to improve sewage treatment and septic systems, as well as curtailing animal waste and fertilizer runoff, making

A journey around Plum Island sometimes turns into a wading trip—remember to check tide tables!

shellfish bed closure a thing of the past. You may see stakes, which biologists place in the marsh so students can study the plant life between the stretch lines to document the myriad types of plants.

Camping: Salisbury Beach State Reservation, Beach Road, off MA 1, 481 campsites; 508-462-4481.

TRIP 26

Ipswich Bay

CIRCUMNAVIGATION OF
CASTLE NECK FROM PAVILION BEACH

Trip Mileage: 9-mile loop

Tidal Range: 8.7 feet at Annisquam

Charts and Maps: NOAA #13247 at 1:42,000

Caution Areas: The mouths of the Essex and Ipswich Rivers can get quite torn up, but neither section is very long. More problematic is avoiding the many motorboats and the confused wakes they create. Fox Creek and the Hay Canal dry out one to two hours on either side of low tide and are impassable. Time your trip accordingly! It is a common error for kayakers to misjudge the timing, ending up stuck in the mud and having to hike out of Fox Creek to the road.

Access: Pavilion Beach, Ipswich

Getting There: To reach Pavilion Beach from MA 128, take MA 1A to MA 133 into Ipswich. Go straight at the town green onto County Road, which will lead into Jeffrey's Neck Road. Follow that road to its end at a parking lot at the beach. Hand-carried boats only are allowed at a passage on the beach's north end.

THE MARSHES ON THIS TRIP are beautiful, the surf created by sand shoals off Crane Beach is challenging, and the view of Castle Hill and Hog Island never wears.

The route is about 9 miles, starting and ending at Pavilion Beach, which joins Little Neck to Great Neck, two summer communities in Ipswich. You put in at Plum Island Sound, and with no stops the trip takes about three hours for the average paddler. It provides an interesting contrast of open water and quiet estuary. In lively surf off Crane Beach, you can pick and choose the waves' steepness and intensity

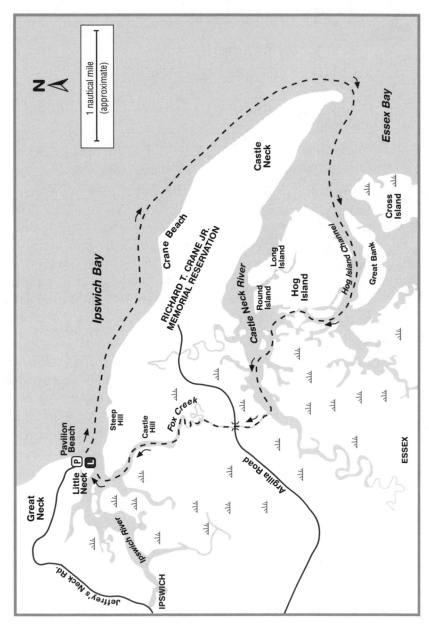

depending on how near you get to the sandbars. Then paddle through the quick current at the mouth of the Essex River, down the back side of Crane in protected water. On the final stretch through the Hay Canal, you're eye level with waving green wands of marsh grass.

The Trustees of Reservations manages about 2,100 acres of beach and marsh including Crane Beach and Castle Hill, the distinct Hog Island drumlin, and four smaller islands in the Essex River Estuary and Bay. That means you can paddle in a fairly settled area in a large tract of open coastal land and a wonderful intersection of past and present. The Trustees allows nonmember visits to Hog Island for a fee. You can also land on the north and south ends of Crane Beach, away from the swimming area.

Shorebirds abound—herons, egrets, sandpipers, lesser yellowlegs, and piping plovers. At Castle Hill, the Great House—a large, English Stuart-style mansion built by Chicago plumbing magnate Richard Crane—alternately recedes into a mass of trees and emerges like the fantasy it was built upon in the early 1920s. The grande allée can be recognized from the water by the abrupt opening in the trees at the top of Steep Hill.

Crane Beach is home to one of the largest numbers of productive pairs of piping plovers. There are about 1,200 breeding pairs that nest on the Atlantic Coast between North Carolina and Newfoundland. In 2002, Crane Beach had twenty-two active nests. Typically, in late April, you can see upwards of thirty plovers. The nests are vulnerable to being washed out by tides and by animal predation, so please respect the closed-off areas. Note the purple tinge to the sand on the north side of Crane Beach. In the world of "sand budgets," this is sand that is sweeping down from the mineral-laden Plum Island to the north. Every decade, the beach changes its profile based on those sand migrations.

You must time this trip with the tides to make it around Hog Island, through Fox Creek, and to the Hay Canal, which empty at low tide. Start from Pavilion Beach and paddle up the 4 miles of Crane Beach. A good picnic spot is the south tip of Crane at the mouth of the Essex River. Pass through the mouth, follow the back side of Crane along the Castle Neck River, then cross to the south of Hog Island toward the barn and Choate House.

Hog Island is a truly magical place. It was the summer home of Masconnomet, chief of the Agawam Indian tribe, who liked the high vantage point and the great fishing and clamming in the area. In 1638,

Circumnavigation of Castle Neck: Fern Usen paddles through Fox Creek.

the Agawams sold the island, which the Choates eventually bought and built a house on in 1725. The prominent dark brown colonial house, named for U.S. senator Rufus Choate, was featured in the film version of Arthur Miller's *The Crucible*, for which an entire colonial-era village was created. For the film, spotters in motorboats patrolled the area to prevent any modern motorboats or kayaks from wandering into the seventeenth-century setting. Cornelius Crane, son of Richard Crane, and his wife, Miné, are buried on top of Hog Island, which overlooks Plum Island Sound. There's a path to the top.

Back in your boat, continue clockwise around the island back to the Castle Neck River until the right (north) turn into Fox Creek, distinguished by the concrete Fox Creek Bridge across Argilla Road, the No Wake signs posted on the marsh, and the view of Castle Hill beyond. You should aim to pass through at least three hours on either side of high tide. Fox Creek leads you out the mouth of the Ipswich River. Cross the Ipswich River swiftly and in a group, as there are strong currents and a multitude of motorboats in summer. Then turn left (north) back to Pavilion Beach.

This trip can also be done in the opposite direction, depending upon the tide. The trip is not advisable on a summer weekend when motorboats roar through the narrow channel of Fox Creek and from about mid-July to mid-August when the female greenhead fly is biting ferociously. The black boxes on stilts that line the channels are put on the marshes come spring to trap the greenheads.

A good, inexpensive refueling spot in Ipswich is the Choate Bridge Pub, four doors down from Choate Bridge, the oldest stone-arched bridge in the United States.

Other Options: The 6-mile paddle from Pavilion Beach to Nelson Island up Plum Island Sound takes you by the Rowley River and beautiful Rowley marshes, some protected by the Essex County Greenbelt Association. A walk down Stackyard Road on Nelson Island, part of the Parker River National Wildlife Refuge, gives you a taste of open meadow, bobolinks, and tidal pools with waders such as the ubiquitous snowy egret and occasional glossy ibis. A good time to paddle here is the first week in September, when shorebird migration is at its peak but duck-hunting season has not yet started. On your way back, cross the sound to Grape Island, site of a former summer hotel.

The views are wide-open marsh vistas across Rowley, Newbury, and Ipswich. Up on the Newbury marshes, you can still see circular "straddles" built during the mid-1800s to keep mown salt marsh hay above water before the hayers floated it to shore on wood platforms. In fall, tractors still mow to sell the weedless marsh hay to the perennial flower garden trade.

Camping: None.

TRIP 27

Essex River

CIRCUMNAVIGATION OF CROSS ISLAND

Trip Mileage: 8 miles round trip

Tidal Range: 8.7 feet at Annisquam

Charts and Maps: NOAA #13274 at 1:40,000

Caution Areas: Strong current at Cross Island

Access: Essex River Basin Adventures, Essex

Getting There: From MA 128 north, take exit 15 (School Street Essex/Manchester). At the end of the ramp, turn left onto School Street. Follow School Street (its name changes to Southern Avenue) for about 2 miles to MA 133. Turn left onto the Essex Causeway; Woodman's seafood restaurant will be on the left. Shortly after, turn right just past Periwinkle's restaurant. Park in public (nonrestaurant) spaces. Overflow parking is available at the fire station, located a short walk up the hill and down MA 22 past the Essex River Basin Adventures barn.

THIS IS A FINE TRIP to take in mid-August or early September when the great blue herons are starting to congregate to fly south. You can see half a dozen or more of these majestic 4-foot-high birds catching fish in the salt water pannes (open water areas) on the marsh or flying low, large wings outstretched, necks folded.

Paddle out from the town dock, past the Essex Shipbuilding Museum, then H. A. Burnham's boatbuilding shop. H. A. Burnham comes from a long line of Burnhams who have been building ships in Essex since colonial times, when this town launched what is known as the chebacco boat—a smaller precursor to the coastal schooners that would soon ply their way up and down the New England coast. In spring 2003, the Burnham Shipyard launched the 65-foot schooner

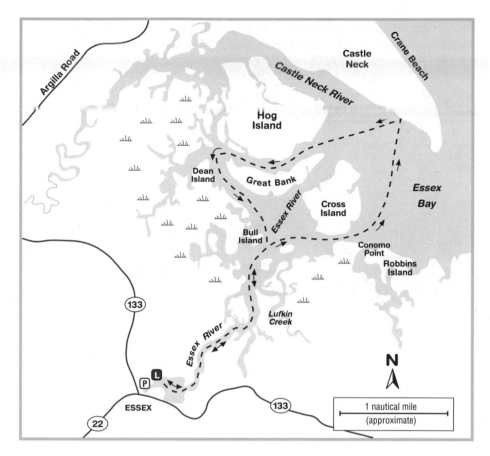

Essex River

Fame. For more information on *Fame* and the history of shipbuilding here, stop in the Essex Shipbuilding Museum (Box 277, 66 and 28 Main Street, Essex, MA 01929; 978-768-7541; info@essexship buildingmuseum.org) with two locations, one at the Waterline Center and the other around the corner next to White Elephant Antiques.

Essex shipyards launched more than 4,000 wooden vessels that sailed to nearly every continent in Essex County's great days of sail and trade. Most ships were built in Essex, then launched into the Essex River and taken to Gloucester for final outfitting of masts and sails. More ships were built in Essex at one time than any other town in New England.

On the right is modern boating—floating docks full of large oceangoing motorboats sporting twin 250-horsepower motors for

The river is the site of the annual Essex River Race in mid-May, a good season opener.

quick fishing trips out the mouth of the Essex River. Beyond is the causeway famous for many seafood restaurants—including Woodman's, where the fried clam was invented.

As you head off into the marshes, to the left, high in a field, is a pink farmhouse known as the Cogswell's Grant, homestead and farm to William Cogswell in the 1650s. The 165 acres, farmhouse, and building are owned by the Society for the Preservation of New England Antiquities (SPNEA) and house one of the most extensive collections of early American folk art, collected for more than forty years by the Bertram and Nina Little.

On anything solid—wood poles, buoys, rocks—you will see the familiar cormorant, drying out its wings before it takes flight. In the water, it floats very low (due to a lack of oil in its wings) with its beak pointing up. Look to the banks on either side for great blue herons.

On the right is a granite outcropping and a bench sitting within a cedar grove, known as Clamhouse Landing; this is part of the Cox Reservation and headquarters of Essex County Greenbelt, a local nonprofit land trust that has preserved more than 10,000 acres of land of ecological, agricultural, and scenic significance within Essex County over the past forty years. It was here, using the granite stones, that the above-mentioned Cogswell operated a ferry from the Gloucester to the Ipswich side of the river where his farm was located in the 1650s.

You can launch a kayak from Clamhouse Landing if you are a member of Greenbelt; the best time is high tide to avoid a mud hike. Stop in the office headquarters for Greenbelt (the white farmhouse as you come in) and let somebody know you are there, then drive down, drop off your boat and gear, and return to the barns to park your car.

Continuing on, in mid-August you will see pale sea lavender wisps growing on the marsh and surviving high tides. Where the tide covers it twice a day, *Spartina alterniflora* is tough and wide. *Spartina patens* grows higher up and only gets covered in the flood tides; it is coarse and was harvested in colonial times for salt marsh hay to be fed to livestock. It is prized by garden clubs as an excellent mulch with lots of nutrients, minus the seed heads of grass and weeds. In October, it turns a beautiful russet-gold color; by the third week in May, the marsh turns green again.

Bear right at Cross Island. The skeleton of a stonework mansion on the point is a curious sight. The story goes that a member of the Cross family built his mansion on top of the island, then let his brother build one below. The new house blocked his view, so he had it dismantled. The two brothers never talked to each other again. The 6-mile route from Essex around Cross Island is the course followed in mid-May every year by the Essex River Race, which is sponsored by the Cape Ann Rowing Club.

The current moves swiftly through "the narrows" here, with much of the flood and ebb tide in the Essex River moving through. You may need to stay in the eddies that run next to Cross Island to get through at midtide during high tide. To the right is an anchorage with several interesting small wood sailboats along with the complement of working aluminum skiffs and pleasure boats. On shore is Conomo Point, with its summer houses pointing to the sea; the town of Essex has given homeowners a twenty-year lease, at which point—according to a recent town vote—they must leave. The houses are not exactly mobile homes, and the task of dismantling that entire community will be daunting.

On a weekday, you will share the channel with the aluminum skiffs of clammers who work out on the productive clam flats at low tide. Returning with burlap bags full of littleneck clams, they are usually in very good moods. Stay to the side of the channel.

You can look over to Hog Island and the Choate House, and to the back side of Crane, known as the inner beach. Paddle over to the beach for a picnic, then head back around the other side of Cross Island for a better view of Hog.

You will also see egrets in the marshes. The smaller white egrets are most likely snowy egrets with yellow feet, also known as "golden slippers." The larger are probably American egrets; they have black feet.

Essex recently voted to put the town under a central sewer system, which should greatly improve water quality here—not that it is bad to begin with, flushed as it is twice a day by the great Atlantic.

For an after-paddle spot, if you are not interested in loading up on fried clams or boiled lobster at Woodman's, try the Conomo Café on the causeway; in summer it has an outdoor deck. In colder months, try the tavern area for light fare and binoculars provided to bird watch from the large picture window or see the kayaks go by from Essex River Basin Adventures.

If you want company on a sea kayak trip here, sign up with congenial Ozzie Osborn at Essex River Basin Adventures, based in the barn at 1 Main Street. (See appendix A.)

Camping: None.

Cape Ann

CIRCUMNAVIGATION

Trip Mileage: 22 miles round trip; alternative half-Cape tour with finish in Rockport, 10 miles

Tidal Range: 8.7 feet at Gloucester; 8.6 feet at Rockport

Charts and Maps: NOAA #13279 at 1:20,000

Caution Areas: You'll often find strong tide and confused wakes from motorboat traffic in Blynman Canal. Refracting waves are off Halibut Point. Confused seas are caused by the heavy traffic of motor, fishing, and whale-watching boats in Gloucester Harbor.

Access: Gloucester town ramp, formerly the Dunfudgin ramp, behind Gloucester High School on the Annisquam River. A ramp fee is charged weekends and holidays, May through September, for nonresidents. There's lots of parking. Another put-in spot is Stone Pier off Atlantic Street in Gloucester, which is free but has a long access walk at low tide.

Getting There: Take MA 128 north, then take the first right on the first traffic circle after the Annisquam River Bridge onto Washington Street. Follow Washington Street to the harbor, turn right onto Western Avenue, then right again on Centennial Street just before the Blynman Canal Bridge, and take the third left onto Blynman Avenue behind the high school to the river.

CAPE ANN THRUSTS a gnarly head into the great Atlantic and makes for dramatic paddling along 20 miles of rocky shore indented by granite coves, deep harbors, and pocket beaches. The Annisquam River, which cuts through Cape Ann on the western perimeter, makes Cape Ann an island—and circumnavigation possible.

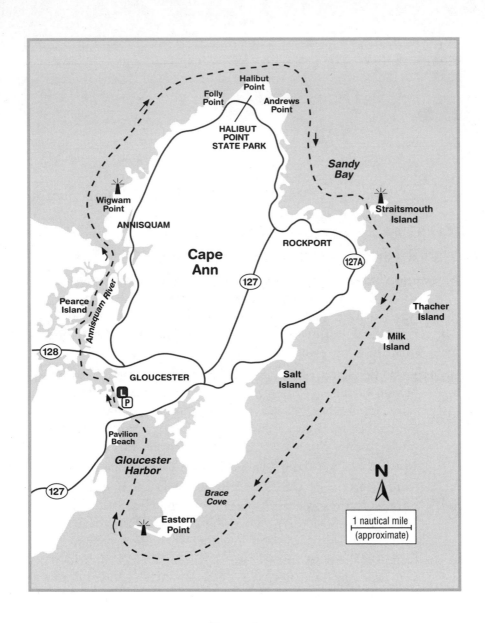

Cape Ann

The clockwise trip around Cape Ann starts and ends in Gloucester in the Annisquam River and combines several paddling environments: the protected Annisquam River with summer houses lining the banks, waves breaking off the desolate but dramatic Halibut Point, ocean swells around Thacher Island, a long, mesmerizing stretch down Gloucester's eastern shore, and the busy and historic Gloucester Harbor.

The Annisquam River has several put-in spots. A good central location with lots of parking is the paved public ramp behind the Gloucester High School. It's about 4 miles from the high school to the ocean through the Annisquam, with wide marshland to the left and old summer houses to the right. Then you enter open ocean and paddle along the rocky coast past Annisquam Lighthouse. You can take shelter in Lane's Cove by entering through the granite seawall. Paddling up, on the right you pass Folly Cove, 100 yards long with a rocky beach at the head of the cove. On a clear day when you aren't concentrating on waves casting spray onto your face, you can see the New Hampshire coastline and Mount Agamenticus in Maine.

Halibut Point is a rocky headland that forms the north tip of Cape Ann and kicks up spectacular spray in northeast winds. Halibut was known historically as Haul-About Point, where sailors changed tack to round Cape Ann on their way to Boston. A jumble of granite slab remains from Halibut Point's historic quarry industry. The area is a public reservation owned jointly by the Trustees of Reservations and the state and is well worth a visit by car. (A boat landing is virtually impossible.)

Pass Halibut, Pigeon Cove, and head on to Rockport, about 10 miles around the cape from the high school. You can put in at Granite Pier just to the north of Rowe Point (a fee is charged for launching in summer). Rockport Harbor is not very hospitable to out-of-town boats landing on its shores. You can, however, paddle around the harbor to view buoy-laden Motif Number One, the red lobster shack that is said to be the most painted and photographed building in the country. Storm waves during the 1978 blizzard destroyed the famous landmark, but townspeople have since rebuilt it.

From Rockport, paddle across Sandy Bay through Straitsmouth Channel to Thacher Island. Straitsmouth is a barren, rocky island with a lighthouse, separated from the mainland by a 50-yard-wide channel, which sometimes gets turned into a washing machine of refracting waves.

Annisquam Light is close to the Annisquam River's mouth.

Once you're through Straitsmouth, head directly south, where sea conditions change fairly dramatically depending on wind direction—from quiet sea, following waves, to large swells, or whatever else. The paddle is about 3.5 miles from Granite Pier to Thacher, marked by the gray stone twin towers.

The alternate route to Thacher is via the Dry Salvages, 2 miles from Thacher and 1 mile out from Straitsmouth Point. These are two rocky ledges know as the Salvages and Little Salvages, a subject of T. S. Eliot's poem "The Four Quartets." Despite their desolation, the Salvages (pronounced *sal-VAGES*) have certain lures for kayakers, not least of which are the seals swimming about.

The Thacher landing is located on the Coast Guard station ramp next to the white shed. To go ashore, catch a wave and slide up the ramp. Sign in at the Coast Guard shed at the top of the ramp. For more on Thacher, see Trip 29.

Continuing on from Thacher to Eastern Point, about 6 miles, the residential coast is indented by Long and Good Harbor Beaches. The beautiful Eastern Point Light marking the entrance to Gloucester Harbor appears. Then you round Dog Bar jetty, pass the Eastern Point Yacht Club, and head the 2 miles into Gloucester Harbor past the mansions of Eastern Point.

To the right, you pass the house of Joseph Garland, a North Shore writer who is perhaps best known for his biography of Howard Blackburn, the fingerless navigator. Blackburn, who lost his fingers to frostbite when his hands froze to the oars on a fishing trip to Nova Scotia, overcame his handicap to break several records for his solo transatlantic crossings long before most sailors gave thought to this idea. Blackburn was one of Gloucester's most famous citizens, and Garland's biography, *Lone Voyager*, can be found in local bookstores.

The Cape Ann Rowing Club has named the premier ocean rowing event it sponsors every July for the famous captain. The Blackburn Challenge, a circumnavigation of Cape Ann, is a good introduction to this trip in the company of other paddlers and rowers. The club's original intent for the challenge was a fun outing with an overnight on Thacher Island, but the event has now turned into a three-to-five-hour race.

Paddling into Gloucester Harbor during summer requires concentration. Fishing vessels, whale-watching ships, offshore racing boats, and other pleasure craft kick up a confusion of waves, and kayakers in their small boats can feel fairly insignificant. One event worth risking the harbor chaos for, however, is the annual Labor Day schooner race. Here the speedy *Adventure*, once Gloucester's most productive fishing schooner, races the likes of the *Harvey Gammage* or *Spirit of Massachusetts*. The large boats in full sail send you back a century or so in history.

You can land at Pavilion Beach in Gloucester Harbor, just past Ten Pound Island near what is known as the greasy pole. This odd structure is a telephone pole hanging sideways, used for a contest something like log rolling in which youths see how far out on the pole they can clamber before slithering off. Another Pavilion Beach landmark is the Fisherman's Memorial, a statue clad in foul-weather gear leaning over a ship's wheel and looking out to sea.

At trip's end, if it is a summer weekend and Blynman Canal Bridge has too much boat traffic, just walk across Western Avenue to return to your car at the high school, then drive back to pick up your kayak and gear.

For pre-paddle fuel, try one of the Italian bakeries on Main Street. Also, don't miss the magnificent Fitz Hugh Lane paintings of Gloucester Harbor in the Cape Ann Historical Society. Another Gloucester citizen, Lane is now considered one of the founders of the American luminist school. The harborside granite house where the polio-stricken artist lived and worked to take full advantage of Gloucester scenes can be seen from the water, not far from Ten Pound Island, one of his most famous subjects. The new Gloucester Maritime Heritage Center on Harbor Loop is also worth visiting for historical waterfront artifacts and boats.

Other Options: The Annisquam River has several put-in spots, and a protected paddle through the marsh tributaries or up into Lobster Cove is an option when the sea is too rough. A good launch spot is from Lane's Cove in Annisquam. From MA 128, cross the Annisquam Bridge. At the bottom of the hill, take the Grant Circle Rotary three-quarters of the way around and get off at MA 127 North/Washington Street. Follow this into Lane's Cove (4.5 miles), then turn left onto Duley Street and follow it to the cove. The ramp is parallel to the seawall; there's parking at the top of the ramp. Expect some mud at low tide. You paddle out the gap in the seawall. Another good access point into the Annisquam River is Long Wharf Landing in the Jones River, with plenty of parking. From MA 128, take Exit 13 (Wingaersheek Beach). Follow Concord Street to Atlantic Street. The launch is on the right, next to the long pier.

Camping: Thacher Island; see Trip 29.

Rockport
to Thacher Island

Trip Mileage: 7 miles round trip

Tidal Range: 8.6 feet at Rockport

Charts and Maps: NOAA #13274 at 1:40,000

Caution Areas: Straitsmouth is a 50-yard-wide channel, which sometimes gets turned into a washing machine of refracting waves. Rolling beam seas are possible on the leg from Straitsmouth to Thacher.

Access: Launch from Granite Pier, Rockport. The fee is $6 for a kayak, $6 for parking. The rest of Rockport parking is by permit only in summer.

Getting There: Take MA 128 over the Annisquam Bridge and go straight through the first (Grant Circle) and second (Blackburn Circle) rotaries, staying on MA 128. At the bottom of the hill at the traffic light, turn left onto MA 127/Eastern Avenue and follow this into Rockport. At the traffic island at the bottom of the hill, turn left onto Granite Avenue. Follow this for about 1 mile to Granite Pier on the right. Launch at the ramp; park on top of the granite breakwater.

———

LESS THAN A MILE off Rockport, Thacher, the 50-acre rockbound island marked by its twin light stone towers, has both history and nature in abundance. The good news is that in 2000, the Coast Guard replaced the wood landing ramp wiped out in 1998's Perfect Storm; after a five-year hiatus it is now possible to land on the island again.

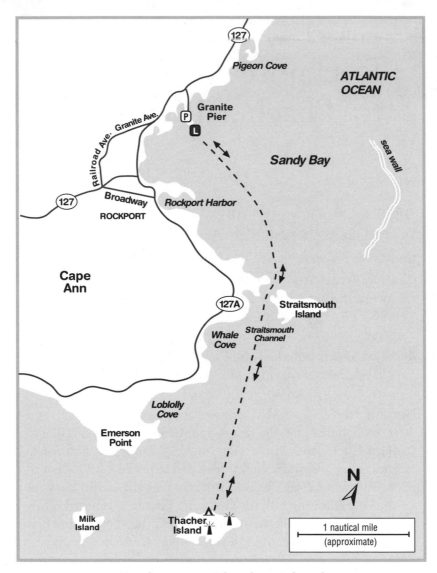

Rockport to Thacher Island

The historic island is named for Anthony Thacher, an early British settler whose ship, the *Watch and Wait*, wrecked on the island in the great storm of August 1635 en route from Ipswich to Marblehead, Massachusetts. Thacher lost all four of his children, twenty-one friends and cousins, and all his possessions. Only his wife, Elizabeth, survived. Even though the British government granted Thacher the island in sympathy for his tragedy, he chose to live in Marblehead.

Still mindful of Thacher's disaster more than a century earlier, colonial officials erected twin 45-foot lighthouse towers on the island in 1771. That was the eleventh light station built in this country and the first built in the United States not specifically for harbor protection.

Officials replaced the old station with taller twin towers (123 feet high) in 1861; those stand today. The Coast Guard shut off the North Tower Light in 1932 as an economy measure and took its last employees from the island in 1980. The Coast Guard automated the South Tower Light and fog whistle, and in 1980 the town of Rockport took over the island by lease from the Coast Guard. In 1983, the Thacher Island Association formed to support and encourage historic preservation on the island. Boardwalks and railways crisscross the island's interior. A well-worn path leads both to the north and to the south parts of the island.

If you visit in summer, you can use this path. In June, the island's lush plant life—pink morning glories, beach rose, and blackberries—blooms effusively. Thousands of fuzzy baby gulls make their parents aggressive and territorial. Some people hike the island with a kayak paddle overhead to ward off marauding parents.

The island receives a lot of care and a lot of visitors, including kayakers and divers. The Coast Guard has turned its property over to U.S. Fish and Wildlife, which now owns the North Tower (closed to visitors). The town of Rockport owns the remaining three-quarters of the island, including the automated South Tower (check to see if visits are allowed).

The Thacher Island Association kept interest alive in the beleagued island for several decades, and finally saw its efforts pay off when officials designated the island a National Historic Landmark in 2001. The Coast Guard replaced the wood landing ramp at a cost of about $300,000 before giving up ownership in 2001. A new outhouse, freshly mowed perimeter trail, and two very nice benches sitting on a promontory overlooking Milk Island to the south—all speak well of the island's upkeep.

Four families, whose job it was to keep up with the relentless schedule of filling the lights with kerosene every eight hours to warn mariners off the rocky shoals, once lived here. You can still see the tracks of the railroad line used to carry the kerosene from the landing area to the towers. An excellent history of the island is *Thachers: Island of the Twin Lights* (Toad Hall, 1985), by Eleanor C. Parsons, available in Rockport and Gloucester bookstores.

Seagulls rule Thacher Island.

To paddle to Thacher, you set off from Granite Pier (you share the ramp with motorboats) and head almost due south (or to the right toward Rockport and Bearskin Neck on top of the granite boulders). It takes about an hour at a leisurely pace to paddle the 3.5 miles. You will share the waters with three sailboat classes racing out of Sandy Bay Yacht Club in Rockport and large oceangoing cabin cruisers whose huge wakes you need to watch.

From Rockport, paddle across Sandy Bay through Straitsmouth Channel to Thacher Island. Straitsmouth is a barren, rocky island with a lighthouse, separated from the mainland by a 50-yard-wide channel, which sometimes gets turned into a washing machine of refracting waves. To find Straitsmouth Channel from your launch, head for the green nun, which marks the entry. The channel is not visible until you are right there.

Distinctly visible to the west are the white-washed Dry Salvages, 2 miles from Thacher and 1 mile out from Straitsmouth Point. Not to be confused with the remains of Rockport's old seawall, these are two rocky ledges known as the Salvages and Little Salvages, a subject of T. S. Eliot's poem "The Four Quartets."

Once in the channel, you can see the two somber stone towers, made from New Hampshire granite. Once through Straitsmouth, head directly south, where sea conditions change fairly dramatically depending on wind direction—from quiet sea to large swells, or whatever else. You can make out the small white Coast Guard shed on the east side of the island.

At the ramp, pop your sprayskirt, get a good speed up, and paddle up as far as you can before hopping out. Those behind should wait until you get out of the way. The first person off can help pull up the others as they arrive. Then carry your boats to the side of ramp, leaving space in the ramp's middle for other users. Sign the guest book and put your $2 donation in the jar. Pick up a map for walking the island's trails.

On your way back, if you still have time, you can poke into Rockport Harbor, a working harbor with many lobster boats. Look for Motif Number One, a red fishing shed hung with lobster buoys, said to be the most painted and photographed building in the country.

To help, join the Thacher Island Association, Box 73, Rockport, MA 01966 ($25 individual, $50 family, $250 lifetime membership).

Camping: Camping is available on Thacher Island near the South Tower for $5 per person per night. Call the island keeper ahead of time to make reservations, 978-546-2326. Camping is June 1 through September 15. Open fires are not allowed; pets are prohibited. You must bring your own water, because there is no drinkable water on the island. The three-bedroom apartment located in keeper's dwelling (it sleeps six) is available for $300 a weekend (Friday noon to Sunday at 6:00 P.M.), or $1,000 a week. Again, bring drinkable water. Call the Thacher Island Town Committee at 978-546-7341 to make a reservation. For more information, visit www.thacherisland.org.

Massachusetts

Salem Sound

DEVEREUX BEACH TO MISERY ISLANDS

Trip Mileage: 15.5 miles round trip

Tidal Range: 9.1 feet at Marblehead

Charts and Maps: NOAA #13274 at 1:40,000

Caution Areas: There are refracting waves off the north side of Tinkers Island and confused waves at Bowditch Ledge. The east-side entry to the passage between Big and Little Misery Islands can develop large breaking waves.

Access: Devereux Beach. A parking fee is charged in summer; you'll find a public restroom and snackbar. You may meet resistance to a beach launch if the beach is crowded. An alternative launch site is directly across the street at Riverhead Beach and Marblehead Harbor. It has ample parking and a paved ramp, which motorboats can't use at low tide. In summer, the town charges a fee.

Getting There: To reach Devereux Beach, take I-95 to MA 128 to Exit 25 (MA 114). Follow MA 114 east through Peabody and Salem into Marblehead. In Marblehead, continue through three sets of traffic lights. At the next blinking light (at the fire station), turn right onto Ocean Avenue. Go straight through the next traffic light and continue to the Devereaux Beach parking lot on the right. The alternative launch site is across the street.

SALEM SOUND'S main attraction is the dozen offshore rocky islands, including the beautiful Misery Islands. Also, on a windy, summer day, the view of hundreds of sailboats gliding across the horizon from Marblehead, Salem, and Manchester Harbors is magnificent.

With the exception of Great and Little Misery Islands and

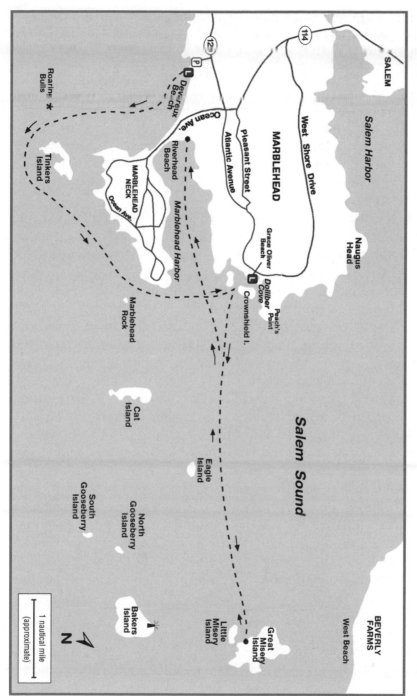

Salem Sound

Crowninshield, the dozen or so islands of Salem Sound are privately owned, and owners refuse permission to go ashore. Bakers Island has a lighthouse on the north point and a host of summer houses. Eagle has a tower. Cat, also known as Children's, has several camp buildings operated by the YMCA in summer, and is hospitable to kayak landings. Others, such as Coney and the Gooseberries, are bald, rocky heads covered with gulls. Boston's financial district towers lie on the horizon to the south. If conditions are particularly settled, paddle south from the Gooseberry Ledges to the big, bald hump of Halfway Rock and, like the ancient mariners, throw a coin onto the rock to signfiy your passing.

The trip starts with a beach launch from Devereux Beach at the west end, where the beach is more level. Don't launch or land inside the swimmer buoys. If the surf is too rough, an alternate put-in spot is across the road at Riverhead Beach, which puts you at the head of Marblehead Harbor. From Devereux, paddle past Marblehead Neck, around the outside of Tinkers Island, then hug the steep and rocky Marblehead Neck past historic Castle Rock and to the inside of Marblehead Rock (a major seabird nesting island), past the Marblehead Light and Chandler Hovey Park to Jack Point at the outermost tip of Marblehead Harbor.

Cross the head of Marblehead Harbor, watching for boats exiting the harbor, to protected Dolliber Cove and Crowninshield Island, also known as Brown Island. The 5-acre oasis is owned by the Trustees of Reservations and is reachable from the mainland at low tide. The small island is surprisingly varied, with a pink granite shoreline, a salt marsh pond, a grassy meadow, coniferous trees, and a sandy beach. In spring, the shores have a lot of winter debris piled up. Quite a few boats stop here, but you can find an isolated spot and good vantage point for the Sunday-afternoon sailboat races out of Marblehead. The booming of the starting gun can be confused with the sound of planes gunning out of Boston's Logan Airport. The island has become quite popular over the years for parties and picnics; a caretaker now keeps on eye on it.

Cross the southern tip of Eagle Island over to Great Misery Island. Paddle into the passage between Great and Little Misery for a landing on Great Misery's wide gravel beach on the south shore, which is less crowded than the coastal-side beach. Be aware that surf sometimes breaks on this bar between the two islands.

The North and South River Watershed

Just 25 miles from Boston's city limits is an oasis for the solitude-seeking paddler in the North and South River watershed. The Nature Conservancy has identified the valley within the watershed as one of the most unique natural areas in southeastern Massachusetts. The North River starts at the confluence of Indian Head River and Herring Brook in Hanover, then travels 12 winding miles to its mouth at Scituate. There it's joined by the South River, which starts somewhat mysteriously from swamps and ponds in the northwest corner of Duxbury and travels 14 miles to its mouth. Paddling in this valley is forgiving yet interesting, peaceful, and full of wildlife. The North River's confluence with the ocean is notoriously risky and should not be attempted except by very experienced kayakers. The North River has many publicly accessible launch sites. The watershed is well looked after by the North and South River Watershed Association, which promotes access and recreation on all the rivers, tributaries, and ponds in the watershed. It produces a map guide and the *NSRWA Canoe and Kayak Guide to the North and South Rivers and the Indian Head River*, which is yours for becoming a member.

You can kayak the freshwater swamp of Herring Brook, kayak in the waves at Sandy Spit, hike through a pine forest, or picnic on Cove Creek. A particularly secluded paddle winds along Herring Brook with its clusters of wild rice, large stands of Atlantic white cedar, Pembroke's Misty Meadows Conservation Area, and abundant birdlife. The Massachusetts Division of Fisheries and Wildlife has made that exploration possible with a kayak-friendly launch ramp on the Indian Head River. The possibilities are endless. To join, contact NSRWA, P.O. Box 43, Norwell, MA 02061-0043; 781-659-8168; nsrwa@juno.com.

Great and Little Misery islands are 0.5 mile off West Beach in Beverly Farms. Both islands comprise 84 acres and make up the second largest landmass between Boston Harbor and Cape Porpoise, Maine. They were once the site of summer cottages, a clubhouse, and a nine-hole golf course. They now host rolling fields, mowed regularly, with scattered stands of oak and pine. Great Misery has several trails that lead you past ruins of the former resort and provide fine views of Salem Sound and Manchester Harbor. It is surprising how uncrowded the island interior is on a busy summer day. Most people moor in their boats around the island but don't go ashore, so you could have the place to yourself. The views are of House Island and Gloucester to the north, the industrial complex of Salem including General Electric's smokestacks to the south, and, beyond that, Marblehead and Boston's skyline.

The Misery Islands Reservation is owned by the Trustees of Reservations, and use of the islands for picnicking and exploring is free to members, with a fee for nonmembers for day use if an official is there to collect (a seasonal boat pass is also available).

Upon returning, instead of paddling south of Marblehead Neck, proceed up the mile-long pouch of Marblehead Harbor to gaze at some of the finest sailing craft in the country. The harbor has 2,450 moorings with a seven-year waiting list for 700 more, attesting to the site's popularity. Launches from the five yacht clubs—Eastern, Corinthian, Dolphin, Marblehead, and Boston—skip around the harbor because using tenders is practically out of the question.

It is possible to disembark at the town's State Street Landing dock at The Landing restaurant. Haul your kayak onto the dock and put it in the middle of the float. The best way to see historic Marblehead, founded in 1629, is on foot: narrow, winding one-way streets and summer crowds make the town hard to drive through.

The sound gets flooded with several thousand boats sailing out of Marblehead (established in 1889, Marblehead Race Week at the end of July has at least 200 competitors a day) as well as hundreds of motorboats emerging from the many marinas close to a thickly settled part of Boston's North Shore. Because of unbelievable traffic and confused wakes, the best bet is to stick close to shore for privacy and protection, or to paddle between Labor and Memorial Days when traffic is minimal.

Finish on Riverhead Beach at the paved launch ramp, then walk across the road to retrieve your car. An alternative launch site is at Grace Oliver Beach, in Dolliber Cove just south of Peach's Point. From MA 114 in Marblehead, bear left on West Shore Drive, which turns into Beacon Street. Follow this to Grace Oliver Beach; there's limited parking on the road.

Other Options: For more direct access to the Misery Islands, launch at West Beach, Beverly Farms, which requires resident sticker parking in summer but is open to the public from Labor Day to Memorial Day. Carry in from the beach. Beverly Harbor has free public access year-round in the Danvers River on the southeast side of the Kernwood Avenue bridge in Salem; Salem Harbor has access at Winter Island in Salem (from Salem, follow signs to Salem Willows, go to Fort Avenue, then turn left onto Winter Island Road and follow signs to Winter Island Park). Farther north, Lynch Park in Beverly has a beach, picnic tables, grills, a playground, bathrooms, an ice cream stand, and a beautiful protected beach for launching. This is a particularly good place for family kayakers. To reach Lynch Park, take MA 128 north to Exit 22E (MA 62). Follow MA 62 through Beverly Center. After passing through town, MA 62 ends and turns into MA 127 at the set of lights. Proceed straight onto MA 127 and take the next right onto Ober Street. Follow Ober Street about 0.3 mile to the park entrance on the right. Fee parking and an overflow lot are available.

Heading north, the coastline past Beverly Farms and Manchester is rugged and rocky, interspersed with privately owned beaches, natural areas, and seaside mansions. From Manchester Harbor, paddle past Singing Beach, Magnolia Harbor and Kettle Island (major heron rookery), Norman's Woe Rock (immortalized by the poet Longfellow), Hammond Castle, to Gloucester Harbor (marked by Eastern Point Light).

Manchester launch spots include the town wharf on Central Street behind the Manchester Police Station (park behind the station in a spot not reserved for police officers). The small beach at Masconomo Park, down Beach Street, is another option (turn right at the playground; limited nonresident parking is in the middle). In summer, you need to arrive very early or after 3:00 P.M. to find a parking spot. Tuck's Point by the Manchester Yacht Club no longer offers official nonresidential parking in the off-season.

Camping: Winter Island, Salem, May through October. Fee. Call the Winter Island Marine Park, 978-745-9430.

TRIP 31

Boston Harbor

HULL TO OUTER ISLANDS

Trip Mileage: Pemberton Point to Georges Island, 1 mile one way; to Great Brewster, 2.5 miles one way at high tide; alternate trip to Hingham Harbor, 5 miles round trip

Tidal Range: 9.5 feet at Hingham

Charts and Maps: NOAA #13270 at 1:22,200

Caution Areas: Hull Gut beween Windmill Point on the Hull Peninsula and Peddocks Island. The current can run out of here at upwards of 3 knots. You will also be paddling over exposed stretches; to check Boston Harbor's tides and weather forecast, log on to www.bostonharbor.com to see what the weather gods plan to throw your way.

Access: Pemberton Point. Parking is free; buy a launching permit at the Pemberton Bait Shop. Or you can launch from the boat ramp at Hingham Harbor Park, also with free parking.

Getting There: To reach Pemberton Point from Boston, take the Southeast Expressway to the Neponset-Quincy exit. Follow signs for MA 3A to Hingham. At the Hingham Rotary, proceed halfway around and follow signs to Nantasket. Once you're in Hull, turn left onto Nantasket Avenue for about 2.5 miles. At the junction of Main Street and Nantasket Avenue, bear left on Main Street and follow it to the end. To reach Hingham Harbor Park, from the rotary follow MA 3A north, go through a set of lights, past a marine store, then turn right at the parking lot by the iron horse statue, just before Hingham Bathing Beach. Free parking.

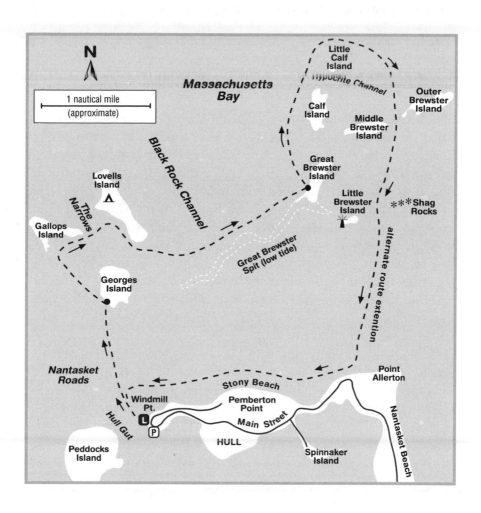

Boston Harbor

THE BOSTON HARBOR ISLANDS provide a wilderness paddling experience within the Boston metropolis and around one of the country's most historical harbors. One of the best put-in spots is at Hull, where the waters are cleaner than other harbor spots, car vandals less likely, and the paddler-friendly Hull Lifesaving Museum nearby.

The 50-square-mile Boston Harbor provides a veritable marine-history museum on and between thirty-four rocky islands that range in character from the truly inviting and lush to the genuinely desolate. From Civil War forts to World War II gun remnants, Indian archaeology sites to mansion ruins, old hospitals to former fashionable hotels, striking lighthouses to rural farmland, the sites make for a dynamic sea kayaking experience. From the water, you can usually see downtown Boston's aqua towers rising above the old Custom House Tower, Boston's first skyscraper. From the inner harbor, the masts of the USS *Constitution* in Charlestown Navy Yard are visible. Several sight-seeing boats that leave from the Boston wharves give narrated harbor tours, and the National Park Service runs a regular trip out to Little Brewster and Boston Light.

The islands are now blossoming from a new appreciation for their scenic beauty. Boston Harbor Islands State Park was formed in the 1970s to help give the public access to nine pristine islands. In 1997, all thirty-four islands became a national park (www.nps.gov/boha or www.bostonislands.com), managed by a unique partnership of the National Park Service and twelve other public and private organizations. At least ten of the islands have marked hiking trails, natural areas, docks, picnic tables, toilets, renovated forts or ruins, and guides in summer. With permission secured in advance, the park allows camping on four islands: Lovells, Peddocks, Bumpkin, and Grape (no longer offered on Great Brewster due to staffing shortages). Camping season runs from early May through the Columbus Day weekend in October. Each island has individual sites and one group site. To reserve a site call Reserve America at 877-I-CAMP-MA or 877-422-6762. You may also register online at www.reserveamerica.com. Fees are $5 for Massachusetts residents, $6 for nonresidents, and $25 for a group camping site. Fresh water is not available, so be sure to bring your own (campers should bring at least 1 gallon of water per person, per day). No pets are allowed. See the Massachusetts Department of Conservation and Recreation website, www.state.ma.us/dcr.

Planes take off from Logan Airport.

The launch from Pemberton Point at the end of the Hull Peninsula allows you a choice between a trip to the outer islands and one to all the good spots in Hingham Bay.

The Outer Harbor includes the cluster of three islands—Georges, Lovells, and Gallops—and the more windswept Brewsters farther out. You have two launch options from Pemberton Point. The official launch is on the south side of Windmill Point, across from the high school parking lot. From here, you put into Hull Bay and paddle through the Hull Gut, between the Hull Peninsula and Peddocks Island. If Hull Gut is too ripped up or has too much boat traffic, launch on the north side of Windmill Point by carrying your boat along the beach. Where you put in depends on how far you are willing to carry your boat.

Peddocks Island, across from the tip of Hull at Pemberton Point, is a series of drumlins connected by sand spits. On the west end is a salt marsh that hosts one of two black-crowned high heron rookeries in the entire state.

Hull Gut is probably the most dangerous spot in Boston Harbor for a novice. The eddies along the shore are passable, but you can't always stay close to shore because of fishermen casting their lines. The gut can be variable, either simple and quiet or complicated by wind, waves, and boat traffic with reflecting and refracting waves and confused wakes. It's best to paddle here at slack and avoid the strongest tidal flow at midtide. Try to anticipate what conditions might be on the return trip. You can always walk your boat back if conditions are too rough or boat traffic too confused.

It's 1.0 miles to Georges Island, a 30-acre island with landing on the southwest side on a beach. Look for the pier. You must cross a shipping channel to reach Georges, so watch for shipping traffic, aim for the red nun, and cross straight, swiftly, and in a group. Also watch for the many commercial boats that bring tourists to Georges. At Georges is Fort Warren, used primarily to house as many as 600 Confederate prisoners during the Civil War. The island is allegedly haunted by the "Lady in Black," a young bride hanged for treason on the island when, after rowing there one stormy night, she tried to free her Confederate husband imprisoned at the fort. Legend has it that she is present when the wind howls through Fort Warren's dank tunnels and dungeons on long, dark nights. During World Wars I and II, officials built guns on the island to protect Boston Harbor, but no action was ever seen except for one German U-boat that approached the harbor, a reminder of how close World War II came to these shores.

During summer, interpreters lead guided tours around Georges for the many visitors who arrive by sight-seeing boats and who also have access to the two neighboring islands by free water taxi. Note that you will not have those islands to yourself.

From Georges, the 16-acre Gallops is a few hundred yards away, identified by a gazebo. Gallops has picnic grounds, paths, and remnants of residential landscaping. It housed a maritime radio school during World War II. Another few hundred yards away, the 62-acre Lovells has camping and clean swimming off the outside of the island. Be aware that you must cross The Narrows. Trails wander though meadows, dunes, salt marsh, woods, and past the bunkers of Fort Standish, built in 1900. To secure camping permission for Lovells, contact the Metropolitan District Commission (see above).

If conditions allow, continue out to Great Brewste (2.5 miles). On your nautical chart, note the mile-long Great Brewster Spit, which dries out to sand at low tide. You must paddle north of it to reach Great Brewster. The spit can get nasty in opposing wind and tide, also to be avoided. Great Brewster's best landing is about midway up the eastern shore. On a summer day, you may see twenty more boats anchored in the small, sandy cove on the leeward side. Officials used to allow camping here, but no longer—day trips only. Great Brewster is a 23-acre island that includes a long sand spit, tidal pools on a rocky beach, and Bug Light, built in 1856. Take the short hike from the beach up the bluff. Views of Boston Light and the outer harbor are spectacular.

About 0.25 mile to the southwest lies Little Brewster, with a Coast Guard station. The best landing is near the dock on the south side. Little Brewster is the site of the first lighthouse in the United States, Boston Light, built in 1716 and still in operation, overseen by the Coast Guard. Retreating British troops blew up that lighthouse in 1776, but the colonial government rebuilt it in 1783, and that is the one you see now. It is the only lighthouse in North America that is still overseen by a lightkeeper. A National Park Service ranger is on the island to give tours; there's a $10 entrance fee for a group to climb the 98-foot tower, well worth the price of admission.

Other Options: An alternative trip is to cut between Green and Little Calf, then back toward Outer Brewster. Calf Island has a narrow stony beach on the southwest tip with a lovely meadow above it. On the edge of the meadow are the ruins of the B. P. Cheney estate. You can still see the initials BP in mosaic over the mantels of the chimneys, which you can also see from miles out to sea. The truly hardy can paddle north to The Graves—it's 2 nautical miles from the north tip of Great Brewster—and visit the windswept and desolate ledge upon which officials built Graves Light in 1903 to mark the entrance to Boston Harbor.

Either way, to return, make your way across the bay back along the top of the peninsula to Hull. Watch out for Shag Rocks, to the east of Little Brewster. If it's late in the day, take heed of the afternoon winds and, in summer, the parade of boats returning to the mainland marinas.

More protected paddling is available in Hingham Harbor closer to shore, exploring the beautiful Hingham Bay Islands of Bumpkin, Grape, and Slate as well as the magnificent peninsula of World's End. You can put in at Pemberton Point or at the iron horse statue area at Hingham Harbor (preferably off-season) and paddle across the harbor to World's End. It's best to avoid putting in an hour on either side of low tide to avoid mud. Restrooms are located at Hingham Bathing Beach, next to the launch. The half-moon harbor surrounding Hingham is particularly attractive and not too built up in an area notorious for congestion. World's End is a 250-acre park of trees rising on four drumlins, joined by a narrow beach of rough sand known as Bar, built by colonists. Here you can land your kayak, arriving from either the harbor or the Weir River side, depending on conditions. Walk around the winding tree-lined drives and enjoy the views of the Weir River, Hingham Harbor, and the Boston skyline. The park was designed by landscape architect Frederick Law Olmsted in 1890 as part of a proposed subdivision of 163 houses, connected by tree-lined roads on the 400-acre farmland belonging to John Brewer (who also owned Sarah and Langlee Islands). The subdivision never occurred, and conservationists later fought off proposals for a United Nations headquarters and a nuclear power plant. The Trustees of Reservations acquired the property in 1967 from Brewer's descendants. You can still see the pastures, the ice pond, and the remains of a seventeenth-century dam in the salt marsh. World's End, aptly named, provides a lovely rural feel in striking contrast to the highly developed Hull shoreline—it's a striking reminder that the peninsula was once a large nineteenth-century farm.

Within Hingham Harbor are small, appealing, town-owned islands called Button, Sarah, Ragged, and Langlee. Camping is by permission from the harbormaster. A nice paddle is across to World's End, over to Bumpkin, then over to the inner islands of Slate and Grape, back along the north shore of Hingham, past Crow Point and the Hingham Yacht Club, and so back to your launch spot at the iron horse statue or Pemberton Point (5.0 miles). Camping is permitted on Bumpkin and Grape Islands. Both landings and docks are located on the islands' south sides. Note that if you're camping on Bumpkin when the tide is out, you will be joined by the residents of Hull, who can walk to the island on a narrow sandbar connector. Bumpkin is bisected by an old military road and crisscrossed by hiking trails. It was once the site of a hospital for quadriplegic children, as well as a World War II outpost. It is now a wild island with new trees, *Rosa rugosa*, bayberry, and meadow. Contact the Department of Environmental Management (see above).

A good source for learning the history of and practical information about the islands is *All About the Boston Harbor Islands* (Hewitts Cove, 1993), by Emily and David Kales. Also, the DEM and MDC publish self-guided trail brochures for all park islands. For more information on Boston Harbor in Hingham, call 781-740-1605.

Hull Lifesaving Museum (1117 Nantasket Avenue, Hull, MA 02045; 781-925-5433; www.bostonharborheritage.org; admission fee; open Wednesday through Sunday June through August, and Friday through Sunday the rest of the year) is a restored lifesaving station whose exhibits capture the skills, courage, and concern of the volunteers who braved storm and sea to save those shipwrecked off Hull in the days before the Coast Guard existed. The museum is well worth a visit not only for its memorabilia but also for the museum keeper's willingness to discuss paddling conditions. It sponsors a youth rowing program, and you may see teenagers out practicing in Hull Bay. Every February, the museum sponsors the Hull Snow Row, a 3.75-mile triangular course that starts from the Museum Boat House, then goes into Hull Bay around Sheep Island and back; sea kayakers are invited. If you're a winter kayaker, this is a great event. Contact the museum.

Thompson Island, located off Columbia Point in Dorchester Bay, is a beautiful island owned by Outward Bound that allows visitors onto its 240 acres on a limited basis for guided tours, hiking, and picnicking. It is the last privately owned island in the harbor, and conservationists breathed a collective sigh of relief when Outward Bound struck a deal in 2002 to keep it wild forever. The island is named for David Thompson, an Indian trader who opened a post here in 1620. It was then farmed for more than 200 years. In 1830, a boys' vocational farming school opened on the island; a summer academy opened in 1974; then Outward Bound took over in 1986 to offer a wilderness experience to inner-city, middle school teenagers. For more information, call 617-328-3900. The best access spot to Thompson Island is from City Point Beach in South Boston. To get there from I-93, take the exit for Columbia Road. Turn left at the bottom of the ramp and go through the rotary to Day Boulevard, which follows the shore. Pass the L and M Street Beaches on the right. City Point is just beyond, south of Castle Island. Free parking.

Camping: Lovells, Peddocks, Bumpkin, and Grape Islands. Call Reserve America toll-free, 877-422-6762, or register online at www.reserveamerica.com.

TRIP 32

Wellfleet Harbor

GREAT ISLAND TO JEREMY POINT

Trip Mileage: 7 miles round trip

Tidal Range: 10 feet at Wellfleet

Charts and Maps: NOAA #13250 at 1:40,000. You can buy a laminated table-mat map in the Mass Audubon store at Wellfleet Sanctuary. It features two favorite trips on flip sides: Nauset Marsh and Wellfleet Harbor. Get a map at the Cape Cod National Seashore headquarters, off MA 6 at Nauset Marsh (508-349-3785) in South Wellfleet.

Caution Areas: A strong southerly can make paddling difficult, especially if you are going against the tide. Early-morning fog can make it difficult for other boaters to see you.

Access: There's a public launch on the Herring River on Great Island in Wellfleet. Parking is available, with additional parking across the street.

Getting There: Head into Wellfleet Center, off US 6, and follow signs for the harbor. Take a right at the marina onto Chequesset Neck Road. After you cross the bridge, to the left is a small turnoff into the access area. If you reach the parking lot for the Great Island Trail, you've gone too far.

GREAT ISLAND in Wellfleet is one of the most remote areas on the Cape. The island, like Nauset Marsh, is part of the Cape Cod National Seashore, federally owned and run, and hence is one of the few places on the Cape with public access year-round. It is also a magnificent shore, undeveloped in an area of creeping summer house settlement. The island has high dunes and pitch pine forests, and the 7-mile round-trip hike along the Great Island Trail, the national seashore's longest, runs through it. The wide expanses of tidal flats at

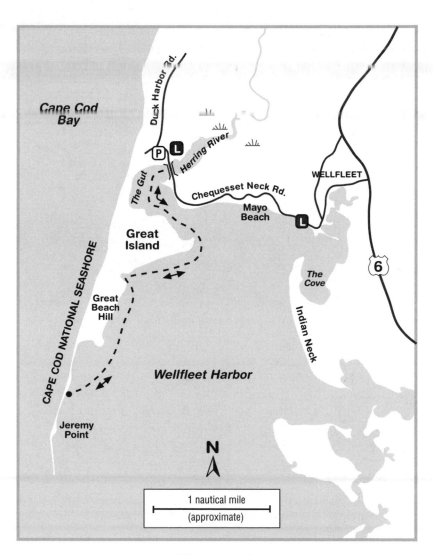

Wellfleet Harbor

low tide are home to the famous Wellfleet oyster, and you can see a great variety of wading birds. Great Island also has historical significance in that it was once the site of an eighteenth-century whaler's tavern when Great Island was an island and not connected by the mainland as it is today. The high bluffs served as a good lookout point for pilot whales when Wellfleet was a major whaling port.

Start from the public launch on Herring River. If it's low tide, don't step on the many fiddler crabs crawling out of their holes. Water

Great Island has high dunes and was once the site of an eighteenth-century whaler's tavern.

floods in and out of the river and creates a rich environment; striped bass may break the surface. About half a dozen bass anglers fish from the bridge at the Herring River Dike. A narrow channel is passable at all tides in the river. Launch at midtide and paddle over to the first wide expanse of beach on Great Island. From here, you can hike through the pine forest to the site of an original whaling tavern.

Back in your boat, continue around Great Island down to Great Beach Hill. You can poke into the marsh, known as Middle Marsh, just beyond Great Island, and do some exploring in the many channels that wind through here. Then paddle onto Jeremy Point, a thin sliver of sand spit with abundant wildlife. Anyplace along the shore, you can pull over and picnic (in summer you will share the beach with numerous powerboaters), and walk over to the Cape Cod Bay side. A dozen miles to the northwest, you can make out Provincetown. Starting in early spring, large interior parts of the beach are fenced off for nesting piping plovers. Jeremy Point is one of the most productive plover breeding grounds in the Northeast. In fall, both harbor and gray seals use the beach as haul-outs.

You can paddle onto the south end of Jeremy Point. A strong current runs around it and the shoals extending south. To the south is Billingsgate Shoal, a sandbar that gets washed over at high tide.

Billingsgate Island was once the site of a fishing community, over-taken by sand and tides. An alternative launch site is the public access beach at Wellfleet Harbor itself, located next to Mac's Seafood. High boat traffic in season may act as a deterrent, however. Other places to explore around Wellfleet Bay, such as Drummer Cove or Loagy Bay, dry out at low tide, and people have been known to get lost in the channels; confine your trip to the top two to three hours of the tide.

Camping: Mass Audubon Society's Wellfleet Sanctuary campground (P.O. Box 236, South Wellfleet, MA 02663; 508-349-2615) is located off US 6 (West Road) in South Wellfleet, on the right if you're head-ing north, just past the movie drive-in. It has nearly thirty campsites for Mass Audubon members. It is fairly easy to get reservations for early summer and fall, but the campground is usually full most of July and August. You have to check in by 5:00 P.M., no exceptions, making a weekend stay difficult. It has inviting headquarters a short walk from the campground, several hiking trails, and a full nature program of walks, cruises, and more in summer for both adults and children. Open 8:00 A.M. to dusk.

TRIP 33

Nauset Marsh

Trip Mileage: 4.5-mile loop

Tidal Range: 6.0 feet at Nauset Harbor

Charts and Maps: You can buy a laminated table-mat map in the Mass Audubon store at Wellfleet Sanctuary. It has two favorite trips on flip sides: Nauset Marsh and Wellfleet Harbor.

Caution Areas: The break at Nauset Beach gets nasty in any opposing wind and running tide. Paddling into a headwind in shallow waters can be difficult.

Access: Hemenway Road launch in Eastham. Please do not use the ramp; instead, leave your car in the parking lot and carry your kayaks down to the water away from the ramp. You can also launch from Town Cove Landing in Orleans next to the Gooose Hummock Outdoor Center, and from Salt Pond Landing Road off US 6 just south of the Cape Cod National Seashore's Salt Pond visitor center, although parking is limited.

Getting There: The Hemenway Road launch is a little less than 2 miles north of the Orleans rotary on the right in the town of Eastham. Follow the road about 0.3 mile down to the put-in.

THE END OF Hemenway Road is a great place to start a trip onto the magnificent Nauset Marsh, one of the most sublime natural places on outer Cape Cod and in New England. The marsh extends south from Coast Guard Beach, the start of a 30-mile stretch of wild, protected beach that Henry David Thoreau wrote about in his 1865 classic *Cape Cod*. The put-in is the province of striped bass fishermen in their modest aluminum skiffs.

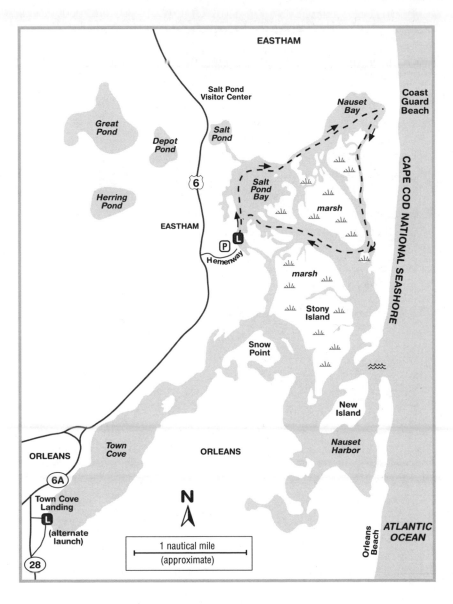

Nauset Marsh

Cape Cod Water Trails

Launched in spring 2003, the new Cape Cod Water Trails is a series of sixteen water routes that circumnavigate the marshes, tidal creeks, rivers, and coastal waters of Cape Cod. The first section covers 15 to 20 miles of shoreline along Orleans/Eastham in Town Cove and Nauset Marsh and includes an interpretive guide map designed for education and safety. The second section covers Waquoit Bay in Falmouth. The reason for the interpretive water trails, according to project coordinator Dick Hilmer (also director of Outdoor Adventure Programs, Goose Hummock Shop, in Orleans), is the exploding recreational use of Cape waterways. The trails are designed to address the potential and actual conflict between recreational paddlers and powerboaters navigating narrow channels, as well as increased use at town landings and impact on the natural environment. The plan is to create an atmosphere in which commercial fishermen, paddlers, recreational boaters, researchers, educators, and water tour operators can all interact positively, according to Hilmer.

During its first year, Cape Cod Trails produced the first trail guide map, that of Nauset Marsh (you can access the map at www.capecodwatertrails.com). The trail organizers hope to increase paddler awareness by enabling them to understand washout plains, identify where boat channels lie, and better grasp winds and currents. They also hope to promote water safety.

Cape Cod Trails has been assimilated into the Center for Coastal Studies "Coastal Awareness" program based at the Center for Coastal Studies in Provincetown. The guides are available at local paddling shops. Cape Cod Water Trails enjoys good company. A few dozen well-established water trails exist throughout the country, and as many as a hundred new ones are being planned.

The marsh is flushed by a powerful break in the long extension of Nauset Beach, providing at once protection and a thin line of defense against the loud booms of the open Atlantic's crashing surf.

The launch site gives you a magnificent panorama of the marsh and tributaries, along with the Coast Guard station, the white towering red-roofed Victorian building perched high on a sand dune. Back in the nineteenth century when this structure was built, the Coast Guard would use surf boats or fire a line to the ship so a breeches buoy could be used and haul the forlorn and terrified mariners in on buckets.

Push out of the town landing and head northeast toward the lighthouse. Paddle through Salt Pond Bay, across the inlet to Salt Pond and the location of the Cape Cod National Seashore Visitor's Station, then along Cedar Bank Creek (lined with red cedars) into Nauset Bay (very shallow) and to the base of the Coast Guard station. It's best to time your trip in this windy, shallow bay with the wind and tide—though these aren't always easy to calculate. The tide is delayed up to three hours in the marsh from the regular tide postings.

The biggest hazard here is getting stuck on sandbars. Push your way out of the muck, using the edge of the paddle blade, which acts more like a knife than a pusher. Brownish-colored water means channel; turquoise water, flats. Avoid the turquoise, although you'll want to decide very quickly whether to go right or left, and avoid any channel in which a gull stands in water up to its knees, a sure sign of grounding. If you get stuck and the tide is coming in, just wait ten minutes and chances are you will be afloat again. It helps to have patience at low tide in Nauset Marsh.

The birdlife is spectacular, and you will see several kayakers just drifting, binoculars and bird book in hand. Nauset Marsh is not a place to get anywhere in but simply to be in.

Nauset Marsh is one of the most important stops of migrating birds along the Atlantic flyway, and interesting birdlife is abundant. The black-bellied plover, one of the longest-distance migrating birds there is, stops by to feed in spring and fall. It is singular in its presence on the mud flats of Nauset Bay, not part of a populous colony like the terns and gulls. In spring, huge colonies of laughing gulls, distinguished by their black heads (they lack the hood in winter) and orange bill rims, call out as if distressed.

What author Wyman Richardson wrote in his 1947 book *The House on Nauset Marsh* (Countryman Press, reprinted 2003) still resonates today:

> The Nauset Marsh at Eastham is an unusual salt marsh. Most such marshes are protected to the seaward by a barrier beach through which an estuary enters. This estuary is widest at its

mouth, and divides into smaller and smaller branches which lead into denser and denser bodies of solid sedge.

Not so the Nauset Marsh. It contains more water than sedge and has large bays at the upper end. Even the Main Channel, while nearly two miles from the Inlet, is a quarter of a mile wide. (The Inlet is the passage through the barrier beach.) The sedge is divided into sections. A large one is the "flat" or "marsh," and a small one "hummock." The largest such piece, Porchy Marsh, is about a mile and a half from north to south. Its nearest, or north, edge is about a mile from the Farm House, and the south end about two and a half miles. We call the outermost tip Cape Horn, and the shallow passageway that makes a tiny island of it, the Straits of Magellan.

One of our best expeditions is "rounding the Horn" in the canoe. To do this, conditions must be just right. In the first place, there must not be so much wind that paddling becomes a task. In the second place, the tide must serve in such a manner that we can drop down the Main Channel on the ebb, meet the flood at the Horn, come up with it, and get home at a comfortable hour for dinner.

It is not too often that all these factors are combined on the same day, so that "rounding the Horn" is a rather infrequent occurrence. And besides all this, let it be said that it requires an expert knowledge of the vagaries of Nauset Marsh tides, as well as a good guess, to hit the "furtherst south" at exactly the right moment.

After you arrive at the Coast Guard station, walk over to Coast Guard Beach. In spring, step around pairs of mating horseshoe crabs when landing and launching. They are all over the shallows of the beaches, and Mass Audubon's Wellfleet Sanctuary celebrates the last weekend in May annually with a horseshoe crab festival.

It is possible to follow these tributaries around and land on Nauset Beach near the break, but by this time next year the location of the break could change. It last shifted in the storms of 2001. Shifting sand is a constant here.

In 1927, Henry Beston took up residence in the small wood cottage he built near the end of Nauset Beach and wrote about it in *The Outermost House* (Henry Holt & Co., 2003). The Audubon Society owned it until the blizzard of 1978, when it was washed to sea.

Stop by the Goose Hummock Shop. This longtime Cape outdoor retail shop has sales and rentals; it offers trips as well. Talk to Dick Hilmer about the newly established Cape Cod Water Trails (see the sidebar on page 236). The shop also has a launch spot for its customers.

The Cape Cod National Seashore was established in 1961 by President John. F. Kennedy. It encompasses 27,000 acres of seashore (including 30 miles of beach), dunes, marsh, pitch pine and scrub oak forest, wetland, and kettles. Salt Pond Visitor Center is open 9:00 A.M. to 5:00 P.M. in summer. It has displays, movies, a bookshop, and an information desk, and offers various nature programs, walks, and sea kayak trips.

The Lighthouse restaurant in Wellfleet, located on Main Street, is casual and friendly. It serves steamers, chowder, burgers, beer, and the like, and is open breakfast through dinner. Memorial Day traffic on Cape Cod is a notorious nightmare. Photos of snarled traffic on the Sagamore Bridge, gateway to the Cape, typically run on the front page of the Saturday-morning edition of *The Boston Globe* that weekend. If you leave before 2:00 P.M. Monday, Memorial Day, you are usually okay.

Camping: Mass Audubon Society's Wellfleet Sanctuary campground is located off US 6 in South Wellfleet (see above).

Monomoy

NORTH ISLAND CIRCUMNAVIGATION
FROM HARDING BEACH

Trip Mileage: 8-mile loop

Tidal Range: 3.7 feet at Monomoy Point; 6.7 feet at Chatham, outside

Charts and Maps: NOAA #13229 at 1:40,000

Caution Areas: A fairly steep beach and dumping surf break off the Atlantic side of South Island and may extend to bars well offshore. Pollack Rips off Monomoy Point at the south tip of South Island, where the Atlantic Ocean meets Nantucket Sound, has swift currents, said to be the most treacherous on the East Coast. The current out of Stage Harbor can run up to 3 knots. The channel out of Stage Harbor also gets a lot of boat traffic; when crossing, do so at a right angle, swiftly, and in a group.

Access: Harding Beach. If a fee is being charged at Harding (in summer), you may want to continue on to Oyster Pond River town landing, where resident stickers are not required. At Oyster Pond, common courtesy urges parking out of the way or parking in the area behind the shops at the corner of Barn Hill Road and MA 28 and leaving only one car at the landing.

Getting There: To reach Harding Beach, make your way onto Cape Cod via the Sagamore Bridge. Follow MA 6 to MA 137. Go south on MA 137 toward Chatham until you reach MA 28. Turn left toward Chatham on MA 28 and travel for 1.5 miles. At the flashing yellow light, turn right onto Barn Hill Road and follow signs for Harding Beach. If you choose to go on to Oyster Pond town landing, instead of turning right on Barn Hill Road, make the next right onto Vineyard Road and follow to its end at the landing.

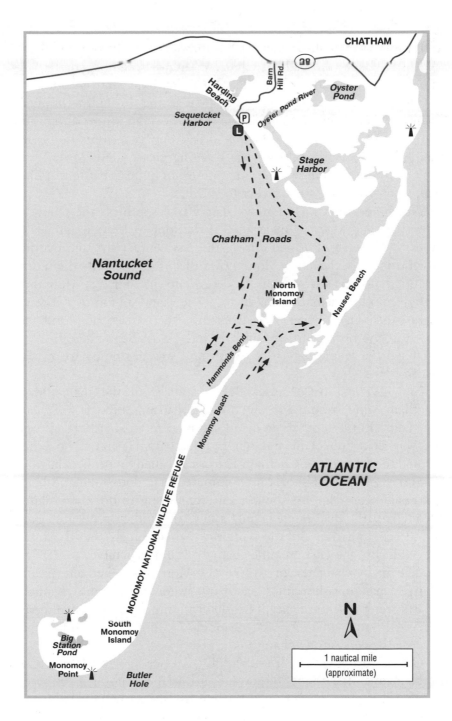

Monomoy

SEA KAYAKING or canoeing at Monomoy usually turns into hiking, said AMC Cape Cod paddler Chuck Wright—if, that is, you're paddling on the west side at low tide. Within an hour after launch from Harding Beach, you may find yourself splashing through a couple of inches of water, towing your kayak, then portaging over about 300 feet of sand to reach the channel break between Monomoy's two islands. You can probably see the opening clearly enough, but you can't get there from here. The situation is not quite as baffling at high tide, when you can paddle closer to shore.

North and South Monomoy Islands trail south off the elbow of Cape Cod and together make one of the longest barrier beaches (9 miles) in the state. Formed during the last century by sand drifting down from north beaches, Monomoy still shifts, eroded by the North Atlantic, and seeks new spots to deposit itself. In 1958, Monomoy parted from the mainland, and in 1978 the island split in two. Twenty years ago, Nauset Beach, which extends to the east of Monomoy, ended at the north end of South Island. As of September 1989, it stretched the whole length of South and was beginning to overlap North Island.

In a 1989 storm, Nauset Beach split from the mainland at Chatham, which resulted in one house collapsing into the water and the removal of two others to avoid a similar fate. That break is now the way boats travel in and out of Chatham Harbor. The beach formed to the south of Chatham Harbor is called South Beach.

Shifting sand and shoals predominate, hazardous for large boats but easily negotiable for the sea kayaker willing to do some hiking. Meanwhile, the tidal range is only a few feet, and currents aren't too bad (except in harbor entrances and the main channels), but the direction, velocity, and current-time change are unpredictable.

The main character of the whole Monomoy-Chatham area is change: changing shorelines, sandbars, water depths, and channels. Charts aren't much use except for determining distance and compass bearings. Buoys, markers, and channels are not marked on charts, because they constantly change.

Owned by the U.S. Fish and Wildlife Service, North Island (closer to the mainland) is about 500 acres; South Island, roughly 2,000 acres. South Island was the site of a former fishing settlement known as Whitewash Village in 1839. Some remains of the village can still be seen at the south tip, as can a lighthouse and some shacks. Vegetation

North Island is owned by the U.S. Fish and Wildlife Service; the east side has a less gradual beach and greater surf.

consists mostly of beach grasses and low scrubby bushes, lots of wild roses, bayberry, beach plum, and poison ivy.

Monomoy is a major flyway for migrating birds. More than 250 species have been sighted here, including nesting and resting fowl and almost every shorebird imaginable; more than 30 are resident colonies. In September, huge flocks of terns blacken the sky. Much of the interior dune area of South Island is closed for nesting terns, although you can land on the shore. Camping is prohibited.

In a very controversial move in 1996, USFWS killed off the gull population in a 75-acre section of South Monomoy to make way for other bird species—dead gulls literally fell from the sky over Chatham. As a result, however, the populations of common terns and piping plovers have ballooned, to the surprise even of the biologists. Monomoy is now the second largest tern nesting site on the East Coast, including the rare roseate tern. Controversy continues over management for traditional uses such as commercial clamming, horseshoe-crab harvesting, moving of buoys, and use of mainland access points; stay tuned. The Monomoys are also a major area for rare gray seals. Nearly 500 live on South Beach year-round. One kayaker spotted more than a hundred hauled off on a spit off the tip of North Monomoy.

A North Monomoy Island circumnavigation is an attainable goal, with stops for birding and surfing. From Harding Beach, head straight south along the west side of Monomoy. Plan to stay at least 1 mile offshore at low tide to avoid extensive sandbars. On the chart, wide sections of common flat at low tide and water levels of 6 inches are indicated. Occasionally, a channel will meander through the sandbars, but you can't count on it going anywhere. The west side usually has a gradual beach and smaller waves than the east side, but a southwest or west wind can create some serious chop.

Paddle down the west side of South Island for as much as time allows. At last check, refuge officials did not allow landings on South Island. Then paddle back and make the turn into the Atlantic at the break. Surfing on the east side of South Island just beyond the break is pretty good. Paddle over to Nauset Beach and walk over to the Atlantic side to see dramatic wave action. Your trip back is on the east side of North Monomoy, with a mild surf because the water is shielded from the Atlantic by Nauset Beach.

Monomoy has desolate beauty. It can be a very moody place when fog shrouds the area. Sometimes haze closes in the islands like a Japanese watercolor in which too much water creates a blurry scene. The sudden appearance of a fish weir takes on an eerie quality. A clanging bell sounds like background sound effects from *Pirates of the Caribbean*. Monomoy's sand dunes become a surreal blur, unable to be located except by the numbers on the compass. The water can be completely flat way out from shore.

Sandbars and dunes appear like mirages. Scale is thrown off by the haze, so a seagull looks to be the same size as a person or a sailboat. The day can be oddly quiet and flat except for a threatening, thundering surf off the Atlantic side. It can be impossible to distinguish huge, rolling waves from sand dunes, melded together like visible heat waves, disorienting and atmospheric. Without fail, a trip to Monomoy is a truly special sea kayaking experience, even on clear days.

Other Options: A total circumnavigation of the Monomoy Islands is about 20 to 25 miles, with very rough water off the south tip at Pollack Rips. The Atlantic side of South Island has a fairly steep beach and dumping surf once you pass the break between North and South Islands. The dumping surf extends all the way to the south end of South Island.

Most people choose shorter trips, of which there are many. One option is to paddle up the east or Atlantic side of North Island, where you don't have to deal with the flats, then cross to the west or Nantucket Sound side at the break and paddle up South Island for a little way, in an S-curve trip configuration.

If the winds are up, you can simply poke around Oyster Pond behind Harding Beach and Stage Harbor. Paddling up to Pleasant Bay is another option. Two launch spots for Monomoy include one on the east end of Oyster Pond off Stage Harbor Road, and another at Stage Harbor at the end of Stage Harbor Road and Port Fortune Lane, both in Chatham. Remember that exiting and entering Stage Harbor can be tricky.

Camping: No established sites on Monomoy. Nickerson State Park in East Brewster has 400 campsites and is usually filled to capacity, but is the closest campground to Chatham and Monomoy. The park is 1,750 acres and has trout-stocked ponds, swimming, sanitary facilities, and picnic facilities; overnight fees are nominal, and reservations are not accepted. Call 508-896-3491 in summer, or 508-896-361 in winter. Family tenting is available to Mass Audubon members of more than a year's standing at Wellfleet Bay Wildlife Sanctuary (see appendix A).

TRIP 35

Osterville Grand Island

CIRCUMNAVIGATION FROM PRINCE COVE

Trip Mileage: 6-mile loop

Tidal Range: 2.5 feet at Cotuit

Charts and Maps: NOAA #13229 at 1:40,000

Caution Areas: The narrow channel at the head of West Bay to Nantucket Sound can kick up confused water with opposing wind and tide.

Access: West Barnstable town landing at Prince Cove. A sticker is needed in season; parking is limited.

Getting There: To reach the West Barnstable town landing, follow MA 28 south, turning onto Prince Avenue at the MA 149 intersection. The landing is next to the marina.

THIS CIRCUMNAVIGATION is ideal for beginning kayakers: it's a short but pleasant tour around Grand Island in protected waters, and you don't need to double back on any sites. There's a lunch spot on Oyster Harbors Beach, and you will pass the historic Crosby Yacht Yard, where a century ago the Crosbys built the famous Cat Boat with retractable centerboard for the Cape's shallow waters.

Geographically, Osterville Grand Island is surrounded by three large, protected shallow bays—Cotuit to the west, North to the north, and West, oddly enough, to the east. They are connected by narrow channels and protected from the ocean by the barrier beach of Oyster Harbors and Sampsons Island, separated from the mainland by the Seapuit River. West Bay and Cotuit Bay both open to Nantucket Sound.

Like other circumnavigations, you will want to plot this one around the tide and wind. Launch at Prince Cove from the landing next to the marina and paddle through the narrow, deep channel that

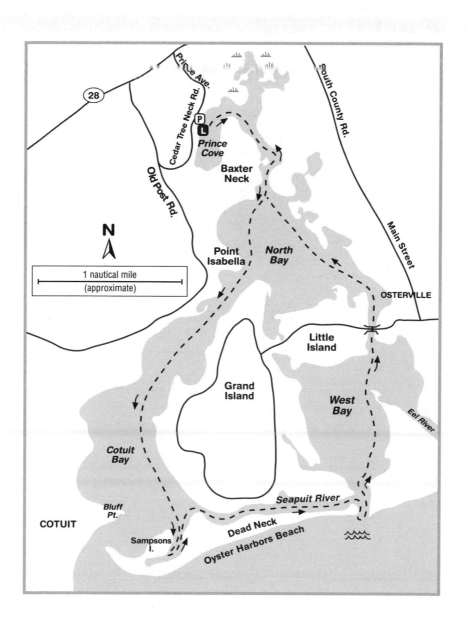

Osterville Grand Island

leads from the ultraprotected cove to North Bay. The channel is used by large yachts.

On a counterclockwise route, head southwest across North Bay to Point Isabella, then through Cotuit Bay. Grand Island to the left has lovely waterfront houses and docks. To the right is Cotuit, a quiet summer residence for the affluent and year-round home for the famous Cotuit oyster. At the entry to the Seapuit River, stop at Dead Neck, which has a lot of *Rosa rugosa* bushes, bearberries, and cedar. Walk across the dunes to Oyster Harbors Beach. On the west end is Sampsons Island Mass Audubon Bird Sanctary, which is free to Mass Audubon members; a fee is charged for nonmembers. Please observe roped-off areas for terns and plovers during nesting season.

Then paddle the mile-long Seapuit River past more mansions, piers, and clubs. Poke your bow into Nantucket Sound at the mouth of West Bay, a narrow channel flanked by rock jetties. Outside the jetties, you can see south to Martha's Vineyard. Back in West Bay, paddle north past Little Island and through the channel to North Bay. At the North Bay entry, you'll again spot historic Crosby Yacht Yard.

The trip can take anywhere from two hours and fifteen minutes with a brief stop and stroll to a full day with a picnic on Oyster Harbors Beach or a paddle into Nantucket Sound.

Other Options: Alternative launch sites include two shallow beach-launching ramps in Osterville. Parking is restricted to town residents in summer, but you can unload, then park on the side streets that aren't posted.

Camping: None.

TRIP 36

Waquoit Bay

**FALMOUTH TOWN (WHITE'S) LANDING
TO WASHBURN ISLAND**

Trip Mileage: 8-mile loop

Tidal Range: 1.5 feet in Falmouth Inner Harbor

Charts and Maps: NOAA #13229 at 1:40,000

Caution Areas: Wind, squalls, and showers can come up suddenly. Conditions on the water can vary, and they change quickly. Be prepared for all weather and sea conditions. Deer ticks are common on the island, so check yourself carefully.

Access: Falmouth town landing (White's) on the Childs River

Getting There: From the Sagamore Bridge (Cape Cod Canal), proceed toward Hyannis on MA 6 to Exit 2—MA 130. Follow MA 130 toward Mashpee for 7.2 miles and bear right onto Great Neck Road just after the Flume Restaurant. Continue to the Mashpee rotary. Halfway around the rotary, take MA 28 toward Falmouth. Reserve headquarters are located on the left 3.5 miles from the rotary; White's Landing is 0.4 mile beyond the headquarters, also on the left, just west of the Edwards Boatyard.

Massachusetts

W$_{AQUOIT}$ B$_{AY}$ is one of several shallow, narrow bays on the south side of Cape Cod created by receding glaciers and protected by barrier beaches. What makes Waquoit so special is its access to the 355-acre, state-owned Washburn Island, the only place you can camp legally on the water on the Cape.

Waquoit is also a National Estuarine Research Reserve (NERR), one of about twenty-five in the country, which is specially protected for research and education. The shallow, warm-water bay averages

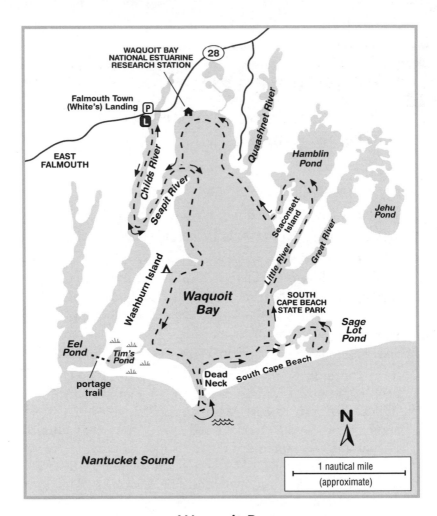

Waquoit Bay

3 feet in depth with a maximum of 9 feet in the channel to Vineyard Sound. It is rich in estuary life and is fed by three freshwater rivers and two saltwater inlets. Many quahog rakers wade waist-high in water, digging their toes into the mud or using a plunger basket to suck and scoop up clams. Shellfish have always been plentiful in this bay. In the past, small sloops also put in at Waquoit Bay to get herring for bait for fishing on the Grand Banks.

Long a private island used with respect by boaters, in 1981 the island became property of the state, thus saving it from its intended fate as the Wind Echo Island development (fifty large houses, a yacht club, and a dock had been planned). Camping is allowed at eleven campsites, most shoreside, on the southwest corner. Camping facilities are primitive, meaning you need to bring everything with you, including water. Take everything with you when you leave. The state park service maintains two compost outhouses.

The camping season runs from Memorial Day through Labor Day. Off-season, after September 1, call the Waquoit Bay National Estuarine Research Reserve headquarters directly to reserve. The campsites are open through Columbus Day. Headquarters are located at an estate just off MA 28 at the north end of Waquoit Bay, but if you reserve in the off-hours, you can pay the ranger who lives on the island seasonally. The cost is $5 per night, per site, for a Massachusetts resident; $6 for a nonresident. Sites 9 and 11 are group sites, with a maximum of twenty-five campers per night. The rest are "family sites," with a maximum of five per night.

Start at the town landing on the Childs River just to the west of the Edwards Boatyard, where a large parking lot accommodates non-resident parking. The launch is the small gravel beach next to the very busy paved ramp. Head down the Childs River past houses, docks, moorings, and boats, making the first sharp left (north) into the Seapit River, then veering right (south) again into Waquoit Bay. Washburn is the large island to the right, distinguished by its woods and complete lack of development in contrast to the rest of the bay's perimeter.

The campsites are about halfway down the east end of the island. Look for the sand cliff, then paddle beyond the next peninsula. Numbers are visible from the water. Some even have reflector posts for visibility for night arrivals. The distance from White's Landing is less than 3 miles.

Campsite 10, located at the south end of the camping area with no one to the south, is a special site. Just a short walk down from height-of-land is a private beach, ideal for swimming and beachcombing. (Our neighbors were a search-and-rescue class from Phillips Academy, Andover, who spent the afternoon practicing wet exits and T-rescues, their fall sport of choice over football.)

At the southwest corner lies a tidal marsh channel into Tim's Pond. You can poke about in here looking for birdlife or follow this up to a suitable landing spot, then hike across the dune to the beach. You can also follow the channel to the west, where you will see a short portage trail to Eel Pond. That allows for a circumnavigation of

The 355-acre state-owned Washburn Island is the only place you can camp legally on the water on the Cape.

Washburn Island. Note the cedar trees all bent to the east by strong northeast winds.

After a rest stop, follow the bay across the entrance channel at Dead Neck and make another stop on Dead Neck Beach, part of state-owned South Cape Beach. Most motorboats picnic on the east side, and you have the west side to yourself for great shell collecting, most notably jingle shells. Walk along the jetty and look across Vineyard Sound to Martha's Vineyard to the south. The current runs swiftly through the jetty.

From here, you can poke around the tidal marshes on the east side. Sage Lot Pond is a pretty place to paddle. It has several active osprey nests. As with all the salt marsh ponds around the bay, the current runs swiftly, but you can usually paddle against it, even in strong winds.

Follow the south shore of Seconsett Island and follow the channel marked by several red and green buoys into the Little River. You can circumnavigate Seconsett and return to the bay by paddling through Hamblin Pond and then through a culvert that passes under the causeway. The water gets very scarce at low tide, so time your trip accordingly. Just south of the Little River is the Great River, also marked by buoys, which leads to another launch site at the Great

River boat landing. From Great River, you can also explore Jehu Pond, another coastal tidal pond, marked by marsh grass and much birdlife. Also worth poking into are the Moonakiss River just north of Hamblin Pond and the upper reaches of the Childs River above MA 28. Kingfishers can usually be seen in those areas.

Shellfishing permits for residents and nonresidents are available for a fee at the town halls in Falmouth and Mashpee. Regulations change frequently and fines are levied, so make a point of knowing what they are. Cape shores have quahogs, soft-shell clams, bay scallops, mussels, oysters, and blue crabs, depending on location. As in the rest of the state, a permit is required for freshwater but not saltwater fishing.

When you get off the water, you may want to visit the reserve and learn more about the special quality of this bay. Reserve headquarters are located on MA 28 in Waquoit, East Falmouth. Further information specifically about Washburn Island and the Waquoit Bay National Estuarine Research Reserve (NERR) can be found at www.waquoitbayreserve.org, by calling the reserve headquarters at 508-457-0495 or by e-mailing waquoit.bay@state.ma.us. General information about all Massachusetts forest and park campgrounds can be found on the Department of Environmental Management's website at www.state. ma.us/dem.

Other Options: Another put-in spot is located down the Waquoit Landing Road off MA 28, but parking is limited.

Camping: Washburn Island, permit required. Permits for the period May 24 through September 2 may be obtained in one of three ways, up to six months in advance. For sites 1, 2, and 9, contact reserve headquarters at 508-457-0495 (www.waquoitbayreserve.org/camp.htm) or in person. For sites 3 through 8, 10, and 11, contact Camp Massachusetts at 877-I-CAMP-MA (422-6762) or reserve online at www.reserveamerica.com. Camp Massachusetts' hours are September through March, 9:00 A.M. to 7:00 P.M.; April through August, 8:00 A.M. to 9:00 P.M. Reserve headquarters are open Monday through Friday 9:00 A.M. to 5:00 P.M. year-round. You are asked to cancel reservations if your plans change.

TRIP 37

Elizabeth Islands

WOODS HOLE TO CUTTYHUNK

Trip Mileage: 32 miles round trip (to Robinsons Hole at end of Naushon, 9 miles; to Cuttyhunk, 16 miles)

Tidal Range: 2 feet at Oceanographic Institute at Woods Hole

Charts and Maps: NOAA #13218 at 1:80,000; NOAA #13229 small-craft chart South Coast of Cape Cod and Buzzards Bay

Caution Areas: Woods Hole Passage between Buzzards Bay and Vineyard Sound is one of the trickiest places to paddle in New England. Fierce currents reach a speed upwards of 8 knots; the average is 4.5 knots on the flood tide and 3.6 knots on the ebb. It is best to time your crossings with wind and tide running in the same direction, at slack tide, and to use side eddies along the main channel. The other holes between the islands can run up to 2.5 to 3 knots.

Access: Great Harbor in Woods Hole. Day parking is usually available around the corner on Bar Neck Road if you get there early, and there are often other spots within two to three blocks of the ramp. If not, you can park in the ferry lot and hop on the shuttle bus back.

Getting There: Take MA 28 south to Woods Hole Road and follow it into town. Near the harbor, turn right on Water Street, then right on Albatross Street. Look for the launch ramp on the left, near the aquarium.

―――――――――――

THE ELIZABETH ISLANDS form a 16-mile archipelago that extends southwest from Woods Hole and effectively divides Vineyard Sound from Buzzards Bay. It is a wonderful place to paddle. However,

Elizabeth Islands

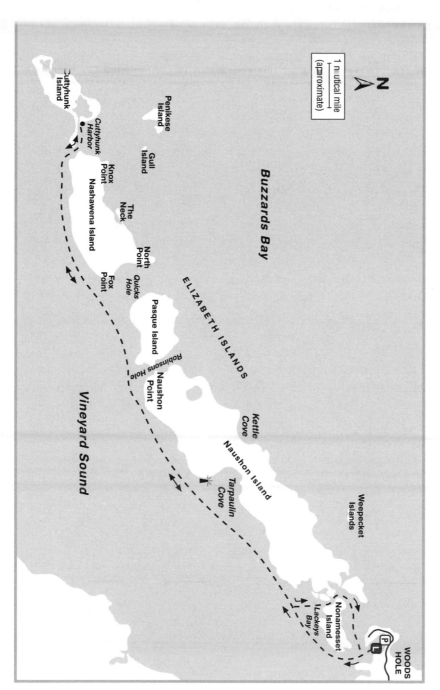

the "holes" between the islands and the mainland where strong currents rip through can make whitewater paddling skills handy.

Between the mainland and Nonamesset and Uncatena Islands, Woods Hole Passage offers some of the most interesting—and challenging—paddling on the Northeast Coast. In the passage, the tidal difference between Vineyard Sound and Buzzards Bay sometimes creates a 6-knot current that pulls huge channel buoys over on their sides in the narrower sections. The water also sweeps over submerged ledges, creating additional speed, whirlpools, and countercurrents. The Woods Hole Passage is about 0.5 mile long and 100 yards wide. Because high-water times differ by several hours throughout Buzzards Bay, Vineyard Sound, and Nantucket Sound, the tidal currents can be fairly ferocious but not insurmountable for the self-propelled boater.

Specifically, Buzzards Bay's 4-foot tide is three hours out of sync with Vineyard Sound's 2-foot tide. Consult the *Eldridge Tide and Pilot Book* and time your trip to coincide with slack tides and fair tides at various narrow channels. Barring perfect planning, prepare to wait out intensity of the rips, use side eddies, or portage over rough spots.

In addition, you can get the constellation of buoys backward. And no matter how detailed the most recent chart may be, many features will inevitably have shifted and changed—buoys removed, buoys added, newly created shoals, and more. Even commercial fishing boats get into trouble in the Woods Hole Passage and have to be hauled off the ledges—insurance does not cover hull damage sustained in Woods Hole, so common are the hazards.

"A strong northwest wind gives rise to probably the worst conditions for the kayaker in the Woods Hole Passage. The wind blowing into the passage from Buzzards Bay against the tide can stir up rather tumultuous conditions at the western entrance," noted Chuck Wright, a longtime Cape Cod paddler.

Check your *Eldridge Tide and Pilot Book*, which gives the daily current tables and also shows an hourly current diagram in the hole. *Eldridge* said the water runs through at 3.6 knots on the ebb and 4.5 on the flood, but local paddlers say it is closer to 8 knots, especially around the rocks and ledges. Another challenge in Woods Hole is large-boat traffic, particularly the Steamship Authority ferries going to Martha's Vineyard and Nantucket. Woods Hole also has a working fishing fleet, one of the few left on the Cape, and research vessels from the Oceanographic Institute, all of which require the kayaker to stay alert. But it's fun to watch the variety of sailboats, from 45-foot transatlantic-crossing ketches to day-tripping Cape Codders. Woods Hole is an entertaining place for the sheer variety of craft.

A scenic and challenging trip is to paddle the Elizabeth Islands' length 16 miles up and back from Woods Hole to Cuttyhunk, last in the chain, which requires an overnight. A paddle to Robinsons Hole at the south end of Naushon is about half that distance.

The archipelago consists of sixteen islands, including ledges and rocks, and is owned by the Forbes family, which began buying the islands during the mid-nineteenth century. The public islands are Cuttyhunk and Penikese. The landscape is mostly wild and windswept, lined by scrub brush and rock walls, and inhabited by sheep, reminiscent of Scottish highlands. Landing and picnics are permitted in specific areas. No dogs are allowed ashore because of the sheep.

First in the chain are side-by-side Uncatena and Nonamesset (all the islands have Algonquian names or variations thereof), visible from the mainland and just a short haul across the Woods Hole Channel. Next is Naushon, 7 miles long and a little more than a mile wide, the largest of the Elizabeth Islands. The Forbes family bought the island in 1850 and has continued to summer here since. Landing is permitted on the south side in Tarpaulin Cove, and on the north side in Kettle Cove.

North of Naushon in Buzzards Bay lie the tiny, rocky landfalls called the Weepecket Islands. One Weepecket has a substantial beach, good for picnicking. The U.S. Navy used the Weepeckets for bombing in World War II, but they are now a nature preserve and major nesting spot for double-crested cormorants (2,000 pairs, by one count). Pasque, just south of Naushon, is a barren square mile of rocks and swamps, followed by Nashawena, also known as Little Naushon, with huge cliffs that drop into Vineyard Sound. The Forbes family bought Nashawena in 1905; a centuries-old farm still operates, with cattle roaming freely. Landing is allowed on a beach on the island's north side, thanks to the Trustees of Reservations.

Penikese, the small island northwest of Nashawena, was the site of one of the world's first marine biology labs, later a leper colony for eighteen years, a bird sanctuary, and now a thirty-year-old alternative vocational school for teenage boys trying to start over. The Penikese Island School (www.penikese.org) is based on a farm-school, extended-family concept to encourage self-reliance and daily structure; it has no electricity or modern heating. It welcomes visitors by prearrangement and is keen on general support of its cause through fundraising. To learn more about this unique experimental school, read Daniel Robb's *Crossing the Water: Eighteen Months on an Island Working with Troubled Boys—A Teacher's Memoir* (Simon & Schuster, 2001). John Moore of Kayaks of Martha's Vineyard has an annual camping trip here to benefit the school (see appendix A).

The caboose is 2.5-mile–long Cuttyhunk, which is the most settled and open to visitors. For three weeks in 1602, it was the first English colony in this country, before colonization in Jamestown and Plymouth. Services are pretty much limited to a general store, a marina, a restaurant, and a gift shop. For an overnight, try the Cuttyhunk Fishing Club Bed & Breakfast Inn (508-992-5585; www.cuttyhunk.com). One hazard mentioned in a New England cruising guide is seaplanes taking off from Cuttyhunk Harbor.

A strong tide flows up and down the Vineyard Sound side of the islands, which can assist in this trip. The tidal current on the Buzzards Bay side is negligible. But beware the strong southwest wind that usually comes up in the afternoon; the islands provide little or no shelter. A retreat to the Buzzards Bay side often proves to be no solution.

Start from the aquarium and paddle out Great Harbor toward the main channel known as the Strait, marked by red and green buoys. When leaving Great Harbor, stay to the west side of the channel, then cross it as you paddle over to Mink Point at the east tip of Nonamesset. The channel leads out of the harbor and also through Woods Hole Passage between the mainland and Nonamesset Island. The Strait is narrow and fast, so you must either go with the tide or stick to the eddies on either side. First stop is Hadley Harbor. If you are rounding Nonamesset's south side, to reach Hadley you have a choice of two guts to paddle through, each marked by a road bridge. It is advisable to pass through the guts at or near slack tide. The west gutter runs less forcefully. The alternative is a portage across the causeway between the two bridges. Paddle around Goats Neck into the inner harbor. Picnicking is allowed on Bull Island.

Hadley Harbor is a beautiful spot. During summer, as many as sixty boats can be moored temporarily in this scenic hurricane hole surrounded by farmland, a large Victorian mansion, and private slip with a small ferry. Amid so many large boats all moored in one spot, you feel very agile in a sea kayak. Hadley has three entrances: the gutters from Vineyard Sound, the main entrance from Woods Hole

In Hadley Harbor, picnicking is allowed on Bull Island.

Passage, and Northwest Gutter from Buzzards Bay. Northwest Gutter is the most direct route to the Weepecket Islands.

You will choose which side to travel down the Elizabeth Islands depending on the wind and tide, possibly passing back and forth between Robinsons or Quick Holes in an attempt to find optimum wind and wave conditions. It is best to be going with both wind and tide, so plan a clockwise or counterclockwise trip accordingly. Good ports can be found at Tarpaulin Cove, Kettle Cove, and the beach on Nashawena. Landmarks to guide you include the lighthouse at the south end of Tarpaulin Cove, the cliffs on the south end of Naushon, Red Buoy #28 at the end of Naushon signaling the end of the island, the green buoy just off Fox Point on Nashawena, and the cliffs. Landing is on the beach at Cuttyhunk Harbor on the north end of that island. Although most of the land is private, visitors can walk on the beaches and stretches of open land. Cuttyhunk is also served by ferry from New Bedford (Cuttyhunk Boat Lines, Inc., Pier 3/Fisherman's Wharf, New Bedford, MA 02740; 508-992-1432; Alert2@Cuttyhunk.com). Kayaks are allowed on the ferry for $10 to $15 each way, depending on size.

One option for your return to Great Harbor is to cross Woods Hole Passage from Hadley Harbor. In that case, make straight for the mainland, then follow the eddies to Penzance Point, paddling around that point, up the side of the Gate of Canso, and across to Devils Foot Island (a good stretch spot) and then back to the aquarium. That is also an option for crossing over initially. The current lessens greatly to the west and east of what is the main channel. The west side is preferable in this case because it is out of the ferry's path. Note that some kayakers never make it out of Great Harbor, preferring to picnic on Devils Foot and watch the boat show at the passage.

Other Options: The crossing from Woods Hole to Martha's Vineyard is recommended for experienced sea kayakers or for locals who can pick their day and the best conditions. The shortest distance between the mainland and Martha's Vineyard is about 3.5 miles from Nobska Point to West Chop. John Moore of Kayaks of Martha's Vineyard and Charles River Canoe & Kayak sometimes offers commercial trips for that crossing.

Some kayakers have referred to this crossing as uneventful, but the trip can be entirely the opposite. You have only to watch the ferry going to the Vineyard to see what a factor the shoals are. The ferry follows channel markers at least 2 miles into the sound before making a left-hand turn for the Vineyard.

The *Island Queen*, which runs out of Falmouth from June through October, is the best bet for transporting a kayak to Martha's Vineyard. If the ferry isn't crowded, officials will allow a kayak on board. The *Island Queen* charges two freight stickers ($10 each) each way. The managers decide at that time if you will be allowed on the boat. The passenger-only *Island Queen* (Falmouth, MA 02540; 508-548-4800; islandqueen@cape.com; www.islandqueen.com) is preferable to the larger Steamship Authority boats (Woods Hole, MA; 508-548-3788; www.islandferry.com) out of Woods Hole because you can keep your boat loaded with gear and provisions at your side rather than having to put it in a car hold. Ferries also go to Martha's Vineyard from Hyannis and New Bedford.

Camping on the Vineyard is not allowed on public beaches (all towns have laws governing that), and there are no public campgrounds. The Martha's Vineyard Family Campground (508-693-3772) in Vineyard Haven is open mid-May through mid-October.

Camping: None. There's a B&B on Cuttyhunk Island; call 508-992-5585.

TRIP 38

Buzzards Bay

NORTH FALMOUTH TO CAPE COD CANAL

Trip Mileage: 13-mile loop

Tidal Range: 4 feet at Pocasset Harbor

Charts and Maps: NOAA #13230 at 1:46,500

Caution Areas: Buzzards Bay chop is always a potential cautionary condition.

Access: Megansett Harbor

Getting There: To reach Megansett Harbor from MA 28 traveling south, bear right onto MA 28A south, then bear right again onto Old Main Road. From Old Main Road, turn right onto County Road. When the roads diverge, take the middle road between the church and the house and follow it to the harbor.

T HE EASTERN SHORE of Buzzards Bay is good day-trip paddling territory. Trips here provide the chance to look out across the 9 miles of bay to Marion and New Bedford or up to the Railroad Bridge at Bourne. The shore is a good vantage point to observe ship traffic headed for Cape Cod Canal.

Buzzards Bay has a score of places to launch that even people who have lived on the Cape for years don't know about. Some are easy to find, but many are difficult. In summer, you can't always tell if the spot is only for residents, but unless you live on the Cape, summer is not the time to paddle here anyway. Spring and fall are the better times, and fall is best—there's good weather through November, along with warm water. The many launch sites give the sea kayaker a great deal of freedom in picking a stretch of shore to paddle.

During spring, the air temperature can be warm, but water is still a chilly 50 degrees. In summer, the Buzzards Bay water temperature is about 68 degrees compared with the Atlantic's 55 degrees.

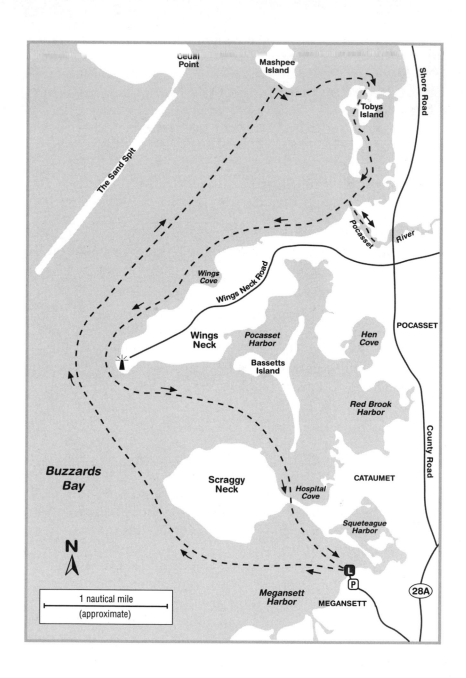

Buzzards Bay

Buzzards Bay is a designated National Estuarine Reserve by the Environmental Protection Agency, one of twenty-five in the United States, including Great Bay in New Hampshire, Waquoit Bay on the Cape, and Narragansett Bay in Rhode Island, all kayak trips described in this book. Buzzards Bay is most famous for its chop, caused by shallow waters over a long fetch and prevailing southwest winds in summer. Typically the heating of the land to the northeast of the bay during the day reinforces the prevailing wind from the southwest to give rise to the 15-to-20-knot winds in the afternoon.

Buzzards Bay is 28 miles long, has a mean width of 9 miles, covers 235 square miles, and has a mean depth of about 36 feet.

A good trip that will give you an idea of the Buzzards Bay shoreline, local real estate, and a glimpse into the Cape Cod Canal starts in Megansett Harbor. Head north across the harbor to Scraggy Neck, then make another crossing to the lighthouse on Wings Neck. Paddle up the north side of Wings Neck, poke around the Pocasset River, and stop at the little sand beach to stretch your legs. Then paddle north to the north tip of Tobys Island, not far from Monument Beach. Next, cross west to Mashpee Island at the edge of Hog Island Channel, then head south to Wings Neck. The trip back has a slight variation. Head toward Bassetts Island, then to the causeway between Scraggy Neck and Cataumet. Portage across the road. Get back into your kayak and paddle back to Megansett Harbor landing.

Other Options: The Cape Cod Canal is a 7-mile–long channel opened in 1914 between Buzzards Bay and Cape Cod Bay as a shortcut to the treacherous 100-mile water route around Cape Cod. The canal was talked about for 250 years and finally completed by New York financier August Belmont, who thought he would become very rich from the venture but instead lost millions of dollars. The Coast Guard permits sea kayakers to paddle through the canal when accompanied by a powerboat.

Other put-in spots for variations on paddling the east shoreline of Buzzards Bay include West Falmouth Harbor, with a put-in next to the town docks on Old Dock Road, and Buttermilk Bay at the town beach and ramp just north of the west-end rotary in the town of Buzzards Bay, for access to the Maritime Academy, western entrance to the Cape Cod Canal, and upper reaches of the bay. The upper reaches include Onset, an old-fashioned resort village that, though somewhat time-worn, still has charm.

Camping: None.

TRIP 39

Westport River (East Branch)

HIX BRIDGE TO HEAD OF WESTPORT

Trip Mileage: 6 miles round trip

Tidal Range: 3.0 feet at Westport Harbor

Charts and Maps: NOAA #13228 at 1:20,000

Caution Areas: The river beyond the bridge at Head of Westport is not passable in low water.

Access: Hix Bridge

Getting There: From I-195, take MA 88 south to Central Village. Turn left, head toward South Wesport, and cross the river over Hix Bridge. Just to the right is a parking and launching area.

THE EAST BRANCH of the Westport River is a good option when 20-to-30-knot northwest winds tear up Westport Harbor and make a trip out the Lions Tongue to the great Atlantic and Halfmile Rock inadvisable.

The East Branch of the Westport River turns around Westport Point, then joins the West Branch at Westport Harbor. The channel passes between Horseneck and Acoaxet (the Indian name for this river) and out into the Atlantic, not far from the Rhode Island border. The view is of Cuttyhunk Island, part of the Elizabeth Island chain.

The East Branch travels inland for nearly 7 miles. A protected, bucolic paddle is the upper half from Hix Bridge to the town of Westport Head. The river starts through the wide-open marshes behind the long Horseneck Beach, then narrows as it travels north. It is a slow-moving river, dark with tannic acid, but straight, without a lot of loops and turns. Westport has about 175 working farmers, and

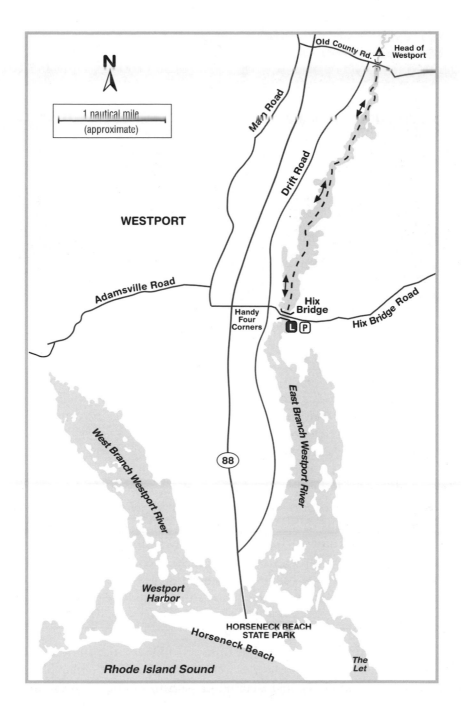

Westport River (East Branch)

Boston Sea Kayak members paddle down from the head of Westport.

thanks to local conservation efforts, open fields, woods, isolated houses, and pasture line the banks, dotted with an occasional picnic table, tree swing, or curious cow. The riverbanks make up a productive working landscape, not a museum.

The Westport River is known for the osprey-recovery program started in the mid-1960s by a local couple, Gilbert and Josephine Fernandez, who built several nesting platforms on tall poles. They theorized that the osprey's comeback might hinge on nesting spots provided by humans to replace all the trees that had been cut down. The federal government's halt of DDT spraying in 1972 really led to the acceleration of the opsrey's comeback, and now the Westport River is said to have the highest concentration of these raptors in the state. The large nests can be seen along the route here. Also, lots of swans, geese, various sea ducks such as goldeneyes and buffleheads, and some mallards flutter about.

Put in at Hix Bridge and paddle upriver 3 miles (about an hour and a half) to Head of Westport. The western shore is gentle marshland punctuated by an occasional channel or path from one of the farms. Use Cornell Point to duck behind in a strong southwest wind for a brief respite. The river then narrows into a lovely corridor of reeds and reaches the small New England town where the river narrows beyond passage at the bridge. The canal in town is lined by neat rock walls. A launch here is possible from the town green at a small gap in the stone fence, right behind the Osprey Sea Kayak Adventures shop (stop in and say hello). You can park anywhere around the triangle.

You can also do this trip in reverse—from Head of Westport to Hix Bridge and back. That direction provides a different sense: as you paddle down, the river continues to widen, and you get a wonderful impression of a theater opening in front of you. Basically, choose the direction based on a favorable wind and tide, at least on the return. To reach Head of Westport, take 1-95 to MA 88, then take MA 88 toward Westport for about 3.4 miles to Old County Road. Turn left and go about 0.8 mile. Cross the bridge and take the driveway just after Osprey Sea Kayak Adventures.

Horseneck Beach is said to be one of the most popular beaches in the state, and traffic along MA 88 can get heavy. The state park has camping along the beach.

Other Options: Horseneck Beach is located at the western end of Buzzards Bay and is breezy all year long. When the winds allow, a trip out to Halfmile Rock is an option.

The West Branch is very shallow, averaging 1 foot in some places, causing the prevailing southwest winds to stir up a bit of a chop. Also, low-tide flats can make it difficult to head where you want to go. The wind-hardened kayakers who paddle around here, however, don't think too much about the chop.

Other launch spots for access to either of the two branches of the Westport include a free state ramp under the MA 88 bridge, which leads instantly into a strong current; and the head of the West Branch in Adamsville, Rhode Island, which requires a high-tide launch. According to local sources, the spot is not very well known, and is not always recognized as being public; a little polite assertiveness may be called for.

Camping: Horseneck Beach State Reservation. From 1-195 east, take MA 88 south to its end. The park entrance is clearly marked. Call 508-636-8816.

Rhode Island

Salt Ponds to Ocean Swells

Rhode Island's 100 miles of coastline offer a wide variety of paddling environments, ranging from high sea cliffs and large swells to sheltered salt ponds, coves, and marshes to long miles of beautiful barrier beach. The state has particularly dramatic paddling at the south end of Narragansett Bay, where the bay meets open ocean head-on and huge waves break against cliffs below Newport's mansions.

Newport reigns as the sailing capital of the East and is the start or finish of many of the world's great sailing races, including the Newport-to-Bermuda Race every other year, the OSTAR single-handed Round-the-World Race, and past America's Cup trials. Between Newport and Mystic, Connecticut, you can probably see the best collection of handsome and historic boats anywhere.

While sea kayaking in Rhode Island can be dramatic, scenic, or feisty, the experience is influenced by several factors, a major one being the U.S. Navy, which has several installations in Newport. The navy prohibits landing or launching on most of Newport-area shoreline and has ships that throw off huge, tricky wakes. Newport is a major shipping port, and barges and freighters the size of apartment buildings go in and out of the bay pulled by tugboats. There are ferries, ocean-crossing sailing craft, fishing trawlers, historic tall ships, lobster and quahog boats, oceangoing pleasure boats, and personal watercraft too. It's usually best to paddle in the off-season or avoid major crossings in summer. All of Rhode Island's bridges are vertigo-inducing high to accommodate large ships.

Physiography

Narragansett Bay carves the state into several peninsulas and extends 28 miles inland, cutting Rhode Island almost in half. Because of the bay's large indentation, most people in the state live within half an hour of the ocean, a perfect setting for sea kayakers.

Three passageways extend from Rhode Island Sound inland as far as Providence and Fall River. The far eastern side is the wide and straight Sakonnet River from Sakonnet Point on the Atlantic to Mount Hope Bay. The west side's large islands of Prudence and Conanicut plus several smaller islands divide Narragansett Bay into a West and East Passage. The East Passage that goes by Newport is the busiest. The island of Aquidneck, with Newport at its tip, divides the East Passage and Sakonnet River.

The south ends of the peninsulas get the full force of the southerly winds and waves that build up over thousands of miles of Atlantic Ocean and into Rhode Island Sound. The farther up the bay you go, the calmer the waters become. Within the bay are thirty major harbors as well as sandy beaches, necks, peninsulas, and several islands that allow endless and varied exploration.

It should be noted that waters around Newport and the Providence River are subject to raw sewage overflows, toxic wastes from industry and households, and toxic runoff from roads, a situation that an environmental organization called Save the Bay is doing much to try to correct. Shellfishing in the northern bay is often closed after rainstorms. In contrast, the mouth of Narragansett Bay is pristine because of lack of industry and daily flushing by the Atlantic.

To the southwest of Narragansett Bay lies the south shore, 20 miles of superb beaches and large saltwater ponds from Narragansett to Watch Hill. The Pawcatuck River, along the Connecticut border, empties into Little Narragansett Bay at Watch Hill.

Camping Considerations

Narragansett Bay is easily accessible from major population centers to the north and south. Even though you are in the thick of the eastern megalopolis, a rural feeling pervades because of the Rhode Island Bay Island Park System, which maintains 23,000 island acres of parkland. The parks are large and generous green swaths plunked down in some of the most built-up areas; boating and views provide wonderful feelings of accessibility to the ocean. Camping facilities, however, are minimal and are restricted to a few municipal campgrounds like Fort Getty on Conanicut Island, the southern beaches, and commercial campgrounds. Dutch and Prudence Islands are closed to camping.

On Rhode Island's south shore, a good camping spot with access to the beaches and salt ponds is Burlingame State Park on freshwater Watchaug Pond (755 well-spaced sites). No tents are allowed at the state beach parks.

Not only does everyone live near the water, but access is plentiful as well, and boating is a way of life. Major parks such as Colt State Park, Fort Adams State Park, and Beavertail all provide generous recreational activities, not only for boating but also for simply enjoying green space in built-up areas.

Access, Launching, and Parking

The Ocean State has a variety of launch spots. Some key boat ramps are managed by the Department of Environmental Management and are well marked, free, open to nonresidents, and loaded with parking space. Towns and cities also maintain ramps—Warwick has three. The biggest problem is the speed with which parking tightens on a Saturday or Sunday morning from June through August.

Also, plenty of spots near the water such as dead-end roads and paths are available by virtue of deeded rights of way, some marked, many not. The Coastal Resources Management Council once gathered a list of rights of way with directions but no mention of whether the spot has a house on it, ends at a cliff, or starts in a marsh. According to one source, Rhode Island has more than one hundred rights of way under state jurisdiction—of which only thirteen are being used. In other words, there is a great deal of access to the water, but it is not very well marked. Most town beaches have special parking for residents but accommodate nonresidents for a slightly higher fee.

A good source of public access points is the Rhode Island Sea Grant's "A Daytripper's Guide to Rhode Island," found on the Web at http://seagrant.gso.uri.edu/daytrip/port_ti.html. The site contains the entire *Public Access to the Rhode Island Coast* guide and includes maps, directions, and information about the state's environmental and coastal recreational resources. To order a copy of *Public Access to the Rhode Island Coast*, send $10 to Rhode Island Sea Grant Communications Office, URI Bay Campus, Narragansett, RI 02882; 401-874-6842; www.seagrant.gso.uri.edu. The 74-page guide describes selected parks, wildlife refuges, beaches, fishing sites, boat ramps, pathways, and views along the state's coast. Another useful book is *A Guide to Rhode Island's Natural Places*, also available from the Sea Grant office for $15. Also, a new access guide is *Kayaking Narragansett Bay: A Precise Guide to 58 Launch Sites with Parking in Rhode Island*. The full-color guide sells for $25 (black-and-white version, $5). Go to www.kayakrhodeisland.com.

Trip Planning

The trips described below focus on Prudence and Dutch Islands as well as the Sakonnet River, all sites handy for day excursions.

When making your way down the long peninsulas, it's best to time your trip with the tides. Long return slogs against wind and tide can be tough. In strong southerlies, you will want to avoid the south ends of peninsulas, which meet the full force of the Atlantic and have few landing spots. According to local sources, the best sea kayaking surf areas are also the best surfboard areas. Those include East Matunuck State Beach near Wakefield, Point Judith, and just north of Narragansett Beach at the mouth of the Narrow River.

The coastal ponds behind the south beaches provide more protected paddling. Charlestown (Ninigret) Pond is more rural than other ponds due to the presence of the Ninigret National Wildlife Refuge and the undeveloped south perimeter. Glacial moraine abuts the north edge, and nice hills descend to the water. Be aware that the narrow breachway out to Block Island Sound from the pond can get very rough with any kind of sea coming in; several motorboats flip over each year.

Point Judith Pond has appealing wooded areas reaching the water's edge on the west side and is a good place for a day trip. The pond is reasonably shallow, and by staying out of the clearly marked channel, kayakers can avoid the maniacal motorboat traffic. While the eastern edge is developed, plenty of little rural islands provide good spots for breaks.

Another trip possibility is Block Island, a 10-mile ride from Point Judith on the Block Island Ferry, 401-789-3502. The paddling can be challenging because of exposure to the Atlantic and the rough conditions of Block Island Sound.

To go anywhere in Rhode Island by sea or by land, you need to know two to four geographic names for the same place. For example, Ninigret Pond is also referred to as Charlestown Pond, and the Pettaquamscutt River as the Narrow River. As one resident explained, "It may be because Rhode Island is a small state and doesn't have enough places, so it has to double up on them."

Helpful Organizations

The Rhode Island Canoe/Kayak Association (see appendix A) is very active in the state. It sponsors trips nearly every weekend in summer, and many in winter as well for those prepared for coldwater paddling. Favorite destinations include Fort Wetherill, Dutch Island and western Jamestown, Brenton Point on Newport Neck, Charlestown (Ninigret) Pond, Greenwich Bay and the Green's River, and Sakonnet Point. Several tour operators run trips from various locations around the bay (see appendix A).

Coastal Wildlife

If you call sleek yachts around Newport coastal wildlife, Rhode Island has plenty, but the Rhode Island Audubon Society also reports 370 bird species in the state. The most famous is the piping plover, a threatened shorebird that nests in dunes, runs down to the water on short yellow legs to feed, and is easily frightened by humans walking along the beach. Plovers and terns nest on most beaches in Rhode Island, and you should stay away from enclosures during nesting season.

Meanwhile, ospreys nest at Charlestown Pond, and harbor seals come into Narragansett Bay in winter. The state has three national wildlife refuges and fifteen Rhode Island Audubon bird sanctuaries (www.asri.org). The pristine waters off Fort Wetherill draw scuba divers from New Jersey to Maine to view the diverse underwater life.

Save the Bay is engaged in an ambitious project to restore eelgrass to Narrangansett Bay. In 2001 to 2002, with state funds, it transplanted more than 21,000 eelgrass plants into more than 0.5 acre in the bay, at three large-scale sites and four test sites. Kayakers aided in the transplanting. Three of the most successful sites included Poplar Point in North Kingstown, the west side of Prudence Island in Portsmouth, and Fogland Point in Tiverton. The species is key to estuaries in that eelgrass beds are a primary source of food and shelter for many types of marine life, including finfish and shellfish such as the bay scallop. Save the Bay estimates that while the majority of historic eelgrass beds in Narragansett Bay are gone, hundreds of acres could once again support eelgrass following full-scale transplanting activities and water-quality restoration.

Safety Considerations

Many Rhode Island paddlers take their first cruise in protected waters of the south beaches' salt ponds or upper, quiet reaches of Narragansett Bay, possibly in a canoe or borrowed sea kayak. It should be noted that the difference between protected water and the swells at Narragansett Bay's south end is perhaps greater than in any other place on the East Coast. Beginning paddlers should proceed with particular caution and make sure that they have the proper boat and equipment when venturing into the more exposed waters.

Sakonnet River

SAKONNET POINT TO TIVERTON

Trip Mileage: 15 miles round trip

Tidal Range: 3.1 feet at Sakonnet

Charts and Maps: NOAA #13221 at 1:47,000 and #13223 at 1:46,500

Caution Areas: At Almy Point, the channel narrows radically, with strong currents of 4 to 5 knots. A quiet eddy line on the east shore is complicated by the risk of entanglement in lines from those fishing from what remains of the Old Stone Bridge.

Access: Sakonnet Harbor, where you'll find free parking on the left; the launch is across the street. The take-out is at The Cove, in the northern part of Portsmouth, with a ramp and plenty of parking.

Getting There: To reach Sakonnet Harbor from I-195, take RI 24 south. At Tiverton before crossing the bridge, bear left onto RI 77. Follow RI 77 through Four Corners all the way to its end at Little Compton. Bear right onto Sakonnet Point Road to the harbor. To reach the take-out at The Cove from Bristol, take the Mount Hope Bridge to RI 24 north to the unmarked dirt road on the right before reaching Hummock Avenue. The road leads to the boat ramp.

Rhode Island

W HILE MUCH OF Rhode Island's coastal zone is densely populated, the eastern shore has by contrast been left to the farmers, dairy cows, and vintners. The Sakonnet River is the most easterly of three passages leading through Narragansett Bay, and many paddlers find it the most inviting because of the rural shoreline and quiet waters removed from the bay's prolific boat traffic of commerce, government, and pleasure.

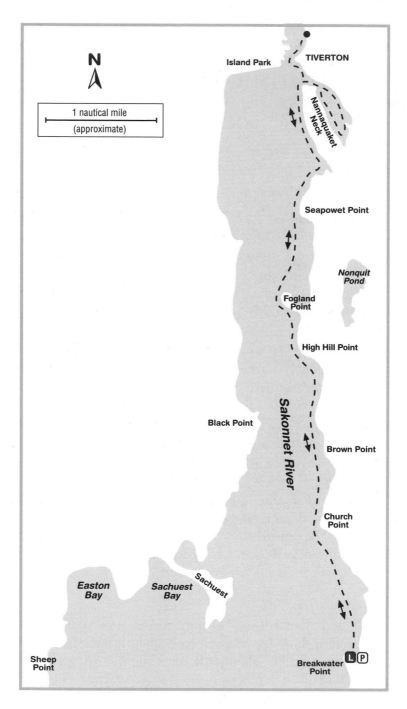

Sakonnet River

A good way to enjoy the Sakonnet River's length without doubling back is to start at Sakonnet Point in Little Compton but spot a car in Tiverton. The view from the river is one of long fields with cows and silos, stone walls and shingled houses, rosebushes and windmills, looking probably much as it did several hundred years ago. The original settlers were a band of explorers from Plymouth Colony seeking to expand; they bought 20 square miles on the peninsula from the Sogkonnite tribe of Indians. Later settlers are famous for having developed the famous Rhode Island Red chicken breed (you can see a monument to the breed in nearly Adamsville). The coastline is broken by beaches and marshy inlets.

Sakonnet Harbor is small and snug, protected from northwest winds by a breakwater. Park in the lot next to the Haffenreffer Wildlife Preserve and carry your boat across the street to the paved launch ramp. The view to the west is to the Sakonnet Point Light on Little Cormorant Rock, built in 1884. Officials discontinued the light in 1955, then relit it in 1997—it flashes white every six seconds with a red sector. Beyond, you can see the cliffs dropping into the sea at Newport. It is tempting to paddle over to Newport, but conditions need to be fairly calm because of the long, exposed crossing.

Sakonnet Point is a dramatic spot but also fairly exposed if the wind is blowing 15 MPH or more from the southwest. From Sakonnet Harbor, hug the shore past Church Cove, Church Point, around Fogland Point to Seapowet Point to Nannaquaket Neck. The shore has several beaches, a few interesting sailboats, and pretty tidal marsh estuaries to poke around in at high tide, such as Nonquit Pond and Seapowet Creek. For a shorter trip, consider paddling as far as Fogland Point Beach, about halfway between Sakonnet and Tiverton.

At the south end of Nannaquaket Neck, turn right (east) into the gut to the quiet Nannaquaket Pond, surrounded by private houses and carefully spotted picnic tables, with ospreys diving overhead.

Back on the Sakonnet River, the view from Nannaquaket Neck is dominated by the large Mount Hope Bridge, a 135-foot-high fixed bridge that spans Mount Hope Bay from Bristol Neck to Aquidneck Island. Beyond is sprawling Fall River. At Almy Point, pass through the narrow passage, which connects the Sakonnet River to Mount Hope Bay. The current rushes through at upwards of 5 knots and is one of the strongest in Narragansett Bay. The jetty on the east side is the former Old Stone Bridge, which used to connect Almy Point to Rhode Island, and from which many fishermen cast their lines. Just to the north is the Tiverton Yacht Club. Cross the river. Paddle under the bridge at Hummock Point into The Cove, then head straight across (west) to the take-out.

On your drive back down RI 77 to Sakonnet Point, stop at one of the many farm stands, check out Gray's homemade ice cream in Tiverton Four Corners (at the crossroads of Main Road/RI 77 and East Road/RI 179), or visit the renowned Sakonnet Vineyards and Winery. The tasting room is open year-round from 11:00 A.M. to 5:00 P.M. off-season, 10:00 A.M. to 6:00 P.M. in summer.

Other Options: Should the water be too choppy at Sakonnet Point, head farther down the peninsula and put in at the Seapowet Point Ramp, which can be reached by turning west onto Neck Road in Tiverton Four Corners at the Provender food market, then north onto Seapowet Avenue. From here, you can explore the Seapowet Marshes. You can also launch from Fogland Beach, which juts out into the river. From Main Road/RI 77, turn west onto Fogland Road and continue to its end at the launch ramp. Ample parking (a fee is charged in season) is available at the town beach to the northwest (right). Fogland Marsh, drained by Almy Brook from Nonquit Pond, is managed by The Nature Conservancy (401-331-7110) and is one of the few unditched marshes in Rhode Island. Most are drained by ditches for mosquito control.

If the water is settled, paddle around the south tip of Sakonnet Point. This is a gorgeous area with several small rock islands, including West and East Islands, and a beautiful beach on the east side of the point (not open to the public). From the point, you are about 4 nautical miles from the Massachusetts border, with the mouth of the Westport River just beyond.

Camping: None.

TRIP 41

West Passage

FORT GETTY TO FORT WETHERILL

Trip Mileage: 8 miles one way

Tidal Range: 3.5 feet at Beavertail Point

Charts and Maps: NOAA #13221 at 1:46,500

Caution Areas: Brenton Reef off Beavertail Point is for experienced kayakers only. The full force of the Atlantic hits this headland with large ocean swells, and the submerged ledges create breaking waves so that it can be difficult to judge a clear passage. If uncertain, paddle around beyond the bell buoy. In any case, you will need to paddle offshore to avoid breakers closer to shore. The area is not for the faint of heart; nor should it be attempted solo. Watch out for the many skin divers off Fort Wetherill.

Access: Fort Getty Recreational Area; Fort Wetherill

Getting There: To reach Fort Getty Recreational Area from the west, cross the Jamestown Bridge (RI 1A) to Conanicut Island, then take RI 138 south to Beavertail Road and follow signs for Fort Getty. From the east, cross the Newport Bridge, turn left into Jamestown, continue to Beavertail Road, and follow the signs.

To reach Fort Wetherill from the bridges, take RI 138 into Jamestown, getting off at the Jamestown exit. Go south past Jamestown Harbor, then turn left at the fork at a sign for Fort Weatherill; continue straight. Take a right into the park, then a left to the boat road. Note that this is a one-way road. You'll find a narrow access to the concrete ramp on the west-facing shore.

Rhode Island

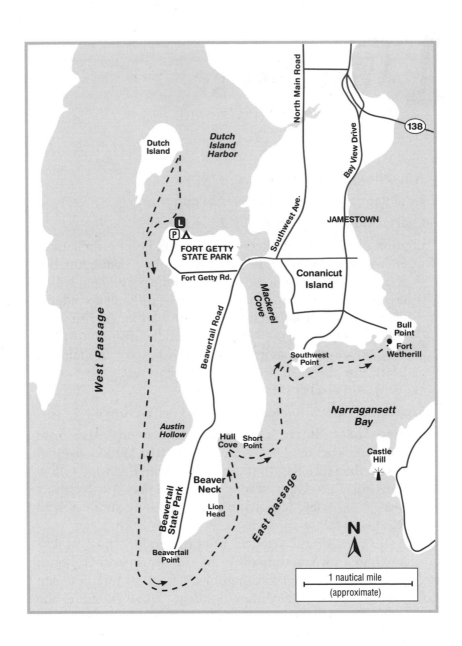

Dutch
Island

Dutch
Island
Harbor

North Main Road

Bay View Drive

(138)

Dutch Island

L
P △

FORT GETTY
STATE PARK

Fort Getty Rd.

Southwest Ave.

JAMESTOWN

Conanicut
Island

West Passage

Beavertail Road

Mackerel Cove

Bull
Point

Fort
Wetherill

Southwest
Point

Narragansett
Bay

Austin
Hollow

Hull
Cove

Short
Point

Beaver
Neck

Castle
Hill

Lion
Head

Beavertail
State Park

East Passage

N

Beavertail
Point

1 nautical mile
(approximate)

West Passage

DUTCH ISLAND is a small state island located in the West Passage just to the west of Conanicut Island and Jamestown. It is located at the bay's south end, where Rhode Island Sound meets the headlands in a powerful encounter. Beavertail Point, about 3.5 miles south of Dutch, is where the West Passage to Narragansett Bay starts and large waves build. With any seas coming out of the south or southeast, conditions can get exciting. This is not a place for the novice. The trip is around the south edge of Conanicut Island and requires spotting a car at Fort Wetherill.

You reach Dutch Island from Fort Getty on Conanicut Island, a little less than 0.5 mile. The launch spot is on the spit on the north end of the island, which puts you into Dutch Harbor. Dutch Harbor is one of several sites in Narragansett Bay where biologists are trying to restore eelgrass to the bay as a nursery for small fish and other creatures, which form the foundation for the larger fish chain. You may need to ferry across the channel marked by the red nun, because the tide runs strongly through here.

You can land on any of the several cobblestone beaches on the east side of Dutch (you may find nude sunbathers) for a picnic before starting your trip. Dutch Island has been a military installation through several wars, and you can see the remains of brick barracks on the north end. It is now managed by the Department of Environmental Management. Unfortunately, it accumulates a fair amount of trash, so you may want to confine your stay to one of the beaches. The rock here is full of mica, and the beach has many crabs. On the south end is Dutch Island Light.

Paddle from Dutch Island to the south tip of Fort Getty, then head down the south side of Beaver Neck. Note how the island resembles a beaver on the chart, with its long flat tail extending to the southern point. Across Austin Hollow, the park starts, the large houses disappear, and you start feeling the effects of ocean swell. You can tuck behind the south tip of Austin Hollow for a wind lee. From Austin Hollow, the shoreline steepens dramatically into a scenic series of miniature coves with a patch of sand and cliff face. Landing in any of these miniature coves is difficult due to swells. From here, you will pick up the flashes of Beavertail Point Lighthouse (it flashes white every six seconds); your view is to the red bell buoy marking Brenton Reef. Paddle offshore around Beavertail Point. If the waves are up, you can be sure to encounter rough conditions here (see above).

Once around Beavertail Point, you can see your destination, the remnants of Fort Wetherill. Paddle toward Lion Head and then Hull Cove (which has a beach), head out around Shore Point, and cross Mackerel Cove. Mackerel Cove is a mile-long narrow horseshoe-shaped cove surrounded by large houses. Don't be fooled by the name *cove*—surfers use this spot to catch some wild rides.

Paddle past Southwest Point. Large swells slurp and refract off the rocky cliffs to the west of Fort Wetherill, and the thrill of lively wave action is sea kayaking at its best. Some coves provide protection.

Fort Wetherill is the most heavily used scuba diving spot in Rhode Island, so watch out for snorkles and diving flags. Also, during a summer weekend, finding a parking spot is nearly impossible. Nonetheless, the fort is a small, scenic public park, and you can climb the cliffs for a picnic and a truly awesome view straight out to sea across the Block Island Sound, down to Point Judith, and over to Newport Neck's green, sloping lawns.

If you still have time, paddle up to Jamestown, just south of the huge expanse of bridge that joins Jamestown to Newport. Jamestown is a lovely little town whose main feature is an old hotel converted into condominiums. Don't miss the Dumpling Islands—large, lumpy rocks—and Clingrock, with one house perched precipitously on the rocky outcrop. Note that Dutch Island may be closed for certain months in spring and summer due to nesting birds. Jamestown has a variety of eateries next to the dock (grab some ice cream or a sandwich while en route) and up Narragansett Avenue.

An alternative after rounding Beavertail Point is to portage from Mackerel Cove across the narrow causeway (marked by telephone poles) back into Dutch. Some do this after encountering rough conditions at Beavertail. Expect mud flats in the marshes at Mackerel Cove at low tide and possibly testy lifeguards; try to land well to either side of the main beach, avoiding swimmers and sunbathers.

Other Options: The northern route around Conanicut to Jamestown and Fort Wetherill from Dutch Island is much longer but a lot more protected than the West Passage.

You can also reach Dutch from the other side. A good launch spot is the University of Rhode Island campus in Narragansett. Take RI 1A in the town of Narragansett, turn east onto South Ferry Road, and watch for signs for URI Bay Campus. Launch from the beach at the end of South Ferry Road. If parking is crowded, leave your car in the lot just above the launch area.

The piping plover is protected along Rhode Island's south beaches.

Camping: Fort Getty Recreational Area (Fort Getty Road, Jamestown, RI; 401-423-7264) is open May 18 through October 1, with sites for twenty-five tents (and one hundred RVs). No reservations. Fort Getty also has a boat ramp and a beach on the south end, frequented by sailboarders, where you can launch and land.

TRIP 12

East Passage

FORT ADAMS TO LANDS END

Trip Mileage: 7 miles one way

Tidal Range: 3.5 feet at Newport

Charts and Maps: NOAA #13221 at 1:46,500

Caution Areas: Waves breaking off the southern tip of Newport Neck in strong southerly winds can be very challenging.

Access: Fort Adams State Park; King Park and Beach

Getting There: To reach Fort Adams State Park from I-195, take RI 24 south to RI 114, then continue on to RI 138 to Newport. Take Broadway to Thames Street. Turn right onto Harrison Avenue, then right onto Fort Adams Drive. Follow signs (black-and-white pennants) to Ocean Drive/ Fort Adams. Turn right into Fort Adams. Go downhill, bearing right down past Sail Newport. Look for a sign for the boat launch, then turn sharply right past the Dr. Fred Alofsin Special Events Building. The launch is straight ahead, with lots of parking. An alternative Newport put-in is at King Park and Beach. From downtown Newport on Thames Street, turn right onto Wellington Avenue. The concrete ramp is just west of the gazebo. Watch for sailboarders. Park on the street (come early in summer). There's a two-hour limit for boats on the beach.

———

THIS TRIP combines a tour of Newport Harbor with a view of the famous Newport mansions on the Cliff Walk. Landing is almost impossible because the shoreline is privately owned; the exceptions are Brenton Point State Park (surge dependent) and Kings Beach (more reliable), just beyond.

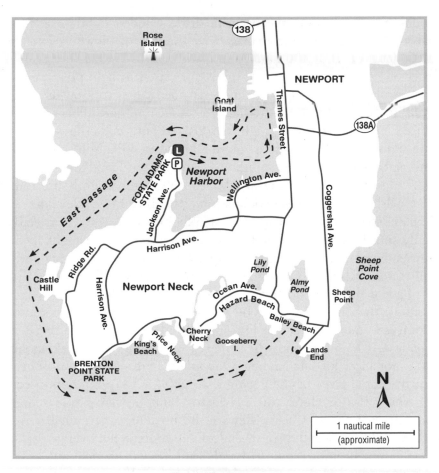

East Passage

From Fort Adams State Park, you'll take in a panoramic view of Newport Harbor and the hundreds of boats moored there, downtown Newport, and the sweeping Newport Bridge to Jamestown. Paddling through Newport Harbor at the waterline of hundreds of beautiful, expensive, and historic sailboats is always popular. Then paddle northeast around Fort Adams. Fort Adams was built between 1824 and 1857 and was active through World War II. The largest coastal fortification in the United States, it commands the entrance to Newport Harbor and Narragansett Bay. It is the site of the Museum of Yachting (you will see large hulls perched on the lawn); in summer the Newport Jazz Festival draws kayakers who dodge hundreds of concertgoing boats anchored offshore.

To the north, note the beautiful little wooden lighthouse, Rose Island Light, owned and managed by the city of Newport and the Rose Island Lighthouse Foundation, and relit in 1993. Every year, as part of Paddle the Bay series, funds are raised to help preserve this historic lighthouse. The lighthouse is open to visitors but is also a wildlife refuge (nesting ground for egrets, oystercatchers, glossy ibises, and black-crowned night herons), so until mid-August, follow the signs that tell you where you're allowed to walk. You can land to the right and left of the lighthouse landing until mid-August only. The closer you stay to the lighthouse, the better. Lighthouse tours (Rose Island Lighthouse Foundation, P.O. Box 1419, Newport, RI 02840; 401-847-4242; www.roseislandlighthouse.org) are available daily July 1 through Labor Day. You can also stay overnight in the museum or volunteer to be the keeper for the week as a paying guest. In winter, seals haul out on Citing Rock on the island's east side.

Paddle along the northwest shore of Newport Neck (mostly residential), then around Castle Hill and down to Brenton Point. Brenton Point is a state park, and at low and midtides you can land there for picnics. At high tide and when the sea is running, the breaking surf does not allow for safe landing. One notable area at Brenton Point is the memorial given by the Portuguese people at the point reminiscent of where Prince Henry the Navigator built his navigation school, Sagres, on Portugal's coast. Beware the breaking waves on Brenton Reef. Paddle along the south end of Newport Neck over to Lands End. From Brenton Point to Lands End, it's 2.3 nautical miles. You can duck into King's Beach, located just before Price Neck. Between Price Neck and Cherry Neck is a pretty little cove; a small culvert runs under the bridge to a marsh on the other side. Pass to the inside of Gooseberry Island, then east to Lands End where the famous Cliff Walk along Newport's mansions ends. It's about 2 nautical miles farther to Easton Beach, an alternative take-out. For a variation on this trip, which takes in the Cliff Walk, the distance from King's Beach to the start of the Cliff Walk, just beyond the Breakers mansion, is 4.5 miles.

This trip is not recommended in a strong southerly wind but can be protected in a northerly one. Summer generates a tremendous amount of boat traffic from Fort Adams to Castle Hill, in which case it feels as though you can walk across the width of Narragansett Bay on boats.

"There are many sailboats and powerboats driven by people who just barely know what they are doing," said a local paddler. "You have to concentrate on the chop generated by the boats; you have to look over your shoulder for the sailboats that aren't making any noise and for the cigarette boats that are making noise. You don't want to be in this vicinity on a summer weekend."

Camping: None.

TRIP 43

Bristol Harbor
to Prudence Island

Trip Mileage: 13-mile loop

Tidal Range: 3.8 feet at Prudence Island

Charts and Maps: NOAA #13221 at 1:47,600

Caution Areas: You will cross a major shipping channel, marked by buoys, through which large ships travel through Narrangansett Bay to Providence. Cross swiftly and at a right angle. The crossing from Poppasquash Point is long and exposed.

Access: Independence Park, Bristol Harbor; there's ample parking. This is also the start of the bike path.

Getting There: To reach Independence Park from Newport (9 miles), take RI 114 north to the Mount Hope Bridge. Cross the bridge and, after about 0.3 mile, bear left onto RI 114, which is also Hope Street (red, white, and blue highway divider for the famous Bristol Fourth of July Parade). Follow this road through Bristol. At junction of RI 114 and Thames Street, turn sharply left to the parking area for Independence Park, across from SS Dion restaurant. The ramp is located right before the walkway.

THE MAINLAND has many put-ins for a paddle to Prudence Island, but a launch from Bristol Harbor gives you a good sense of what the island is about. Prudence is 6.5 miles long and 1.6 miles wide. It is home to about 150 people and many deer—which, while they're beautiful to look at, have made Lyme disease notorious on the island.

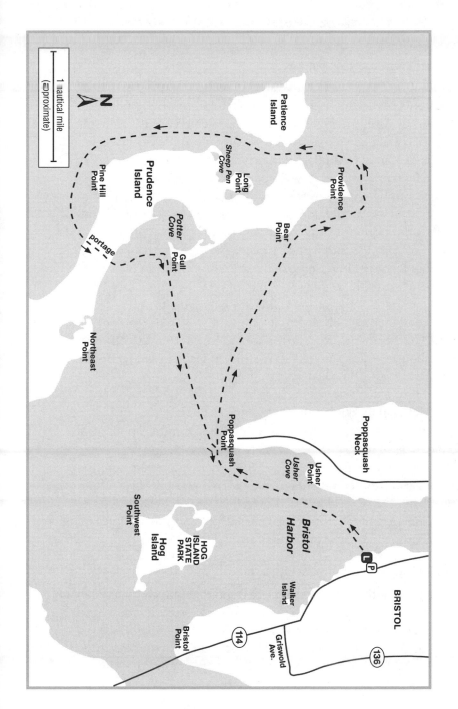

Bristol Harbor to Prudence Island

The Seals of Narragansett Bay

The Why, Where, and When

Surprisingly to many Rhode Islanders, harbor seals are common inhabitants of Narragansett Bay from October through April. Each fall, harbor seals migrate south from Maine and the Atlantic provinces of Canada to winter in the warmer waters and protected harbors of Narragansett Bay. Harbor seals are the most commonly seen marine mammal in New England.

Seals can be seen from shore resting on rocks or haul-out sites that are exposed at low tide. Seals use approximately fifteen haul-out sites throughout Narragansett Bay from as far north as Barren Ledge in Warwick and Usher Cove in Bristol to the rocks off Sakonnet Point in Little Compton and Brenton Point in Newport.

Volunteers from Save the Bay, Inc. of Providence, RI have been recording the number of seals at these haul-out sites since 1994. The largest number observed at one time was on the rocks off Rome Point in North Kingstown—a total of 169 seals! The seal population in Narragansett Bay reaches its peak in late February through the month of March.

How Many Seals Winter in Narragansett Bay?

To try to answer this question, Save the Bay organizes annual seal counts. The highest number of seals observed during a baywide seal count was on February 27, 1999, when volunteers counted 268 seals at thirteen haul-out sites. The number of seals in Narrragansett Bay has increased over the last few decades due to the Marine Mammal Protection Act of 1972 and the ending of a bounty on seals in the early 1960s.

Other Seals in Narragansett Bay

In recent years, there have been more sightings of harp and hooded seals in Narragansett Bay and along the southern Rhode Island shore. Juvenile harp and hooded seals, usually found in the Canadian Arctic and sub-Arctic waters, often arrive in southern New England malnourished and exhausted, and may strand on shore.

—From *Save the Bay, Inc. of Providence, Rhode Island*
www.savebay.org

From Indpendence Park in Bristol Harbor, paddle south and west to Poppasquash Point. From here, you are looking at the low-lying Prudence Island to the west and south. You can head southwest and hit the east side of Prudence at the ferry dock at Homestead (a general store is located here). If you paddle south, in about a mile you will come to Sandy Point Lighthouse, built in 1851, next to a small beach. You can paddle all the way to the South End State Park, located at the old naval base, then turn around.

You can also paddle northwest from Poppasquash Point to the island's east side and around the north tip of Prudence at Providence Point. Then paddle either around Patience Island or between Patience and Prudence Islands and down the opposite shore before turning and coming back. The west side has many stopping points, especially between Prudence and Patience. A small gut at the narrowest section of Prudence just south of Pine Hill Point is passable at high tide. Paddle to the end of the marshy area, walk a little bit, then portage your boat across the road and put in on the beach on the other side, negating the need to retrace your route. You have about half an hour on either side of high tide for this option, so time your trip accordingly. From here, it's about 4 miles to the take-out.

The only area where tides are a factor is between Prudence and Patience, where the current runs about 1 knot. An outgoing tide will speed you down the west side; an incoming tide will slow you down a bit but is not insurmountable. It could be a factor in rushing to reach the crossover gut by high tide.

In summer, the crossing from Bristol and Prudence (and vice versa) can be hazardous because of all the boat traffic through here, especially on weekends. You need to cross a commercial shipping lane that travels up to Providence, but most of that traffic is slow-moving freighters you can see coming from a long distance. The weekend powerboats are the ones to be concerned about, because they go very fast, don't watch where they are going, and probably don't know where the channel is, let alone use it, according to longtime Rhode Island paddler Mike Martin. On a very busy day, cross at the narrowest part and run from buoy to buoy. It is advisable to make this trip in the off-season or during the week in summer.

The center of Prudence Island is a 475-acre nature preserve, the Heritage Foundation of Rhode Island parkland, for hiking, bird watching, and photography. Charts indicate that the west side is a restricted torpedo range, and the government gives ample warning of any activity. You can also take the ferry (401-245-7411) to Prudence Island from Bristol to Homestead. Reservations are necessary for taking cars.

An alternative launch spot is Colt State Park. From Newport, take RI 114 north to the Mount Hope Bridge. Cross the bridge and, after about 0.3 mile, bear left onto RI 114, also Hope Street. Follow this road through Bristol. Pass Poppasquash Road on the left. Just beyond, enter at gates flanked by two bulls (one way). Follow signs for the park; the boat launch is to the right on the water (follow the sign). It has two concrete ramps and lots of parking. Park admission is $1 for Rhode Island residents, $2 for nonresidents.

While you're in Bristol, don't miss a trip to the Herreshoff Marine Museum, the Herreshoff Manufacturing Company's collection of yachts—including a Herreshoff-designed sea kayak, the Attu. The museum is at 1 Burnside Street, Bristol, RI 02809; 401-253-5000; www.herreshoff.org. It's open daily from May through October. The SS Dion restaurant is a locals' favorite.

Camping: None.

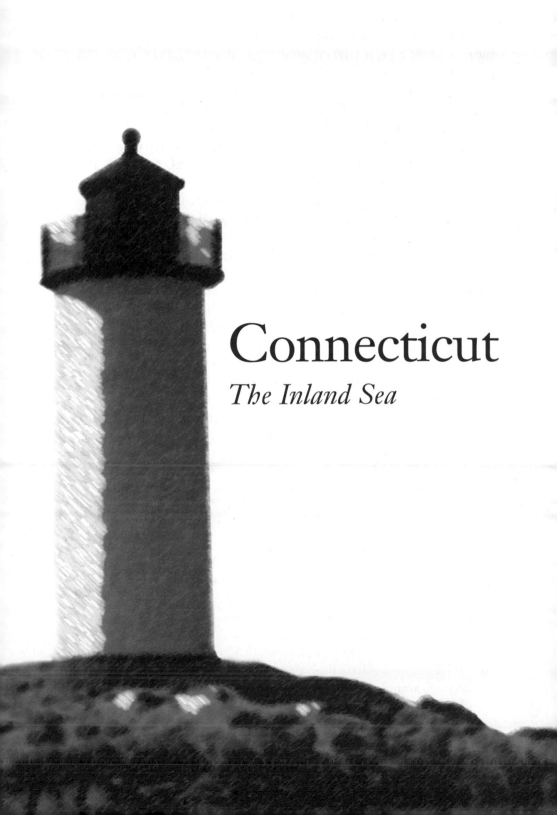

Connecticut
The Inland Sea

ALTHOUGH THE Connecticut coast is densely populated, the sea kayaker has the great advantage of being able to launch cartop boats in Long Island Sound without the high fees charged for putting powerboats or sailboats in the water. Other benefits include no need to get tied up in boat traffic while waiting for bridge openings, and no reservations required months in advance for moorings.

The kayaker also has the benefit of the sheer variety of paddling. Along the 250 miles of Connecticut coast, every kind of water is available: from sound to bay; river to cove; salt marsh to creek—from fully exposed water to winding passageways you could lose yourself in. The main interaction is with Long Island Sound, which is generally protected because the arm of Long Island acts as a buffer to the Atlantic. An east or west wind, however, can bring up some strong currents.

The shoreline offers quiet refuges wedged between industrial activity. Smaller towns such as Stonington, Mystic, Clinton, and Guilford with white colonial houses and one-way streets lie between the commercial sprawls of Stamford, New Haven, and New London. The shoreline offers the only visual access to some of Connecticut's more exclusive neighborhoods, if you're interested in a coastal real estate jaunt. It is pleasant to use the many white church steeples as onshore navigation aids.

Many houses, beaches, marinas, fish piers, jetties, lighthouses, power plants, and harbors all blend together in a dynamic mix of past and present, tourism and commerce, primary residences and weekend houses. Nuclear submarines motor into Groton. Lobster boats and dragger fleets work away. The last commercial fishing fleet in the state operates out of Stonington and has its annual Blessing of the Fleet in July. Antique boats sail in and out of Mystic. All are reminders of the strong historic maritime economy from the days when New London, Mystic, and Stonington were major whaling ports.

Generally, the farther east you go, the less crowded the shoreline becomes, until you arrive at the beautiful Barn Island marshlands at the end of Fishers Island Sound. Many local Connecticut sea kayakers tend to paddle east instead of west.

Off-season trips before Memorial Day and after Labor Day are highly recommended to beat the confusion of wakes produced by motorboats and the traffic crush, which some paddlers say is worse than the Connecticut Turnpike.

Dynamics of Long Island Sound

Long Island acts as a buffer for Long Island Sound against ocean waves, which can be three times the size of those in the sound, according to one veteran local paddler. The sound is also shallower than the ocean, so waves are not as large. The big ocean waves are diminished by the ledge running from Montauk to Block Island. They are further reduced by ledges running from Orient Point to Watch Hill.

Once you pass New London going west, you no longer have the ocean swells. By the west end, all you have are wind waves. Generally, the water moving through the sound runs in slow motion, and the tide is a factor only in spots, although it can be used to advantage because of a delay in tide change close to shore.

Not all is benign in terms of tides, however. From the Great Gull Islands northeast of Orient Point on Long Island to the west end of Fishers Island is a 4-mile stretch of water known as The Race, through which the Atlantic surges into and out of Long Island Sound. Tides can run 4 to 6 knots, creating 5-to-6-foot waves while the rest of Long Island Sound is flat calm. If you are circumnavigating Fishers Island, you need to reckon with The Race, which is well marked by navigation signals. The *Eldridge Tide and Pilot Book* publishes an hourly tidal current chart for Long Island Sound, using The Race as the start for tidal ebb and flow.

Physiography

The Connecticut shoreline starts at the Rhode Island border at the Pawcatuck River, which empties into Little Narragansett Bay, the eastern end of Fishers Island Sound. The fully exposed ocean beach of Rhode Island is left behind and the more protected waters of the Long Island Sound begin.

The shoreline from Stonington to Mystic is craggy and full of ledges. Running roughly parallel to that shoreline is the long 8-mile lump of Fishers Island. At Mystic is the mouth of the Mystic River, followed by several miles of shoreline to the 1-mile–wide mouth of the Thames River. Tankers, barges, and nuclear submarines enter Groton and New London, making for some serious boat traffic.

Next you pass Waterford and Millstone Point, a nuclear power station, and cross 1.5-mile–wide Niantic Bay, which gets some interesting wave conditions from reefs and powerboat wakes. Then

Connecticut

you're at Black Point and soon at the mouth of the 1-mile–wide Connecticut River, with the towns of Lyme and Old Saybrook on either side. The mouth is the halfway point of the coast, and the shallow delta causes some potentially choppy conditions.

From here west, beaches and residential communities alternate, such as Clinton Harbor and the state beach at Hammonasset. At Stony Creek, you pass the granite Thimble Islands, the largest concentration of islands on the coast. Then you reach the mouth of the Housatonic River at Stratford and the scenic Norwalk Islands, scattered along the shore for 6 miles, about 0.5 mile out. The Connecticut coast ends at Captain Harbor in Greenwich, just to the east of the New York border.

You get a concentration of islands at Stony Creek and Norwalk. The islands in Long Island Sound are glacial rock deposits, and wave action has created cobble beaches.

Trip Planning

Trip variations are endless. The problem is limited landing spots because of so much privately owned and carefully guarded coastline property, so you may have to stay in your boat most of the time. You can paddle along the sound, then up one of four major Connecticut rivers that empty into it—the Mystic, Thames, Connecticut, and Housatonic—and back down. Or you can steam straight up and down one of those rivers just for the exercise.

Several offshore islands close to the mainland are good spots to travel to. A Mystic launch gives you a trip to Fishers Island to ogle the mansions of this wealthy New York summer community. Guilford, farther down the coast, is a convenient put-in for a 4-mile paddle to Faulkner Island, a National Wildlife Refuge and major tern nesting site, which is closed to landing. Stony Creek gives you access to the hauntingly beautiful Thimble Islands. The state boat ramp in Westport is a launch spot for the sixteen Norwalk Islands, with landing allowed on the U.S. Fish and Wildlife Service islands of Sheffield and Chimon (except during bird nesting season) as well as town-owned Cockenoe, Shea, and Grassy Islands. Greenwich gives you access to the Captain Islands.

Connecticut law states that the shore is public below the mean high-tide line. So if you need to land, you can walk on a beach below that line without trespassing.

An investment in two NOAA charts covers coastal Connecticut: #12364 (Long Island Sound—West End) and #12372 (Watch Hill to New Haven Harbor). Spot a car and make a long day trip along the coast, perhaps from Barn Island to Groton or Groton to Old Saybrook, both popular trips. Sew day trips together and travel the long seam of the Connecticut coast from Watch Hill, Rhode Island, to Greenwich. I-95 skirts the edge of the coast and has several put-in spots under its bridges.

Other alternatives include moonlight paddles, a dock-side restaurant in Stonington or the many ethnic restaurants in South Norwalk, and breakfast stops at an old, colonial waterside inn like the Griswold Inn in Essex.

Camping Considerations

A free brochure, "State Parks and Recreation Areas," includes a checklist of both the parks' camping facilities and availability of boat-launch ramps, from the Department of Environmental Protection, State Parks Division, Bureau of Outdoor Recreation (79 Elm Street, Hartford, CT 06106-5127; 860-424-3200;http://dep.state.ct.us/stateparks/camping). Coastal state parks open for camping include Hammonasset Beach State Park (nearly 600 sites) on US 1 in Madison (203-245-1817), and Rocky Neck State Park (160 campsites) on CT 156 in Niantic (860-739-5471), both $15 per night per campsite.

The Connecticut River has several camping spots starting about 9 miles up from the river's mouth. Camping is also available on three Norwalk Islands.

Access, Launching, and Parking

The Department of Environmental Protection owns or leases sixteen public boat-launch sites on Long Island Sound from Barn Island in Stonington to Westport. All are free, but parking places fill quickly on summer weekends.

Write for the *Guide to State Boat Launch Areas*, which includes launch sites on Long Island Sound with directions, from the Department of Environmental Protection, Office of State Parks and Recreation (Connecticut DEP, Boating Division, P.O. Box 280, Old Lyme, CT 06371-0280; 860-434-8638; dep.boating.division@po.state.ct.us; http://dep.state.ct.us/rec/boating/guide.htm; look for part 5, "Boating Launch Information"). The Connecticut Coastal Access Guide (2001) is an oversized map divided into four coastal regions, each shown on a separate panel. It describes more than 276 coastal public access areas with a wide variety of uses. To request a copy, call the Department of Environmental Protection's Office of Long Island Sound Programs at 860-424-3034 or e-mail your request to coastal.access@po.state.ct.us.

Join a club! ConnYak, Connecticut Sea Kayakers (see appendix A), lists "Launch Site Directions" to major sites in Connecticut, which can accommodate many people and cars. Here's what ConnYak says about paddling and launching etiquette:

> Due to the increased amount of paddlesports using launch facilities, please double up cars (one in front of the other) in areas where cars and trailers park whenever possible. This reduces our parking usage to 50 percent. In other areas park tight so other launch site users have a spot.
>
> We share the launch sites with others who need much more space than us. Park efficiently and launch to the side of launch ramps that are in use whenever possible. Shove off and fasten your spray skirt on the water if possible to make way for others during group launches and to not hold up any waiting trailer boats. Please stay out of channels and be aware of boating traffic especially around launch areas. Paddle boats do not have right of way—it's our responsibility to stay clear of larger craft.

Coastal Wildlife

One of the best places to see ospreys on Long Island Sound is in the east-side marshes at the mouth of the Connecticut River, where they nest on many platforms built by the Department of Environmental Protection. The ospreys start to arrive in April just after the wintering bald eagles have left.

Mute swans are plentiful, particularly at the mouths of the Connecticut and Mystic Rivers, and have multiplied to the point that population control of this European species is hotly debated, according to the Connecticut Audubon Society. Swans proliferate because they are extremely defensive in protecting their eggs and chicks against all predators, including humans, and their long necks provide access to a lot of food that many ducks can't reach.

Faulkner Island is a nesting sight for the common tern and roseate tern. The island is part of the Stewart B. McKinney National Wildlife Refuge, founded in 1984 and managed by the U.S. Fish and Wildlife Service, which posts signs to warn you away during nesting season. Also part of that refuge are two of the Norwalk Islands, Sheffield and Chimon, which have a substantial heron population. Even though it is a heavily populated spot, the Norwalk Islands also attract many waterfowl such as American oystercatchers because the water is prolific with shellfish, according to one source.

The Connecticut Audubon Society has opened the Coastal Center at Milford Point (1 Milford Point Road, Milford, CT 06460; 203-878-7440) at an 8-acre barrier beach known as the Smith-Hubbell Wildlife Refuge at the mouth of the Housatonic River. The area is rich in wildlife, including piping plovers and least terns. Milford Point is said to be one of the top ten birding sites on the East Coast.

Many harbor seals migrate south in winter and can be seen hauled out on rocky ledges throughout the sound. One source has reported paddling into a whale off Watch Hill in Block Island Sound.

Safety Considerations

In Long Island Sound, survival of the fittest certainly applies to sea kayakers, given the huge volume of powerboats, fishing boats with their lines extended, water-skiing boats, and entire fleets of many yacht clubs, not to mention partially submerged nuclear submarines and enormous oil barges. Since sea kayaks can operate in just a few inches of water, hassle-free journeys can be enjoyed under peaceful and scenic conditions, even in summer, by staying in shallow water.

It is important to stay out of channels marked by buoys, which boats needing deeper water use. When crossing these busy traffic corridors, do so at a right angle, in a group, and swiftly.

Because of the exploding number of kayakers taking to Long Island Sound, the state Department of Environmental Protection now offers a voluntary, two-hour Canoe and Kayak Safety Class. It is designed for beginning paddlers who may or may not have taken other U.S. Coast Guard Auxiliary courses. For more information, visit http://dep.state.ct.us/rec/boating.

Also, since the events of September 11, 2001, other safety issues have surfaced. New laws concern the proximity of pleasure boats to various large vessels, bridges, and shore facilities. The government is also asking pleasure boaters to assist in homeland security by observing and reporting certain activities. To find out about regulations in the harbor you plan to paddle, look up U.S. Coast Guard Security Zones on the Web at http://cryptome.org/uscg-sz.htm.

One of the sport's early sea kayak symposiums—when kayakers were few and hungry for every bit of information they could find—took place at the Mystic Community Center, sponsored by Mystic Valley Bikes. Now large kayak retailers such as the Small Boat Shop and North Cove Outfitters have their own demo days, and Mystic Seaport offers several kayak-building courses, in wood or skin-on-frame. ConnYak provides many social and educational opportunities. Join ConnYak on one of its frequent outings (every weekend and Tuesday nights in summer), or enjoy its workshops, classes, and newsletter.

One final word of warning: several islands on the Connecticut coast claim to be the place where Captain Kidd buried his treasure. It is just not possible that he had enough treasure to bury in all the places that locals claim he did.

TRIP 44

Fishers Island Sound

MYSTIC SEAPORT TO STONINGTON

Trip Mileage: 12.5-mile loop

Tidal Range: 2.3 feet at Noank; 2.8 feet at Stonington

Charts and Maps: NOAA #13214 at 1:20,000 or NOAA small-craft chart #12372 at 1:40,000, Long Island Sound, Watch Hill to New Haven

Caution Areas: A great deal of motorboat traffic travels into and out of Mystic Harbor.

Access: Mystic Seaport; Groton town ramp; I-95 bridge; Esker Point Beach, Groton Long Point

Getting There: To reach Mystic Seaport from I-95, take Exit 90, then follow CT 127 south. Pass the seaport entrance just beyond, and turn right onto Isham Street. Use the ramp at the end of the street. Park on the museum side of the road next to the chain-link fence. If there are no places, leave your vehicle in the Mystic Seaport's parking lot across the street.

To reach the Groton town ramp, follow CT 127 south past the seaport, turn right onto Willow Street, and then turn right again onto East Main Street, which turns into West Main Street across the drawbridge. Turn left onto Water Street just across the bridge. Bear left at the Captain Daniel Packer Inne restaurant. The town boat ramp is on the left. Parking is nonexistent without private arrangements with a marina or restaurant.

Another put-in site is found under the I-95 bridge on the Mystic River's west side. From West Main Street, turn right onto Pearl Street and then left onto Grove, which turns into River Road. The parking area is on the right just north of the I-95 overpass; there's room for eight cars.

To reach Esker Point Beach, follow CT 215 (Groton Long Point Road) south of Mystic to its junction with

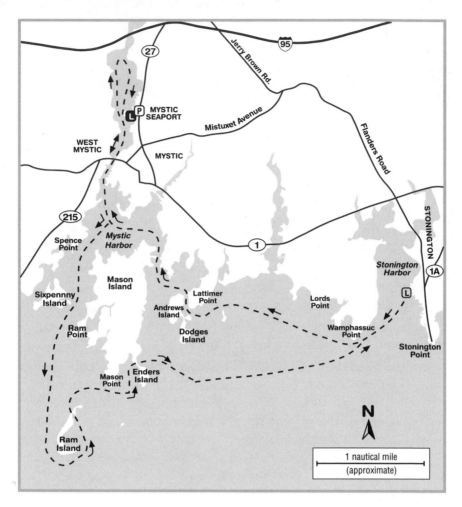

Fishers Island Sound

Marsh Road. Here you'll find restrooms, a snack concession in season, and a picnic area with hibachis and picnic tables. Parking costs $1 per car.

THIS TRIP takes you out past the inviting rocky islands in Fishers Island Sound to scenic Stonington Harbor. You'll paddle by the historic boats of Mystic Seaport, a replica of a nineteenth-century waterfront community and the largest maritime museum in the country.

Start at Mystic Seaport and paddle north under the bows and sterns of more than thirteen historic tall ships and vessels. Then paddle down the Mystic River toward Fishers Island Sound, a distance of about 3 miles.

Paddle under the Mystic's famous bascule drawbridge, which opens at quarter past the hour, every hour, on summer days. Then paddle under the railroad bridge, which announces in digital numbers when it will next open. You may hear Amtrak roaring by. Pass several marinas and slips, waterside condos, and restaurants. Stay to the right (west) of Mason Island, the end marked by a sand spit. To the right is the Mystic Shipyard, with hundreds of vessels; just beyond, marked by a white church steeple, is Noank. The town's great distinction during the 1880s was being home to the largest fisheries business in Connecticut. Also, Abbotts in Noank is the biggest lobster pound in southern New England and a good place to eat seafood after paddling. At the south tip is the deactivated Morgan Point Light, a private summer house renovated in 1991, including a new lantern room fashioned by the U.S. Lighthouse Service. The granite structure, looking more like a house than a tower, is similar to those found in Greenwich and Norwalk.

Paddle past the beach at Ram Point, a nature preserve—look for oystercatchers. Then head straight out to privately owned Ram Island, site of a large contemporary wood house and greenhouse. Your view is dominated by the long hulk of 8-mile–long Fishers Island to the south and the brown-striped lighthouse on Latimer Reef to the east. Built in 1884, the cylindrical spark-plug-shaped lighthouse marks Fishers Island Sound. While there may be wild conditions nearby at The Race just off the west end of Fishers Island, within Fishers Island Sound conditions can be benign. Strong southeast winds can make the going a little rough, however, as you struggle to avoid taking the waves straight on a beam. Use the peninsulas and points for wind lees in such conditions.

Paddle past Enders Island, with its rock-reinforced point. A few Edmunites—a Roman Catholic order of brothers and priests—live on the island and welcome those seeking spiritual sabbaticals. It is also home to the St. Michael Institute of Sacred Art and offers master classes in stained glass. You can paddle under the stone causeway to the east side of Mason Island. In winter, you may spot seals on Cormorant Reef, just south of Dodges Island. Steer a course toward the Red Reef green buoy and enter Stonington Harbor between the jetty and Wamphassuc Point. Stonington is one of the prettiest coastal villages in Connecticut, well preserved from its days as a major ship-building and whaling center during the nineteenth century. Stonington Point is the site of the state's first lighthouse, and the large town dock was originally built for steamboats from New York that connected with the Stonington & Providence Railroad. Park your kayak and head into town to one of the seafood restaurants or to the Old Lighthouse Museum.

To return, pass back through the jetty entrance and head for bald and rocky Lyddy Island. Paddle to the south of Lyddy, avoiding rocks, and between Andrews Island and Latimer Point—a passable route despite all the rocks marked on the chart. Paddle under the bridge joining the north of Mason Island to the mainland. Just to the right of the bridge, note the active osprey nest. Leave the shoreside trailer park to the left and bear left (west) back into the Mystic River.

In February, you will have the sound to yourself except for the presence of a few fishing trawlers and lobster boats. In mid-May, you will also have the sound to yourself—but be acutely aware that the literally thousands of berthed boats will soon be set free. In summer, you probably won't be able to hear yourself talk over the roar of motor-boats.

An alternative trip, for beginning kayakers as well as youngsters, is to go down the Mystic River and circumnavigate Mason Island, a total distance of 7 miles.

At Mystic Seaport, collections of old buildings and sheds, boats and artifacts, and a working shipyard are included in the 17-acre complex of more than sixty buildings. The North Boat Shed exhibits the small-craft collection, including several catboat models; well worth a look. Also, the museum keeps up to date with modern maritime activities—a dinghy sailing fleet for classes of old and young alike, a rental fleet of traditional sailing and rowing wooden craft, a dock full of sculls—and in general welcomes kayakers. Note that it is nearly impossible to both see the seaport museum and accomplish a day's paddle. Mystic Seaport (www.mysticseaport.org) is open from 9:00 A.M. to 5:00 P.M. from April through October and 10:00 A.M. to 4:00 P.M. the rest of the year. Admission is $17 (2003); less for children and seniors.

Downtown Mystic has become a lot more lively in the past dozen years. A good apres-paddle spot is The Captain Daniel Packer Inne, an old tavern on Water Street in West Mystic with fires burning in cold weather. Mystic Pizza was the subject of a movie by the same

At Mystic Seaport, you can paddle under the bows of more than 13 historic ships.

name, starring Julia Roberts. For a good breakfast, try 41 North, near the drawbridge.

Other Options: Another good access spot to Fishers Island Sound farther east is Barn Island Management Area on Little Narragansett Bay, not far from Watch Hill, Rhode Island. Barn Island is the only major boat ramp in the area that is protected and that gives you access both to Block Island Sound and to Fishers Island Sound. Sandy Point Island and Napatree Beach help provide the buffer zone.

Barn Island is an 800-acre state wildlife preserve with lots of tidal marsh, great bird watching, clear salt water, and good swimming and exploring. Many paddlers make a day trip out of paddling from Barn Island to Stonington, Mystic, and Groton on the Thames River; one Connecticut paddling group often puts in here during a full moon and paddles up to Stonington for dinner and back.

The free, state-owned public launch attracts many motorboats. On a summer weekend, cars are parked for at least a mile up the road, and early-morning arrival is necessary. You may be able to grab a parking place from a departing fisherman. The bay channel sees extremely heavy motorboat use during summer, particularly water-skiing boats. Always choose the shortest crossing possible. The best plan is to visit in spring and fall.

To reach the launch ramp from US 1, turn off at Greenhaven Road, then turn again within 50 feet onto Palmer Neck Road. Take this road all the way to the end, following signs to Barn Island.

Camping: None.

TRIP 45

Lower Connecticut River

GREAT ISLAND TO OLD LYME

Trip Mileage: 7-mile loop

Tidal Range: 3.5 feet at Saybrook Breakwater

Charts and Maps: NOAA #12375 at 1:20,000 or NOAA small-craft chart #12372 at 1:40,000

Caution Areas: Shallow water at the mouth of the river can create large standing waves in conditions of opposing wind and tide. It is inadvisable to cross the river on a hot summer weekend at high tide because of the high volume of motorboat traffic.

Access: Great Island state ramp, with parking for thirty-five cars; Old Saybrook has room for seventy-five cars.

Getting There: To reach the Great Island state ramp from I-95, take Exit 70 to CT 156 south at Old Lyme, then turn right onto Smith's Neck Road and follow it to the end at the ramp. To reach Old Saybrook from I-95, take Exit 69 to CT 9 north. Take either Exit 1 or Exit 2 off CT 9. At the end of the exit ramp, turn right onto Ferry Road and follow this to the launch area, located under the Baldwin Bridge, on the west side of the river.

THE GREAT ISLAND area provides paddling in the secluded back channels, side rivers, and coves that parallel the lower Connecticut River near the mouth on the east side. You wind through 10-foot-tall marsh reeds and generally avoid the voluminous summer boating traffic. Whereas deeper-draft boats have to pay attention to the charts, kayaks can wander all over the place in the shallow waters here.

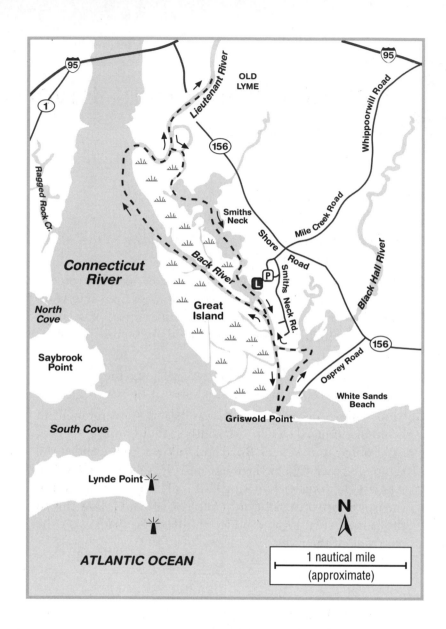

Lower Connecticut River

Another advantage of the lower Connecticut is that three-quarters of the 1-mile–wide mouth averages a few feet in depth, which serves to keep motorboats to a minimum or forces them into the west channel, which exits through two stone breakwaters beyond Saybrook Point Lighthouse. The water just off the breakwaters is also very shallow—even small boats sometimes get grounded.

Great Island offers good summer sea kayaking amid marsh grass, seaside goldenrod, glasswort, sea lavender, and water hemp. As at many other Long Island Sound spots, however, the most serene time to paddle is before Memorial Day and after Labor Day.

The 410-mile Connecticut River, the longest in New England, starts in the Fourth Connecticut Lake in northern New Hampshire and travels through Vermont, Massachusetts, and Connecticut before ending in Long Island Sound. It winds through many types of terrain, from rural idyllic to heavily industrial, but near the mouth it is known for its many marinas, tall sailboats heading to the sound, the famous shipbuilding town of Essex, and the lighthouses—the Saybrook Lighthouse at Lynde Point and the Saybrook Breakwater Light marking the channel between the two stone jetties that lead to the sound.

A sandbar at the 1-mile–wide entrance makes the Connecticut River the only major river in the United States without a city at its mouth. Because of constantly shifting shoals, the river's estuary has remained relatively rural. Instead of industrial development, visitors find the two colonial villages of Old Saybrook, founded in 1635, and Old Lyme, founded in 1665.

Put in at Smith's Neck, which has a large parking area and is used heavily by fishermen because no fishing license is required below the railroad bridge. Many osprey nest platforms line the east side of Great Island, and in April literally dozens of ospreys can be seen (they are present March through fall). From December to early April, you can usually see bald eagles in the Great Island area, but when you see the first osprey in spring, the eagles have gone. Other birds include mute swans, great blue herons, snowy egrets, rails, thousands of migrating shorebirds in spring and fall, and many duck species. The last make duck-hunting season an inadvisable time for paddling here.

Great Island was renamed the Roger Tory Peterson Wildlife Area in 2000. The famous naturalist—he first published *A Field Guide to the Birds* in 1934—and his wife, Virginia, lived in Old Lyme, and the family of Virginia Peterson recently donated their tidal-front property to The Nature Conservancy. Peterson was one of the first naturalists to

Connecticut

observe the osprey decline due to the use of DDT, and he erected the first nest platform at Great Island in 1962. The entire Connecticut River watershed is the Silvio O. Conte National Fish and Wildlife Refuge, and the tidewaters in particular are recognized and protected through several agencies.

Paddle upriver a short distance to the Back River, actually a connecting channel, which bears to the left (west) to the Connecticut. Aim for the Amtrak bridge, whose drawbridge looks to be in an up position even when the train rushing from New York to Boston passes over.

Many fishermen have found a way on foot through the tall marsh grass and line the banks to angle for panfish. Other species in the river's lower portion include largemouth bass, northern pike, catfish, eel, carp, white perch, and sometimes striped bass.

Once called the nation's most beautifully landscaped sewer, the Connecticut River received a boost when federal water-quality legislation in the 1970s helped to turn the river around from its polluted state. It now has a B classification, safe for fishing and swimming, and in some places an A classification, safe for drinking, according to the Connecticut River Watershed Council.

Just before the Amtrak bridge, bear right (east) into the modest Lieutenant River and pass under several bridges until you eventually reach a large cove. The Lieutenant and other side rivers are navigable by sea kayak at low tide. You paddle by many fine riverfront houses of Old Lyme, marked by the white Congregational Church steeple.

Upon returning, head into the large cove north of Great Island, then to the barrier beach at Griswold Point. Walk across the point, being careful not to walk through bird nesting areas, to see how the sound looks. Your view is to the north end of Long Island.

A sandbar extends across the river at Griswold Point, a potentially turbulent area when tide and wind oppose each other. Standing waves of 7 to 8 feet are not uncommon. If you want to play in the surf with your kayak, this is a good place to practice. Meanwhile, all the motorboats converge in the west-side channel. From here, you may want to paddle east up the sound to Rocky Neck Park, a state camping area on the shore.

After leaving Griswold Point, wander into the Black Hall River, whose banks are sites for more osprey nests. Both the Lieutenant and Black Hall Rivers are spring fed, not tidal. Right away you will notice the intricate currents, sandbars, and tides the lower river has. Tidal current is a factor as far as Middletown, and the combination of river current and ebb tide can be strong, occasionally 3.5 knots. One long-time paddler reported that he's never seen the tide overpower the force of the river, which means you always have a downcurrent.

The Connecticut River Watershed Council publishes two useful guides. *The Complete Boating Guide to the Connecticut River* has maps and mile-by-mile descriptions. The price of $15 includes postage and handling, available to members only. *Tidewaters of the Connecticut River: An Explorers Guide to Hidden Coves and Marshes* is a guide to touring some of the most beautiful areas of the lower river. It includes twelve self-guided tours with descriptive text, route maps, and launch points. The $20 fee again includes postage and handling. Send your order with payment to CRWC, 15 Bank Row, Greenfield, MA 01301; 413-772-2020; crwc@crocker.com; www.ctriver.org.

ConnYak has a regular schedule of campouts and river trips on the lower Connecticut River.

Other Options: Many trip variations are possible. For example, head north of the I-95 bridge to Nott Island and Lord's Cove, where you can paddle in side channels out of harm's way. The environment is similar to that of Great Island, and much birdlife can be observed.

On the west side, it's 6 miles from Old Saybrook Lighthouse to Essex, which has been a major shipbuilding port since 1675 because of its excellent harbor. Essex is said to be one of the busiest yachting centers on the East Coast, and some very large and luxurious sailboats and motorboats line the marinas. You can launch at the town ramp at the end of Main Street. From Exit 3 off CT 9, go to a stoplight and proceed east on West Avenue into Essex Center. Continue to the rotary at the head of Main Street, then go north (left) on North Main Street for one short block, turning right onto Bushnell Street. Just before entering the Dauntless Boat Yard, there is a dirt road to the left, leading a short distance to the boat launch and parking area. Paddle Middle Cove to South Cove, circumnavigating Thatchbed Island, then past the slips into North Cove (beware current into North Cove).

On Main Street in Essex is the Griswold Inn, which has been operating since 1776 and on Sundays serves a popular English Hunt Breakfast, complete with cod cakes and creamed chipped beef. Have breakfast, then paddle upriver to Gillette Castle or possibly the Goodspeed Landing, cross the river on the Chester–Hadlyme Ferry, and come back down. Gillette Castle, built by actor William Gillette, who made his fortune playing Sherlock Holmes, resembles a cloned medieval castle high on the bluffs characteristic of this part of the river. The Chester–Hadlyme Ferry has operated here since 1769. Next to the ferry landing is Gillette Castle State Park, where you can launch a kayak from the grassy riverbank, picnic, or camp. Plan to decamp by 9:00 A.M.

Finally, from Essex it's about 3 miles to Selden Neck State Park (about 10 miles from Old Saybrook), with campsites in four separate areas available from May through September for boaters only. Your length of stay is limited to one night. The primitive riverside park has fireplaces, a pit toilet, a water supply, and ten sites. Note that hunting season on state land near Selden Neck starts the day after Labor Day (no hunting on Sundays). The fee for both camping areas is $4 per person per night (2003). Reservations for both Gillette and Selden should be made in person or by letter at least two weeks in advance with Gillette Castle State Park, 67 River Road, East Haddam, CT 06423; 860-526-2336; http://dep.state.ct/us/stateparks/camping. There's also camping for twelve people at Hurd State Park, 9 miles upriver from Gillette Castle State Park (same information applies). For more information on these areas, refer to the *AMC River Guide: Massachusetts, Connecticut, and Rhode Island.*

Camping: Rocky Neck State Park in Niantic, as well as higher up the river at Gillette Castle and Selden Neck State Parks.

TRIP 46

Stony Creek
to Thimble Islands

Trip Mileage: 9.5-mile loop

Tidal Range: 6 feet at Branford Harbor

Charts and Maps: NOAA #12373 at 1:20,000 or NOAA small-craft chart #12372 at 1:40,000

Caution Areas: The main channel runs between Pot and High Islands and can get fairly rough in strong wind and opposing tide.

Access: Stony Creek. Launch from the paved ramp at the public dock, and park around the corner on Thimble Island Road, but be sure to arrive early on summer weekends to find a parking place.

Getting There: To reach Stony Creek from I-95, take Exit 56, turn south toward the water on Leetes Island Road for 2 miles, then continue through the stop sign onto Thimble Island Road. This road takes you directly to the town dock (follow the signs).

THE THIMBLE ISLANDS are a picturesque spot on the Connecticut coast. It's as though the pink-granite-ringed islands of the Maine coast migrated south just off the quiet town of Stony Creek.

On the marine chart, a rough count yields about 20 Thimbles lying just offshore pointing southwest, but in fact there are 365, of which 32 are habitable, according to Duncan and Ware. All of those have summer houses, most without heating, electricity, or running water. Some islands have just one house, while others make up clubby

Stony Creek to Thimble Islands

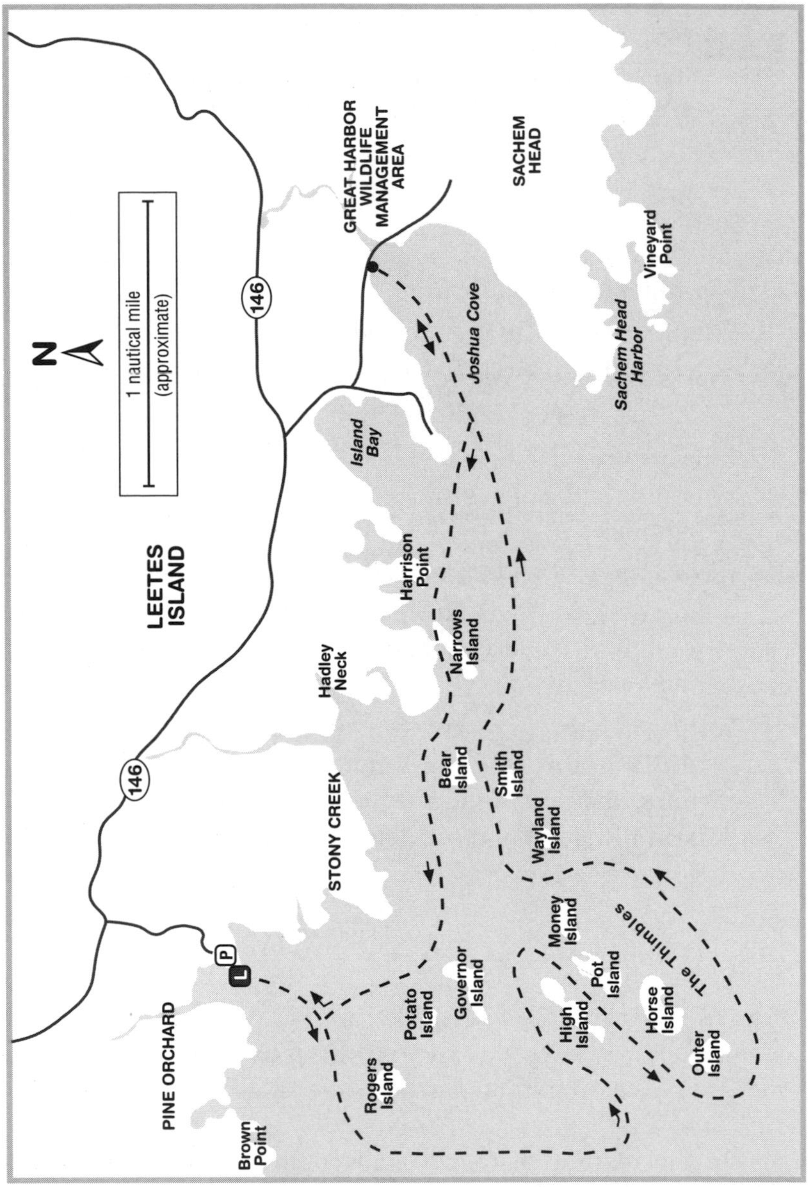

1 nautical mile
(approximate)

N

146

146

LEETES
ISLAND

STONY CREEK

PINE ORCHARD

Brown
Point

Rogers
Island

Potato
Island

Governor
Island

Hadley
Neck

Harrison
Point

Narrows
Island

Bear
Island

Smith
Island

Wayland
Island

Money
Island

High
Island

Pot
Island

Horse
Island

Outer
Island

The Thimbles

Island
Bay

GREAT HARBOR
WILDLIFE
MANAGEMENT
AREA

Joshua Cove

SACHEM
HEAD

Sachem Head
Harbor

Vineyard
Point

communities with special island associations. Commercial launches run between the islands during summer, transporting people, pets, and groceries.

The Stony Creek Indians named the islands for the thimbleberry, a lesser cousin of the gooseberry. The largest island is Horse (17 acres) and the smallest is Dogfish (0.75 acre). Captain Kidd is said to have had a lookout on High Island and buried treasure on Money Island. All the islands are private, so landing is not possible.

As you head out of Stony Creek, your view is dominated by the huge pink Tudor mansion on Rogers Island. Loud, barking guard dogs keep watch. If you paddle west, you pass by some of the Thimbles, whose lucky owners have entire islands to themselves. Next you reach the Blackstone Rocks, with a view down to Indian Neck and Branford Harbor. New Haven is right around the corner.

Paddle back toward the Thimbles and dodge between the islands. They lie as three vertical ridges running southwest to northeast, so you pass up and down the passages, weaving in and out among the islands trying to identify each one from the chart—a difficult task, as some are mere ledges. The main current runs between High and Pot Islands, and this passage can get fairly turbulent in opposing wind and tide. High Island has very large granite cliffs with houses perched on top; Money Island most resembles a town. Outer Island is part of the Stewart B. McKinney National Wildlife Refuge and is used by Southern Connecticut University for research; Horse Island is owned by Yale University for marine biology research.

Lying on the outer eastern edge of the Thimbles is a rock ledge whose owner has built what can only be termed a wooden "nest" on stilts with the exact latitude and longitude bearings painted on the welcome sign. The ledge is barely large enough for a group of seagulls. Such is the architectural ingenuity on the Thimbles and the value of local real estate, even rocks. Famous residents include TV host Jane Pauley and her cartoonist husband, Garry Trudeau. Kayaker Gail Ferris used to be the caretaker for a house on Rogers Island.

Rock formations make it fun to poke around outcroppings. Some islands are joined by small bridges, and a multitude of circumnavigations are possible. In early March, you can see thousands of ducks raft up offshore, a spectacular sight.

After you leave the Thimbles, work your way up the shoreline in an eastern direction to Joshua Cove, where landing is permitted on a state-owned beach. A 6-foot-wide opening in a rock jetty from the

Harry White does the real estate tour of the Thimble Islands.

sound to a marshy cove creates a remarkably powerful reversing falls of up to 6 to 8 knots—quite a phenomenon to witness, let alone paddle. From Joshua Cove, you can also continue east to Sachem Head or Guilford, both attractive paddling areas.

Two or three tour boats motor around the islands to give you the area's history, and children will jump off the rocks when you throw coins at them.

Other Options: From Guilford, it's 4 miles to Faulkner Island, part of the Stewart B. McKinney National Wildlife Refuge and a major tern nesting site. Landing on Faulkner is not allowed. The state maintains a boat launch and parking area at the mouth of the East River, which empties into Guilford Harbor. From US 1, go south on Neck Road about 2 miles. The launch entrance will be on the right. From the Thimbles, it's about a 6-mile paddle to Faulkner.

Camping: None.

TRIP 47

Norwalk Islands

Trip Mileage: 13-mile loop

Tidal Range: 7.1 feet at South Norwalk

Charts and Maps: NOAA #12364

Caution Areas: The islands' south shores can get strong wind and wave action in southwest winds and are less protected than the northern shores.

Access: Calf Pasture Beach, where a nonresident seasonal fee of $15 weekdays, $20 weekends, is charged, usually after July 1. An alternative launch site is the Saugatuck River in Westport. A seasonal fee is charged, and there's parking for twenty-five cars.

Getting There: To reach Calf Pasture Beach from I-95, take Exit 16, East Norwalk, and head south on East Avenue. Turn left at the cemetery, then right (south) onto Gregory Boulevard, left onto Marvin Street, and right onto Calf Pasture Beach Road; follow this road to its end at the beach. The launch is on the southeast side of the park. An alternative launch site is in Westport on the Saugatuck River. From I-95 south, take Exit 18, and turn right at the end of the ramp. Turn left at the second light onto Greens Farms Road. Go through two stop signs, then turn left at the first light. The boat ramp is past the sewage treatment plant.

THE NORWALK ISLANDS are a splendid retreat just 40 miles from downtown Manhattan. On a clear day, you can see the skyscrapers from the top of Sheffield Island Light. The chain of a dozen islands stretches for 6 miles beyond Norwalk Harbor. Three of them—Chimon, Goose, and most of Sheffield—are part of the

Connecticut

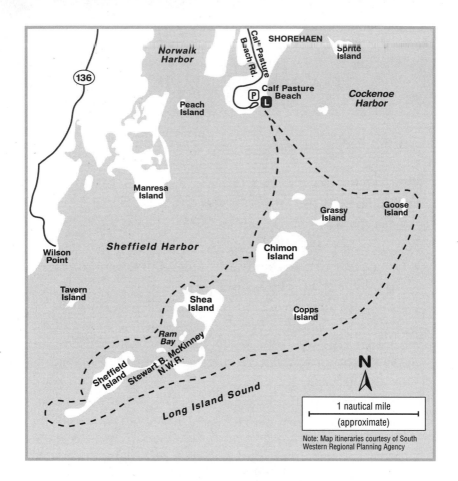

Norwalk Islands

Stewart B. McKinney Wildlife Refuge and are sanctuary to an impressive host of waders and shorebirds, including the endangered roseate tern. Most notably, three of the islands provide overnight camping: Cockenoe, owned by the town of Westport; and Shea and Grassy Islands, owned by the town of Norwalk. To get the full effect of urban wilderness while camping, turn your back on the Manresa Island Power Plant's smokestack on the mainland in Rowayton.

When launching from Calf Pasture Beach, note the Kayak Trail Map posted on the bulletin board at the launch area. The map includes trail locations, soundings, and public access points and indicates a half- and full-day itinerary for the Norwalk Islands. Thank the South Western Regional Planning Agency (203-316-5190;

www.swrpa.org), which used a grant from the Long Island Sound Fund to produce that map and also 6,000 smaller laminated copies. You can pick one up at the Small Boat Shop in Norwalk or the Outdoor Sports Center in Wilton.

The route passes by Chimon Island's wildlife sanctuary, Grassy and Shea Islands' campsites, and several private islands. Take a snack or lunch break on Sheffield, then work your way back. The people who live here have the advantage of being able to kayak around on all sorts of different itineraries.

"The private islands of Tavern (like Lago di Como in Italy) and Sprite (a yacht club—heavily wooded, lovely beach on the east shore) are quite beautiful. The little islands in Ram Bay between Shea and Sheffield are picturesque the way they rise out of the water, almost as if on stilts. The Sheffield lighthouse is picturesque. I like the south shores of Cockenoe, Chimon, Shea, and Sheffield Islands—they face the open sound, are more rocky and therefore less tramped upon," said Michele Sorensen, who runs Kayak Adventure out of Norwalk.

"I like the mainland coastline for dramatic scenery—especially off Greenwich, Darien, and Rowayton (reminiscent of Newport or Acadia). I launch from the Community Beach on Five Mile River in Rowayton and explore either east or west. The launch at Greenwich is under I-95 near the historical site parking lot."

Shea Island is 45 acres; the shoreline is strewn with rocks and boulders. It has sixteen campsites available by reservation from the Norwalk Recreation and Parks Department, 125 East Avenue, Norwalk, CT 06851; 203-854-7806. Norwalk residents pay $5 a night; nonresidents, $15. Grassy Island is 7.3 acres made up of gravel sand and silts. Camping is permitted at four sites (again, contact the Norwalk Recreation and Parks Department).

Cockenoe is directly off Calf Pasture Beach, beyond Sprite Island. The C-shaped Cockenoe's two ends encompass a lagoon; four campsites are spread throughout the island. Most of the island is off-limits to human traffic due to a heron rookery. For camping on Cockenoe Island, contact the Westport Conservation Department, Town Hall, Room 205, Westport, CT 06880; 203-341-1170. The fee is $7 a night.

Due to bird nesting, landing on USFWS-managed Chimon is restricted April 1 through August 15, but you can land on the 3-acre beach on the northwest shore year-round (no camping and no walking in the interior, though). Most of Sheffield is also a U.S. Fish and

Wildlife Service island. You can, however, land at the Sheffield Island Lighthouse (built in 1868), next to the pier on the west end of the island. Privies are available, if you ask politely. The lighthouse and picnic grounds, whose architecture is similar to the lighthouse in Niantic, are open for visits in summer for a fee ($4 in 2003); a short trail takes you inland. The Norwalk Seaport Association operates the lighthouse (www.seaport.org). You may want to avoid Norwalk during the first weekend in September, when the Norwalk Seaport Association's annual fund-raising Oyster Festival at Veteran's Park on the mainland draws up to 70,000 people.

Another itinerary, starting in Westport—one that Atlantic Kayak Tours (see appendix A) uses—is to head out the Saugatuck River to Long Island Sound and cross over to Cockenoe Island. The next stop is Chimon Island. Then paddle around some of the other islands in the area, possibly around Sheffield to get a glimpse of the lighthouse. On the return trip, head into Bermuda Lagoon before paddling back up the river. It's a little more than a mile from Calf Pasture Beach to the north shore of Chimon.

Camping: Cockenoe, Shea, and Grassy Islands.

APPENDIX A

Resources

Outdoor and Instructional Organizations

American Canoe Association (ACA)
7432 Alban Station Boulevard, Suite B-232
Springfield, VA 22150
703-451-0141
www.acanet.org

Appalachian Mountain Club (AMC)
5 Joy Street
Boston, MA 02108
617-523-0636
www.outdoors.org

British Canoe Union—
North America
320 West Saugerties Road
Saugerties, NY 12477
info@BCUNA.com
www.bcuna.com

Leave No Trace (LNT)
P.O. Box 997
Boulder, CO 80306
800-332-4100
www.lnt.org

Trade Association of Paddlesports (TAPS)
P.O. Box 84
Sedro Woolley, WA 98284
800-755-5228
info@gopaddle.org
www.gopaddle.org

Magazines

Atlantic Coastal Kayaker
P.O. Box 520
Ipswich, MA 01938
978-356-6112
ackayak@comcast.net

Canoe & Kayak
P.O. Box 3146
Kirkland, WA 98083
www.canoekayak.com

Messing about in Boats
29 Burley Street
Wenham, MA 01984
978-774-0906

Paddler
P.O. Box 775450
Steamboat Springs, CO 80477
970-879-1450
www.paddlermagazine.com

Sea Kayaker
7001 Seaview Avenue
Northwest, Suite 135
Seattle, WA 98117
206-789-9536
www.seakayakermag.com

Sea Kayak Clubs and Associations

Maine

Maine Association of Sea
Kayaking Guides & Instructors
685 Headtide Hill Road
Alna, ME 04535
info@maineseakayakguides.com
www.MaineSeaKayakGuides.com

Penobscot Paddle and
Chowder Society
1115 North Main Street
Brewer, ME 04412

Southern Maine Sea
Kayaking Network
P.O. Box 4794
Portland, ME 04112-4794
207-874-2640
www.smskn.org

Massachusetts

Boston Sea Kayak Club
47 Nancy Road
Newton, MA 04267
617-246-1337
www.bskc.org

Cape Ann Rowing Club
P.O. Box 1715
Gloucester, MA 01930
978-281-2642
www.blackburnchallenge.com

North Shore Paddlers Network
www.nspn.org

Rhode Island

Rhode Island Canoe/Kayak
Association
299 Gleaner Chapel Road
Scituate, RI 02857
chorbert@juno.com
www.ricka.org

Connecticut

Connecticut Sea Kayakers
(ConnYak)
P.O. Box 197
Ellington, CT 06029
connyak@connyak.org
www.connyak.org

Sea Kayak Outfitters: Trips and Instruction (Listed north to south)

Maine

Machias Bay Boat Tours
and Sea Kayaking
P.O. Box 42
Machias, ME 04654
207-259-3338
www.machiasbay.com

Sunrise County Canoe & Kayak
80 Main Street
Machias, ME 04654
207-255-3375
877-980-2300
rob@robguide.com
www.sunrisecanoeandkayak.com

Tidal Trails Eco-tours
P.O. Box 321
Leighton Point Road
Pembroke, ME 04666
207-726-4799
www.tidaltrails.com

Schoodic Tours
General Delivery
Corea, ME 04624
207-963-7958

Coastal Kayaking Tours
P.O. Box 405/Cottage Street
Bar Harbor, ME 04609
207-288-9605
800-526-8615
www.acadiafun.com

Krismark Outfitters
Box 349
202 US Rte. 1
Falmouth, ME 04105
1-888-746-CAMP
www.krismarkoutfitters.com

Island Adventures Sea Kayaking
141 Cottage Str eet
Bar Harbor, ME 04609
207-288-3886
www.islandadventures
  kayaking.com

National Park Sea Kayak Tours
39 Cottage Street
Bar Harbor, ME 04609
207-288-0342
800-347-0940
www.acadiakayak.com

National Park Outdoor
Recreation Center
P.O. Box 120
Mount Desert, ME 04660
207-288-0007

Maine State Sea Kayak
Guide Service
P.O. Box 97
Southwest Harbor, ME 04679
207-244-9500
www.mainestatekayak.com

Castine Kayak Adventures
P.O. Box 703
Castine, ME 04421
207-326-9045
www.castinekayak.com

Old Quarry Adventures
RR 1, Box 700
Stonington, ME 04681
207-367-8977
www.oldquarry.com

Granite Island Guide Service
66 Dunham Point Road
Deer Isle, ME 04627
207-348-2668
www.graniteislandguide.com

Sea Kayaking with New
England Outdoor Centre
Dennet's Wharf
Castine, ME 04421
800-766-7238
www.neoc.com

Water Walker
152 Lincolnville Avenue
Belfast, ME 04915
207-338-6424
www.touringkayaks.com

Maine Sport Outfitters
Route 1
Rockport, ME 04856
207-236-7120
888-236-8797
www.mainesport.com

Duck Trap Sea Kayak
RR 3
Box 3315
Lincolnville, ME 04849
207-236-8608

SeaEscape Kayak
RR1, P.O. Box 758A
Vinalhaven, ME 04863
207-863-9343
www.seaescapekayak.com

Hurricane Island
Outward Bound School
75 Mechanic Street
Rockland, ME 04841
207-594-5548
www.hurricaneisland.org

Breakwater Kayak
PO Box 627
Rockport, ME 04856
1-877-559-8800
www.breakwaterkayak.com

Sea Spirit Adventures
1140 State Route 32
Round Pond, ME 04564
207-529-4SEA
www.seaspiritadventures.com

Salt & Stone Kayaking
620 Dutch Neck Rd.
Waldoboro, ME 04572
207-832-4265
SaltandStone@hotmail.com

The Chewonki Foundation
485 Chewonki Neck Road
Wiscasset, ME 04578
207-882-7323

Compass Rose Expeditions
P.O. Box 552
Wiscasset, ME 04578
207-549-3270

Tidal Transit
P.O. Box 743
Boothbay Harbor, ME 04538
207-633-8329

Poseidon Kayak Imports
Box 120, Route 129
Walpole, ME 04573
207-644-8329

Seaspray Kayaking
Brunswick, ME 04011
www.seaspraykayaking.com

L.L. Bean
Outdoor Discovery School
Casco Street
Freeport, ME 04033
888-552-3261
www.llbean.com/odp

H2Outfitters
P.O. Box 72
Orrs Island, ME 04066
207-833-5257
800-20-KAYAK
h2o@h2outfitters.com
www.H2Outfitters.com

Maine Island Kayak Co.
70 Luther Street
Portland, ME 04108
207-766-2373
800-796-2373
micko@maine.rr.com
www.maineislandkayak.com

Into the Wild Expeditions
PO Box 4564
Portland, ME 04112
www.wildexpeditions.com

Kittery Trading Post
US 1
Kittery, ME 03904
207-439-2700
www.kitterytradingpost.com

Harbor Adventures
P.O. Box 345
York Harbor, ME 03911
207-363-8466
www.harboradventures.com

Coastal Maine Outfitting Co.
1399 US 1
Cape Neddick, ME 03902
207-363-0181
www.excursionsinmaine.com

New Hampshire
Country Canoeist
1005 School Street
Dunbarton, NH 03046
info@Countrycanoeist.com
www.CountryCanoeist.com

Portsmouth Kayak Adventures
185 Wentworth Road
Portsmouth, NH 03801
603-559-1000
bill@portsmouthkayak.com
www.portsmouthkayak.com

Portsmouth Rent & Ride
37 Hanover Street, Suite 2
Portsmouth, NH 03801
603-433-6777
jonah@portsmouthrentandride.com
www.portsmouthrentandride.com

Seacoast Kayak
210 Ocean Boulevard
Seabrook, NH 03874
603-474-1025
www.seacoastkayak.com

Kayak New England
Durham, NH 03824
603-312-0094

Massachusetts

Adventure Learning
67 Bear Hill
Merrimac, MA 01860
978-346-9728
800-649-9728
alc@greennet.net
www.adventure-learning.com

Essex River Basin Adventures
1 Main Street
P.O. Box 270
Essex, MA 01929
978-768-ERBA
800-KAYAK-04
info@erba.com
www.erba.com

Ipswich Bay Ocean Kayaking
(IBOK)
121 Jeffrey's Neck Road
Ipswich, MA 01938
978-356-2464
www.ipswichma.com/ibok/index
.htm

Outdoor Explorations
(for adaptive paddling)
98 Winchester Street
Medford, MA 02155
781-395-4999
www.outdoorexp.org

Charles River Canoe
and Kayak Center
2401 Commonwealth Avenue
Newton, MA 02459
617-965-5110
www.paddleboston.com

Eastern Mountain Sports
1041 Commonwealth Avenue
Boston, MA 02215
617-254-4250
(also outlets throughout New
England)
www.ems.com

REI
279 Salem Street
Reading, MA 01867
617-944-5103
(also outlets throughout the
United States)
www.rei.com

Billington Sea Watercraft
41 Branch Point Road
Plymouth, MA 02360
508-746-5644
800-286-0083 (MA only)
www.billingtonseakayak.com

Canoe Passage Outfitters
Route 44 (Dean's Plaza)
Raynham, MA 02767
508-824-1146
800-689-7884
www.canoepassage.com

Osprey Sea Kayak Adventures
489 Old County Road
Westport, MA 02790
508-636-0300
adventures@ospreyseakayak.com
www.ospreyseakayak.com

Cape Cod Coastal
Canoe & Kayak
36 Spectacle Pond Drive
East Falmouth, MA 02536
508-564-4051
www.capecodcanoekayak.com

Cape Cod Kayak
P.O. Box 1273
North Falmouth, MA 02556
508-563-9377
www.capecodkayak.com

The Paddler's Shop
Rivendell Marine
420 Shore Rd.
PO Box 926
Monument Beach, MA 02553
508-759-0330
www.thepaddlersshop.com

Snug Harbor Kayak
North Falmouth, MA 02556
500-610-3216

Waquoit Kayak
1209 East Falmouth Highway
East Falmouth, MA 02536
508-548-9722
www.waquoitkayak.com

Cape Cod Museum of
Natural History
Route 6A
Brewster, MA 02631
508-896-3867
800-479-3867 (toll-free in
Massachusetts)
www.ccmnh.org

Cape Cod National Seashore
Salt Pond Visitor Center
Route 6
Eastham, MA 02642
508-255-3421
www.nps.gov

Goose Hummock Shop
Route 6A
Orleans, MA 02653
508-255-0455
www.goose.com

Off the Coast Kayak
237 Commercial Street
Provincetown, MA 02657

Kayaks of Martha's Vineyard
P.O. Box 840
Martha's Vineyard, MA 02575
508-693-3885
www.kayakmv.com

Berkshire Outfitters
Route 8
Adams, MA 01220
413-743-5900
www.berkshireoutfitters.com

Rhode Island

The Kayak Centre
9 Phillips Street
Wickford, RI 02852
888-SEA-KAYAK
(also locations in Watch Hill
and Charlestown)
www.kayakcentre.com

Ocean State Adventures
99 Poppasquash Road
Bristol, RI 02808
401-254-4000
www.kayakri.com

Sakonnet Boathouse
169 Riverside Drive
Tiverton, RI 02878
401-624-1440
www.sakonnetboathouse.com

Connecticut

Outdoor Sports Center
80 Danbury Road
Wilton, CT 06897
203-762-8324
800-782-2193
www.outdoorsports.com

The Small Boat Shop
144 Water Street
South Norwalk, CT 06854
203-854-5223
www.thesmallboatshop.com

Collinsville Canoe & Kayak
41 Bridge Street (Route 179)
P.O. Box 336
Collinsville, CT 06022
860-693-6977
www.cckstore.com

Stony Creek Kayak
Stony Creek, CT
203-481-6401
www.stonycreekkayak.com

Atlantic Kayak Tours
320 West Saugerties Road
Saugerties, NY 12477
845-246-2187
KayakTours@aol.com
www.AtlanticKayakTours.com

North Cove Outfitters
75 Main Street
Old Saybrook, CT 06475
860-388-6585
www.northcove.com

Kayak Adventure, LLC
Norwalk, CT
888-454-0300
mskayak@attglobal.net
www.kayak-adventure.net

Land/Island Owners and Stewards (Listed north to south)

Maine

Acadia National Park
Superintendent
P.O. Box 177
Bar Harbor, ME 04609
207-288-3338
www.nps.gov/acad

Bureau of Parks and Lands
22 State House Station
Augusta, ME 04333-0022
207-287-3821

Bureau of Parks and
Lands/Camping
800-332-1501 (within Maine)
207-287-3824 (out of state)
www.state.me.us/doc/parks/
programs

Department of Inland Fisheries
and Wildlife
41 State House Station
Augusta, ME 04333-0041
207-287-8000
www.state.me.us/doc/parks/
programs/boating

Gulf of Maine Council on the
Marine Environment
Maine State Planning Office
184 State Street, 38 State
House Station
Augusta, ME 04333-0038
207-287-1491
www.gulfofmaine.org

Island Institute
386 Main Street
Rockland, ME 04841
207-594-9209
800-339-9209
inquiry@islandinstitute.org
www.islandinstitute.org

Knubble Bay Camp
Dave Wilson, AMC Registrar
5 Indian Lane
Wakefield, MA 01880
617-245-5714
www.outdoors.org/lodging/
camps

Maine Audubon
20 Gilsland Farm Road
Falmouth, ME 04105
207-781-2330
info@maineaudubon.org
www.maineaudubon.org

Maine Coast Heritage Trust
Bowdoin Mill
1 Main Street, Suite 201
Topsham, ME 04086
207-729-7366
info@mcht.org
www.mcht.org

Maine Department of
Conservation
Station #22
Augusta, ME 04333
207-289-4900

Maine Island Trail Association
41A Union Wharf
Portland, ME 04101
207-761-8225
mita@ime.net
www.mita.org

Marine Animal Lifeline
P.O. Box 621
Portland, ME 04104
207-773-7377
851-6625 (do not dial 207 in
Maine)
mal@stranding.org
www.stranding.org

Marine Environmental
Research Institute (MERI)
55 Main Street
Blue Hill, ME 04614
207-374-2135
MERI@downeast.net
www.meriresearch.org

Project Puffin
159 Sapsucker Woods Road
Ithaca, NY 14850
607-257-7308
puffin@audubon.org
www.audubon.org/bird/puffin

The Nature Conservancy
14 Main Street, Suite 401
Brunswick, ME 04011
207-729-5181
www.tnc.org

U.S. Fish and Wildlife Service
Moosehorn National Wildlife
Refuge
RR 1 Box 202, Suite 1
Baring, ME 04694
207-454-3521
www.fws.gov

U.S. Fish and Wildlife Service
Petit Manan National Wildlife
Refuge
P.O. Box 297
Milbridge, ME 04658
207-546-2124
www.fws.gov

New Hampshire

Audubon Society of
New Hampshire
3 Silk Farm Road
Concord, NH 03301
603-224-9909
asnh@nhaudubon.org
www.nhaudubon.org

Great Bay National
Wildlife Refuge
100 Merrimac Road
Newington, NH 03801-2903
603-431-7511
www.fws.org

New Hampshire Fish and
Game Department
Division of Marine Resources
225 Main Street
Durham, NH 03824
603-868-1095
www.wildlife.state.nh/us

New Hampshire Fish and
Game Department
Great Bay National Estuarine
Research Reserve
Region 3
Durham, NH 03824
603-868-1095
www.greatbay.org
http://inlet.geol.sc.edu/GRB

New Hampshire Division of
Parks and Recreation, Seacoast
P.O. Box 606
Rye, NH 03871
603-436-1552
www.nhparks.state.nh.us

New Hampshire Office of
State Planning
Coastal Program
152 Court Street
Portsmouth, NH 03801
603-431-9366
www.seacoastnh.com
www.state.nh.us/coastal

Massachusetts

Boston Harbor Islands National
Recreation Area
Boston Harbor Islands
Partnership
408 Atlantic Avenue, Suite 228
Boston, MA 02110-3350
617-223-8667
www.nps.gov/boha

Department of Conservation
and Recreation—Division
of State Parks and Recreation
251 Causeway Street, Suite 600
Boston, MA 02114-2104
617-626-1250
www.state.ma.us/dem

Essex County Greenbelt
Association
82 Eastern Avenue
Essex, MA 01929
978-768-7241
ecga@ecga.org
www.ecga.org

Massachusetts Audubon Society
208 South Great Road
Lincoln, MA 01773
781-259-9500
www.massaudubon.org

Massachusetts Coastal Zone
Management
251 Causeway Street, Suite 900
Boston, MA 02114-2151
617-727-9530
www.state.ma.us/czm

Massachusetts Environment
Police—Boat and Recreation
Vehicle Safety Bureau
www.state.ma.us/d.fwele/dle/
BoatRVSafe.htm

Merrimack River
Watershed Council
600 Suffolk Street, Fourth
Floor
Lowell, MA 01854
978-275-0120
www.merrimack.org

The North and South Rivers
Watershed Association
P.O. Box 43
Norwell, MA 02061-0043
781-659-8168
www.nsrwa.org

Public Access Board
1440 Soldiers Field Road
Brighton, MA 02135
617-727-1843
www.state.ma.us/dfwele/PAB/
Pab_table2.htm

Thacher Island Association
Box 73
Rockport, MA 01966
978-546-2326
www.thacherisland.org

Trustees of Reservations
572 Essex Street
Beverly, MA 01915-1530
978-921-1944
www.thetrustees.org

Wellfleet Bay
Wildlife Sanctuary
P.O. Box 236
South Wellfleet, MA 02663
508-349-2615
wellfleet@massaudubon.org
www.wellfleetbay.org

New England Aquarium
Central Wharf
Boston, MA 02110
617-973-5200
www.neaq.org

Rhode Island

Audubon Society of
Rhode Island
12 Sanderson Road
Smithfield, RI 02917
401-949-5454
www.asri.org

Burlingame State Park
Route 1
Charlestown, RI 02882
401-322-7337
www.riparks.com/burlinga.htm

Colt State Park
Colt Drive
Bristol, RI 02809
401-253-7482
www.riparks.com/colt.htm

Division of Parks and
Recreation
2321 Hartford Avenue
Johnston, RI 02919
401-222-2632
www.riparks.com

Save the Bay
434 Smith Street
Providence, RI 02908
401-272-3540
www.SavetheBay.org

Save the Bay
Narrangansett Bay Station
Seamen's Church Institute
18 Market Street
Newport, RI 02840
800-NARR-BAY

Connecticut

Connecticut Audubon
2325 Burr Street
Fairfield, CT 06430
203-259-6305
www.ctaudubon.org

Connecticut River Watershed
Council
15 Bank Row
Greenfield, MA 01301
413-772-2020
crwc@crocker.com
www.ctriver.org.

Department of Environmental
Protection
Office of State Parks and
Recreation
Boating Division
P.O. Box 280
Old Lyme, CT 06371-0280
860-434-8638
http://dep.state.ct.us/rec/
boating/guide.htm

Department of Environmental
Protection
79 Elm Street
Hartford, CT 06106-5127
Office of Long Island Sound
Programs
860-424-3034
http://dep.state.ct.us
Bureau of Outdoor Recreation
860-424-3200
http://dep.state.ct.us/stateparks

Gillette Castle State Park
67 River Road
East Haddam, CT 06423
860-526-2336
http://dep.state.ct/us/stateparks

Stewart B. McKinney National
Wildlife Refuge
Silvio O. Conte National
Wildlife Refuge
www.fws.gov

Ferries

Casco Bay Lines
P.O. Box 4656
Portland, ME 04112-4656
207-774-7871
www.cascobaylines.com

Cuttyhunk Boat Lines
Pier 3/Fisherman's Wharf
New Bedford, MA 02740
508-992-1432
Alert2@Cuttyhunk.com

Island Queen
75 Falmouth Heights Road
Falmouth, MA 02524
508-548-4800
www.islandqueen.com

Maine State Ferry Service
P.O. Box 645
517 A Main Street
Rockland, ME 04841
207-596-2202
800-491-4883
www.state.me.us/mdot/opt/ferry/
ferry.htm

Woods Hole Steamship
Authority
Falmouth, MA 02543
508-548-3788
www.islandferry.com

Map Sources

DeLorme
2 DeLorme Drive
P.O. Box 298
Yarmouth, ME 04096
800-511-2459
www.delorme.com

Maptech
10 Industrial Way
Amesbury, MA 01913-3223
888-839-5551
www.maptech.com

The Map Shack
253 North Avenue
Wakefield, MA 01880
800-617-MAPS
www.baldwinmapshack.com

NauticalCharts.com
866-6-CHARTS
www.nauticalcharts.com

NOAA
www.noaa.gov/charts.html

Weather and Marine Sites Online

www.maineharbors.com
www.gomoos.org
www.nws.noaa.gov
www.uscgboating.org

APPENDIX B

Equipment Checklist

Safety Items

- [ ] PFD (personal flotation device), required by federal law
- [ ] Towrope
- [ ] Spare two-part paddle
- [ ] Repair kit for either fiberglass or plastic boat
- [ ] Paddle float
- [ ] Air horn
- [ ] Smoke signals
- [ ] Flares
- [ ] Whistle
- [ ] Waterproof flashlight
- [ ] Trip float plan
- [ ] Hand pump
- [ ] Sponge
- [ ] Wet/drysuit
- [ ] Spare warm, dry clothes
- [ ] Compass
- [ ] Marine charts and chart case
- [ ] Weather radio
- [ ] Thermos
- [ ] Stove
- [ ] Matches
- [ ] First-aid kit
- [ ] Fresh drinking water
- [ ] Sunglasses
- [ ] Sunscreen
- [ ] Hat for rain/sun

Boat Gear

- [ ] Kayak
- [ ] Paddle
- [ ] Sprayskirt
- [ ] Float bags for both ends if you don't have bulkheads
- [ ] Waterproof storage bags
- [ ] Deck lines

Clothing

- [ ] Drysuit or wetsuit jacket and farmer john/jane
- [ ] Neoprene booties
- [ ] Paddling jacket
- [ ] Neoprene gloves, mittens, or pogies
- [ ] Polypropylene or fiber pile jacket
- [ ] Polypropylene or fiber pile pants
- [ ] Long underwear
- [ ] Complete change of clothes
- [ ] Swimsuit and towel
- [ ] Rain jacket and pants
- [ ] Security strap for glasses or sunglasses
- [ ] Hiking shorts
- [ ] T-shirt

Day-Trip Items

- ☐ Waterproof matches and container
- ☐ Emergency shelter
- ☐ Insect repellent
- ☐ Sitting pad
- ☐ Drinking cup
- ☐ Handkerchief
- ☐ Camera/film and dry bag or box
- ☐ Toilet paper
- ☐ Litter bag
- ☐ Windbreaker
- ☐ Lunch/snacks

Overnight Items

- ☐ Tent
- ☐ Sleeping bag and pad
- ☐ Stove and fuel
- ☐ Cooking pot
- ☐ Pot holder
- ☐ Eating utensils
- ☐ Pocketknife
- ☐ Personal toilet items
- ☐ Biodegradable soap
- ☐ Extra batteries
- ☐ Portable toilet

Other Items

- ☐ Sneakers
- ☐ Binoculars
- ☐ Fishing gear
- ☐ Bird identification guide
- ☐ Camp seat
- ☐ Notebook

APPENDIX C

Emergency Contacts

The Coast Guard serves as search-and-rescue coordinator for all maritime emergencies and is the appropriate point of contact whenever you are concerned for your safety. In a distress situation, use flares or any other distress-signaling device to catch the attention of another boater who can assist you or call the Coast Guard for you. The Coast Guard monitors channels 16 VHF/FM and 2182 khz HF/SSB, which are dedicated distress and calling frequencies at all times.

The following is a list of cities and towns with Coast Guard stations. The First District, headquartered in Boston, covers New England, New York, and New Jersey; call 800-848-3942. For all stations, call on your cellular phone *CG. See also the *Eldridge Tide and Pilot Book* for all phone numbers.

Maine: Southwest Harbor, Jonesport, Rockland, S. Portland, Boothbay Harbor

New Hampshire: Portsmouth

Massachusetts: Boston, Merrimac-Newburyport, Gloucester, Point Allerton-Hull, Scituate, Cape Cod Canal, Woods Hole, Chatham, Provincetown, Menemsha-Martha's Vineyard, Brant Point-Nantucket

Rhode Island: Newport, Point Judith

Connecticut: New Haven, New London

What to tell the Coast Guard:

- Your location or position
- Exact nature of the problem
- Number of people in your party
- Description of your boat
- Safety equipment on board
- Any special problems

Beaufort Wind Scale

Force	Wind (knots)	WMO Classification	Appearance of Wind Effects On the Water	On Land
0	< 1	Calm	Sea surface smooth and mirror-like	Calm, smoke rises vertically
1	1–3	Light Air	Scaly ripples, no foam crests	Smoke drift indicates wind direction, still wind vanes
2	4–6	Light Breeze	Small wavelets, crests glassy, no breaking	Wind felt on face, leaves rustle, vanes begin to move
3	7–10	Gentle Breeze	Large wavelets, crests begin to break, scattered whitecaps	Leaves and small twigs constantly moving, light flags extended
4	11–16	Moderate Breeze	Small waves 1–4 ft becoming longer, numerous whitecaps	Dust, leaves, and loose paper lifted, small tree branches move
5	17–21	Fresh Breeze	Moderate waves 4–8 ft taking longer form, many whitecaps, some spray	Small trees in leaf begin to sway
6	22–27	Strong Breeze	Larger waves 8–13 ft, white-caps common, more spray	Larger tree branches moving, whistling in wires
7	28–33	Near Gale	Sea heaps up, waves 13–20 ft, white foam streaks off breakers	Whole trees moving, resistance felt walking against wind
8	34–40	Gale	Moderately high (13–20 ft) waves of greater length, edges of creasts begin to break into spindrift, foam blown in streaks	Whole trees in motion, resistance felt when walking against wind
9	41–47	Strong Gale	High waves (20 ft), sea begins to roll, dense streaks of foam, spray may reduce visibility	Slight structural damage occurs, slate blows off roofs
10	48–55	Storm	Very high waves (20–30 ft) with overhanging crests, sea white with densely blown foam, heavy rolling, lowered visibility	Seldom experienced on land, trees broken or uprooted, "considerable structural damage"
11	56–63	Violent Storm	Exceptionally high (30–45 ft) waves, foam patches cover sea, visibility more reduced	
12	64+	Hurricane	Air filled with foam, waves over 45 ft, sea completely white with driving spray, visibility greatly reduced	

APPENDIX E

Float Plan

Name, age, paddling experience (beginner, intermediate, advanced), type and color of kayak, color of life jacket, and pertinent medical information for each person in your group!

_____

_____

_____

_____

Emergency contacts: _____

_____

_____

Launch time and location: _____

_____

Take out time and location with latest expected return date: _____

_____

_____

Intended route:_____

_____

_____

Safety equipment you have with you (include tent color and style): _____

_____

_____

_____

Plan of action if not back by latest expected return date: _____

_____

_____

_____

Vehicle type: _____ License Plate: _____

Location: _____

Float plan courtesy of _The Maine Association of Sea Kayak Guides and Instructors_

APPENDIX F
Leave No Trace

 The Appalachian Mountain Club is a national educational partner of Leave No Trace, Inc., a nonprofit organization dedicated to promoting and inspiring responsible outdoor recreation through education, research, and partnerships. The Leave No Trace Program seeks to develop wildland ethics—ways in which people think and act in the outdoors to minimize their impacts on the areas they visit and to protect our natural resources for future enjoyment. Leave No Trace unites four federal land management agencies—the U.S. Forest Service, National Park Service, Bureau of Land Management, and U.S. Fish and Wildlife Service—with manufacturers, outdoor retailers, user groups, educators, organizations like the AMC and the National Outdoor Leadership School (NOLS), and individuals.

The Leave No Trace ethic is guided by these seven principles:

- Plan ahead and prepare.
- Travel and camp on durable surfaces.
- Dispose of waste properly.
- Leave what you find.
- Minimize campfire impacts.
- Respect wildlife.
- Be considerate of other visitors.

The AMC has joined NOLS—a recognized leader in wilderness education and a founding partner of Leave No Trace—as the sole national providers of the Leave No Trace Master Educator course through 2004. The AMC offers this five-day course, designed especially for outdoor professionals and land managers, as well as the shorter two-day Leave No Trace Trainer course at locations throughout the Northeast.

For Leave No Trace information and materials, contact:
Leave No Trace, Inc.
P.O. Box 997
Boulder, CO 80306
800-332-4100
www.LNT.org

GLOSSARY

baidarka Originally a boat designed by the Aleuts of Alaska, having two seats and great storage capacity for long, exposed voyages, and given a third cockpit by Russian fur traders.

beach rips Otherwise known as riptides or rip currents; narrow seaward-flowing currents that extend from the shore out through the surf zone.

beam sea A sea in which waves approach your boat from the side, often over the gunwale.

bore A steep-fronted wave caused by the tide entering a shallow channel of an estuary or river and building up to overcome a seaward-directed current. (There are both tidal bores and wave bores.)

broach The turning of a boat parallel to the waves, when running at an angle to the waves. Could result in a capsize if the paddler is unskilled or unprepared.

bulkheads Built-in walls of fiberglass or closed-cell foam to create watertight compartments in the bow and stern sections of the kayak, which provide structural support, buoyancy, and dry stowage, with access through deck hatches.

chine The sharp edge on some hulls that is formed by the intersection of a flat bottom and sides of a boat, which provides extra stability and aids in turning.

clapotis The zone of interference between incoming and reflected waves, usually found adjacent to headlands, islands, cliffed shores, and near-shore structures such as breakwaters, seawalls, and jetties.

coaming The rim around the cockpit opening to which the sprayskirt is attached.

dead reckoning Position on the water, deduced from the distance and direction paddled away from a known location.

draw stroke A maneuver to move the kayak sideways in which you pull the driving face of the paddle blade toward you in a vertical position.

drogue A device dragged astern to check the boat's speed or to keep the stern up to the waves in a following sea.

drysuit A one- or two-piece nylon-coated waterproof suit with latex seals at neck, wrists, and ankles to keep water out, usually worn with pile underneath for insulation.

ebb tide A falling tide.

eddy A current of water running contrary to the main current; in its bigger, more intense form, a whirlpool.

Eskimo-bow rescue An assisted rescue in which a capsized victim grabs on to the bow of another boat and raises himself or herself to the surface.

Eskimo roll A self-rescue in which the capsized victim rights himself or herself without leaving the boat by a sweeping and pull-down movement of the paddle blade with hip thrust. Many variations exist.

estuary A passage where the tide meets freshwater current.

fair tide Going in the direction of the tidal current.

feathered paddle Blades positioned at angles of 60 to 90 degrees to each other to reduce windage when paddling into the wind.

ferrying Paddling a course upstream or upwind of your destination, which will result in a straight tack across either a current or an opposing wind.

fetch The distance over which wind can blow, causing waves.

fjord A narrow inlet of sea that is caused by ocean flooding of a former glacially scoured valley.

flood tide A rising tide.

folding boat A boat with a canvas or nylon hull that can be collapsed into one or more carrying bags.

following sea A sea in which waves approach the stern of your boat.

foul tide Going against the direction of the tidal current.

gunkholing Wandering into and out of coves and inlets.

head sea A sea in which waves approach the boat's bow.

Kevlar A carbon-fiber material used in rigid kayaks for lightness and strength.

knot A measure of speed equal to 1 nautical mile, about 6,080 feet an hour.

lee shore The shore toward which the wind is blowing.

nautical mile About 6,080 feet, or one-eighth longer than the statute mile of 5,280 feet.

overfall An area where tidal current streams collide; often a wave is formed when one current falls over the other.

paddle brace A technique that allows a paddler to remain upright in a breaking wave on the beam by leaning the boat and placing the paddle into the wave.

paddle float A portable flotation device, slid over the end of the paddle, that acts as an outrigger in a self-rescue.

paddle leash A piece of cord that attaches the paddle to the wrist of the paddler to ensure that the paddle isn't lost.

PFD Personal flotation device, otherwise known as a life jacket.

pitchpole The action in which the boat is thrown end over end in very steep seas or breaking surf.

pogies Tubular mitts attached around the paddle shaft by Velcro tabs to protect the hands from cold and spray yet maintain direct hand contact with the paddle shaft.

reversing fall Estuarine-water tidal current that reverses flow at the same location during flood and ebb current and at some stage of the tide flows over bedrock ledge with the usual features of whitewater.

rotomolded A kayak molded by melted plastic, generally stronger and less expensive but heavier than fiberglass models.

rudder A vertical metal plate used to steer the boat; it's attached to the stern and operated by cables running forward to foot controls.

sea anchor Any device used to reduce a boat's drift before the wind (also see *drogue*).

sculling A paddle stroke in which you draw the paddle back and forth in small arcs or a Z-formation, used to move a kayak sideways or for support when the boat is leaning sideways on the water.

shoal Shallow area in the sea, often a sand bank or rock ledge.

skeg A tracking device that comes in three types—removable, molded into the hull at the stern, or a retractable blade that can be lowered from the keel.

slack water Slow-flowing or still water that occurs briefly between ebb and flood currents at extremes of high and low tides.

sprayskirt A skirt made of neoprene or nylon designed to be worn by the paddler and attached to the coaming to prevent water from entering the cockpit.

sweep stroke The paddle is swept in an arc out and away from boat to turn the boat to the left or right, usually accompanied with boat lean in the direction opposite the intended direction of the turn.

tidal rip An area of fast, turbulent water with steep waves that occurs when a strong current is abruptly altered, occuring on shoals, at points of land along the shoreline, and in opposing currents.

West Greenland kayak Originally a swift, single-seat kayak designed by the Natives of northern Canada and Greenland for hunting and travel.

wetsuit Generally, a tight-fitting two-piece suit made of 0.13-inch-thick neoprene foam that serves to trap a thin layer of water warmed by the body while providing a protective barrier from cold ocean water.

windward shore The wind is off the land.

BIBLIOGRAPHY

Here are some sea kayak books, other boating manuals, guides, and personal accounts that might be of interest the New England paddler:

Bascom, Willard. *Waves and Beaches.* Garden City, N.Y.: Doubleday, 1980.

Burch, David. *Fundamentals of Kayak Navigation.* Guilford, Conn.: Globe Pequot Press, 1993.

Broze, Matt, and George Gronseth. *Deep Trouble: True Stories and Their Lessons from* Sea Kayaker *Magazine.* Camden, Maine: Ragged Mountain Press, 1997.

Daniel, Linda. *Kayak Cookery.* Menasha Ridge Press, 1997.

Dowd, John. *Sea Kayaking: A Manual for Long Distance Touring.* Seattle: University of Washington Press, 1997.

Foster, Nigel. *Nigel Foster's Sea Kayaking.* Guilford, Conn.: Globe Pequot Press.

Hutchinson, Derek. *Eskimo Rolling.* Camden, Maine: Ragged Mountain Press, 1992.

———. *The Basic Book of Sea Kayaking.* Guilford, Conn.: Globe Pequot Press, 1999.

Johnson, Shelley. *The Complete Sea Kayaker's Handbook.* Camden, Maine: Ragged Mountain Press, 2002.

Lessels, Bruce, and Karen Blum. *Paddling with Kids.* Boston, Mass.: AMC Books, 2001.

Nordby, Will, ed. *Seekers of the Horizon.* Chester, Conn.: Globe Pequot Press, 1989.

Rowe, Ray, ed. *Canoeing Handbook: Official Handbook of the British Canoe Union.* The Chameleon Press Limited, 1990.

Schumann, Roger, and Jan Shriner. *Sea Kayak Rescue.* Guilford, Conn.: Globe Pequot Press, 2001.

Washburne, Randel. *The Coastal Kayaker's Manual: A Complete Guide to Skills, Gear, and Sea Sense.* Guilford, Conn.: Globe Pequot Press, 1998.

Boating Manuals

Duncan, Roger F., and John P. Ware. *The Cruising Guide to the New England Coast.* New York: W. W. Norton & Co., 1995.

Taft, Hank, et al. *A Cruising Guide to the Maine Coast.* Peaks Island, Maine: Diamond Pass Publishing, 1996.

White, Robert Eldridge. *Eldridge Tide and Pilot Book.* Boston: Robert Eldridge White, 2003.

River Guides

AMC River Guide: Maine, 2nd ed. Boston: AMC Books, 1991.

AMC River Guide: Massachusetts, Connecticut, Rhode Island, 2nd ed. Boston: AMC Books, 1990.

AMC River Guide: New Hampshire, Vermont, 2nd ed. Boston: AMC Books, 1989.

Borton, Mark C., ed. *The Complete Boating Guide to the Connecticut River.* Easthampton, Mass.: The Connecticut River Watershed Council, 1987.

Connecticut River Watershed Council. *Tidewaters of the Connecticut River: An Explorers Guide to Hidden Coves and Marshes.* Greenfield, Mass.: CRWC, 2003.

Paddling Guides

Bull, Shirley, and Fred Bull. *Paddling Cape Cod: A Coastal Explorer's Guide*. Woodstock, Vt.: Countryman Press, 2000.

Bumsted, Lee. *Hot Showers! Maine Coast Lodgings for Kayakers and Sailors*. Brunswick, Maine: Audenreed Press, 2000.

Evans, Lisa Gollin. *Sea Kayaking Coastal Massachusetts*. Boston: AMC Books, 2000.

Hodgins, Richard, and Erika Racz. *Connecticut Kayaking: A Paddler's Guide*. Even Keel Publishing, 2002.

Johnson, Shelley, and Vaughan Smith. *Guide to Sea Kayaking in Maine*. Guilford, Conn: Globe Pequot Press, 2001.

Maine Island Trail Association. *2003 Stewardship Handbook & Guidebook*. Rockland, Maine, 2003.

Miller, Dorcas. *Kayaking the Maine Coast: A Paddler's Guide to Day Trips from Kittery to Cobscook*. Woodstock, Vt.: Countryman Press, 2000.

Mullen, Ed. *Kayaking Narragansett Bay: A Precise Guide to 58 Launch Sites with Parking in Rhode Island*. Warwick, R.I., 2003

Paigen, Jennifer Alisa. *The Sea Kayaker's Guide to Mount Desert Island*. Camden, Maine: Down East Books, 1997.

Weintraub, David. *Adventure Kayaking: Trips on Cape Cod*. Berkeley, Calif.: Wilderness Press, 2000.

Related Reading

Beston, Henry. *The Outermost House*. New York: The Viking Press, 1928.

Bolster, Jeffrey W., ed. *Cross-Grained & Wily Waters: A Guide to the Piscataqua Maritime Region*. Portsmouth, N.H.: Peter Randall Publisher, 2002.

Conkling, Philip C. *Green Islands, Green Sea: A Guide to Foraging on the Islands of Maine*. Rockland, Maine: Hurricane Island Outward Bound School, 1980.

———. *Islands in Time*. Camden, Maine: Down East Books, 1999.

Jewett, Sarah Orne. *The Country of the Pointed Firs*. New York: Doubleday, 1956.

Gibbons, Euell. *Stalking the Blue-Eyed Scallop*. New York: D. McKay, 1964.

Greenlaw, Linda. *The Lobster Chronicles: Life on a Very Small Island*. New York: Hyperion Books, 2002.

Kales, David, and Emily Kales. *All about the Boston Harbor Islands*, 3rd ed. Hingham, Mass.: Hewitts Cove Publishing Co., 1989.

McCloskey, Robert. *One Morning in Maine*. New York: Viking Press, 1952.

Parsons, Eleanor C. *Thachers, Island of Twin Lights*. Canaan, N.H.: Phoenix Publishing, 1985.

Pratt, Charles. *Here on the Island*. New York: Harper & Row, 1974.

Richardson, Wyman. *The House on Nauset Marsh*. Boston: The Atlantic Monthly Co., 1947.

Robb, Daniel. *Crossing the Water: Eighteen Months on an Island Working with Troubled Boys—A Teacher's Memoir*. New York: Simon & Schuster, 2001.

Thaxter, Celia. *Among the Isles of Shoals*. Fort Lauderdale, Fla.: Wake-Brook House, 1873.

Thoreau, Henry David. *Cape Cod*. Boston: Ticknor and Fields, 1865.

Instructional Videos and DVDs

The Brent Reitz Forward Stroke Clinic. Brent Reitz. Moss Landing, Calif.

Capture Kenneries of Rescue Procedures. Wayne Thornbush. Santa Barbara, Calif. University of Sea Kayaking.

1st Roll: Rolling Video for Sea Kayakers. Branford, Conn.: Outer Island Kayak.

The Kayak Roll. Durango, Colo.. Performance Video.

Nigel Foster Sea Kayaking Series, Vol. 1–6. Nigel Foster. Orlando, Fla.: Starling Productions.

Sea Kayaking Performance Sea Kayaking: The Basics and Beyond. Durango, Colo.: Peformance Video.

Seamanship for Kayakers: Getting Started. John Dowd. Sea Kayak Videos. Gabriola Island, Washington.

In the Surf! Performance Surf Kayaking: The Basics and Beyond. Durango, Colo.: Performance Video.

ABOUT THE AUTHOR

Tamsin Venn is a longtime outdoor writer. As travel editor for *Skiing Magazine*, she wrote more than one hundred articles about ski resorts throughout the world and compiled its annual guide to ski resorts in the United States, Canada, and Europe. As an editor for North Shore Weeklies, she won an award for best newspaper of the year from the New England Newspaper Association. She started *Atlantic Coastal Kayaker* magazine twelve years ago after completing the first edition of this guidebook. She lives with her husband and two children in Ipswich, Massachusetts.

GET OUT & GET ACTIVE WITH THE AMC

Since 1876, the Appalachian Mountain Club has promoted the protection, enjoyment, and wise use of the mountains, rivers, and trails of the Northeast. We encourage people to enjoy and appreciate the natural world because we believe that successful conservation depends on this experience.

Join Us!

With the AMC, you can participate in virtually every Earth-friendly outdoor activity there is. Connect with new people, learn new outdoor skills, and feel good knowing you're helping to protect the natural world you love. In addition to hundreds of adventures offered by your local AMC chapters, you'll also enjoy discounts on AMC skills workshops, lodging, and books.

Outdoor Adventures & Workshops

Develop your outdoor skills and knowledge! From beginner backpacking and family canoeing to guided backcountry trips, you'll find something for any age or interest at spectacular locations throughout the Northeast.

Destinations & Accomodations

From the North Woods of Maine to the Delaware Water Gap, AMC offers destinations tailored for every kind of traveler. Experience outdoor adventure at its best as our guest.

Books & Maps

AMC's hiking, biking, and paddling guides lead you to the most spectaular destinations in the Northeast. We're also your definitive source for how-to guides, trail maps, and adventure tales.

Contact Us Today!

Appalachian Mountain Club
5 Joy Street
Boston, MA 02108
617-523-0636

www.outdoors.org